Charles Alston Messiter

Sport and adventures among the North-American Indians

Charles Alston Messiter

Sport and adventures among the North-American Indians

ISBN/EAN: 9783742898685

Manufactured in Europe, USA, Canada, Australia, Japa

Cover: Foto ©ninafisch / pixelio.de

Manufactured and distributed by brebook publishing software (www.brebook.com)

Charles Alston Messiter

Sport and adventures among the North-American Indians

CONTENTS.

CHAPTER I.

Leave England.—Voyage and arrival at Quebec.—Proceed to Toronto and then to St. Paul's.—Threatened rising of the Sioux. Its causes. The storm bursts.—We start for Fort Carlton.—Description of journey.—Arrival at Fort Abercrombie.—Hostile Indians.—Reach Georgetown.—Attack on Fort Abercrombie.—Barbarity of the Indians.—Retreat in canoes.—Awful storm.—Arrival at Pembina. —Arrival at Fort Garry.—Our Guide and preparations to start.— "The early bird catches the worm."—A Red-River cart.—Leave Fort Garry.—Crossing the Saskatchawan.—Arrival at Fort Carlton. —Fight between bloodhound and wolf.—I astonish the Indians.— A boxing-match. Its consequences.—Murder at council of Indians. Its results 1

CHAPTER II.

Leave Fort Carlton.—Swimming horses.—Our first buffalo.— Laronde's method of killing buffalo.—Our first meeting with wild Indians.—Attempt to stalk antelope.—Immense herds of buffalo. —A run with buffaloes.—I run down a wolf.—Sudden appearance of three Indians.—An unpleasant adventure.—A night in an Indian lodge.—Rejoin my companions.—The advantages of steel hobbles.—Studying a buffalo at close quarters.—Prairie-dogs.— Return to Fort Carlton.—Our Party breaks up.—I leave for Thickwood Hills.—Sleigh-dogs 16

CHAPTER III.

Scenery in the Thickwood Hills.—Building huts.—Tom Boot. His size and strength.—Our nearest neighbour.—Visit the South Saskatchewan.—Large Camp of Crees.—A Sioux Indian prisoner. His trial and fate.—Attempts to save him.—We leave the Camp.—Return journey. — Dreadful spectacle. — Setting in of winter. Severe cold.—Description of trapping in winter.—Unpleasant adventure with Indians. Tom Boot to the rescue. His prowess.—A-ta-ka-koup makes friends.—Snow-shoe travelling.—A visit from Driver 29

CHAPTER IV.

A moose-hunt.—Description of my tent.—A-ta-ka-koup in camp.—Hunting moose on snow-shoes. Deaths of a bull and a cow.—Lynx-hunting.—Tom Boot a nuisance.—F——'s history. His miserable condition. I take him with me.—Beautifying the hut.—F—— and I visit my late companions. Our journey.—The wolverine.—Getting F—— home.—Badger neglects the traps.—Narrow escape of being murdered. My precautions for the future.—An invitation to a stealing-party 45

CHAPTER V.

How to make a plum-pudding.—Our Christmas party.—Nocturnal visits of F—— and myself to the plum-pudding.—Our daily routine.—F—— does not enjoy winter.—I am summoned to a Cree council.—A night apparition.—The Cree camp. Accusations against me. Enmity of some of the Indians.—Rescued from a dangerous position by "White Hawk."—A new religion.—Impunity of lunatics.—Leave Cree camp.—Mis-ta-wa-sis corrects his wife with an axe.—Attempt to marry me.—A-ta-ka-koup propitiates the hunting god.—Camping in the snow.—A dog-sleigh described.—Behaviour of dogs 57

CHAPTER VI.

A bear-hunt.—Curious story of a bear.—A wolf-hunt.—Indian dogs.—Visit Fort Carlton.—Recipe for Rubbiboo.—A ball at Fort Carlton.—Ponies wintering in the snow.—Intelligence of sleigh-dogs.—Ingratitude of Ki-chi-mo-ko-man.—Tom Boot a thief. Determine to punish him. A-ta-ka-koup joins me in the enterprise. Surprise Tom Boot. Tremendous struggle. Tom Boot receives a thrashing.—Leave our hut for Fort Carlton.—Serious difficulty at the river. Nearly starved. Rescued by boat. My feet frozen.—The manufacture of pemmican.—Frozen fish.—A professional bear-hunter.—F—— and I part.—Effect of eloquence on Indians 70

CHAPTER VII.

An Indian swims the Saskatchawan.—Start from Fort Carlton.—Prairie fire and narrow escape.—Unpleasant surprise.—A Sioux camp. Interview with the chief. Suspicious circumstances. A parley with the chief.—A fight and race for life.—Our mode of travelling.—Arrival at Fort Garry. Our miserable appearance.—The composition of galette.—The Sioux outbreak and cause.—Threat to sack Fort Garry.—Enmity between English and French half-breeds.—My new guide, and his character.—Kindness of the citizens.—Start for Fort Garry and mode of travelling.—Desolation of the country.—My first night in a bed, and consequences.—Taken for a half-breed scout.—Expedition against the Indians. Its utter failure.—Death of "Little Crow".—Execution of Indians.—Start for England 85

CHAPTER VIII.

Return to America.—Start for Kansas.—Warning against obliging strangers.—The town of Troy.—Horse-racing. A soft thing.—A breakdown.—A wrestling-match.—My new man Fox. His objection to sheriffs.—The settlement of White Rock. Its history.—A happy hunting-ground.—A Tenderfoot's first run with buffalo. He prefers walking.—A wonderful mare. I buy her.—Trying Brown's courage.—Appearance of Indians near camp 105

CHAPTER IX.

Find a Sioux camp-ground.—The omnivorous horse.—A Rocky-Mountain moose.—A large turkey-roost.—A deserted settlement.—Fox thinks he is going to die.—Crossing the river under difficulties.—A fast buffalo-calf.—Adventure with a buffalo.—Camp deserted. Another made. Row with the men. Brown discharged. Remove to old camp.—More buffalo-hunting.—Surprised by Indians. Cut off from camp. Plan of getting through. Its success and safety.—Neighbourhood getting too warm.—Fox declines going near a sheriff.—Return eastwards 115

CHAPTER X.

Another expedition to White Rock.—A fighting butcher.—The fate of Fox.—Excitement about Indians.—Advised to turn back.—Settlement No. 10 at White Rock.—Bold settlers.—Examine buffaloes at close quarters.—The bold settlers demoralized.—A large herd of elk.—Desperate struggle with a horse. Laid up from a kick.—The fate of our buffalo-tongues.—Settlers about to avenge themselves. Their indifferent armament. A serious consultation. The expedition given up.—I intend going alone to Fort Kearney 126

CHAPTER XI.

Start on my journey.—Miserable weather.—Appearance of three Indians. I compel them to breakfast with me. An uncomfortable breakfast-party. I bid them adieu.—Reach the ranche.—

Report of our having been murdered.—Mr. Martin. His history.—Visit to Fort Kearney.—Interview with Major North. His recent fight with Sioux.—Start on my return journey.—Uncanny sight.—Dense fog.—Camp on Little Blue River.—Horse missing. Vain efforts to track him.—Weary journey back to ranche. Quite done up. Kindness of the Martins.—Return journey to camp.—A pleasant surprise.—Narrow escape from Indians.—A horrible sight 136

CHAPTER XII.

Awful thunder-storms.—Bad water-supply.—Life in camp.—I leave for St. Joe.—Come across two Indians.—Arrive at Lake Sibley.—Swarm of grasshoppers.—Apprehensions of the settlers.—A man wishes me to engage him. I decline.—I make the acquaintance of a detective.—A plan to rob me. I manage to frustrate it.—Meet F—— at Martin's.—Sioux steal Pawnees' horses. Pawnees and Whites try to recover them. A fight and repulse of Pawnees.—Mrs. Martin's reminiscences of her husband.—Poor sport.—Return to St. Joe.—Intend to winter in Texas.—Billy Breeze. His history 153

CHAPTER XIII.

Voyage down the Missouri.—Wild-fowl shooting.—Objectionable freed slaves.—New Orleans.—My companion dies of cholera. I also am attacked. I recover.—Meet some Confederate generals.—Gambling-saloons.—Galveston.—Several shooting-trips.—An expensive night's lodging.—A young Englishman joins us.—A New Yorker and his supper-party.—The lone tree.—Difficulties with the waggon.—The town of Richmond.—We are fined. But do not pay.—F—— has an accident.—A useful doctor.—General Sheridan's horse.—Buy a wild horse.—A stream in flood.—Racing in Texas.—A racing mule 164

CONTENTS.

CHAPTER XIV.

PAGE

Move to Clear Lake.—A bankrupt railway.—Abundance of game.—Stalking wild geese.—Invitation to a bear-hunt.—A norther. Story of a norther.—Lynch law.—Bear-hunting poor sport.—Great abundance of snipe.—Good shooting.—Extortionate landlord.—Semi-wild hogs.—Wild bulls. Narrow escapes from them.—Our dog Booze. His fighting capabilities.—Invitation to a plantation. Melancholy appearance of it.—A good afternoon at the ducks.—A Masonic tip.—A Texan ball.—Buying mules.—Fishing in Texas. 180

CHAPTER XV.

San Antonio and Texas in 1868.—Horse-stealing. Its punishment.—Shoeing and breaking wild ponies. Negroes the best breakers.—Mexicans and their mode of life.—Part with Billy Breeze.—Move to Fredericksburg.—Too hot for dogs. Death of one.—Trying the men's courage.—Halliday, his history.—A real frontiersman. He declines to go with us.—H—— has an adventure while on guard. —Fort Mason.—Indians catch and torture a man.—Big-foot Wallace. Refuses to go with us.—Leave Fort Mason.—Fight between horses.—A refractory mule. His cure.—An over-confident Major. —Start for Fort Belknap.—A plundered waggon.—I meet with Indians. I am pursued. Shoot an Indian's horse and escape.—Difficult country 194

CHAPTER XVI.

Fort Belknap.—Buffalo-dance by Tonkaways.—A-sa-ha-be. We agree to his coming with us. His suspicious conduct. He leaves us by night.—We turn back.—Appearance of Indians.—A-sa-ha-be comes to propose terms. They are rejected.—The Comanches attack us.—We still move on.—We kill and scalp an Indian.—A reinforcement of Indians.—Downfall of A-sa-ha-be.—Arrival of three Caddo Indian scouts. We send one of them for help. He is pursued, but escapes.—Our casualties.—Halliday's courage.—Arrival of troops.—We reach Fort Arbuckle 211

CHAPTER XVII.

The Caddo Indians.—Story of their chief and the Comanches.—An insolent blacksmith. His punishment.—Our camp fired into.—Discovery of the culprits. Their punishment.—Leave Fort Arbuckle.—Chase of a wolf by a pointer.—Difficulty of crossing the Red River.—I return for provisions.—Difficulty of carrying eggs on horseback.—An Indian reservation.—Incivility of an Indian. We become better friends.—Thirsty oxen.—Our party breaks up   228

CHAPTER XVIII.

Account of Julesburg. A specimen of the manners of Julesburg. Our lodgings. Seeing the town. Its inhabitants.—Gambling-saloons.—We start for Sheyenne.—Description of hotel accommodation.—A citizen shot by an officer.—Start for Elk Mountain.—Reach Willow Springs.—All Houston.—Camp at Willow Springs.—Woodchoppers, bad characters.—Story about Houston.—Obliged to hunt singly.—We go together to hunt.—A deserted hut and grave of occupant.—A visitor.—Polly's behaviour.—F—— starts for Sheyenne.—Snowed in.—Villainous-looking visitors. They are induced to go.—Precautions.—F——'s return.—I return to Sheyenne.—F—— goes to Virginia Dale   238

CHAPTER XIX.

Move to Virginia Dale.—Meet my old driver.—Stage drivers.—Abundance of antelope.—Reach Sheyenne.—Vigilance committee.—Election for Mayor.—An unpleasant neighbour. Play a practical joke on him.—Life in Sheyenne.—Action of the Vigilance committee.—Stories of various desperadoes.—Joe Riley, the prize-fighter.—Racing at Sheyenne.—A railway quickly made.—Leave for England and sell "Polly."   254

CHAPTER XX.

Intend to go up the Wichita and Red Rivers.—Grouse-shooting.—Creasing a horse.—Poor settlers.—A money-lending parson.—Danger of Mexican cooks.—Henrietta in 1874.—A norther.—Rough cowboys.—Lose my horse.—Return towards Henrietta.—Indians about.—A suspicious horseman.—Reach Henrietta.—The settlement raided by Black Kettle.—The settlers cowed.—A preacher. The preacher and I put up in the same room. The first night he scores; the second I do.—Life of a cowboy.—A new class of cowboy.—A gentleman cowboy.—A good shooting-ground.—I shoot a puma.—A lucky sportsman 266

CHAPTER XXI.

Camp on Buffalo Creek.—Awful thunder-storms.—Two cowboys visit our camp. We return the visit.—Description of a shack.—Stories of attacks by Indians.—A buck-jumper.—A curious shot.—A refractory mare.—Loss of a horse.—A herd of wild horses. Old Bridger's opinion of them.—Camp nearly destroyed by fire.—Poisoning wild animals.—A ghost story 278

CHAPTER XXII.

Resolve to go to the Judith Basin.—Colonel P—— agrees to accompany me.—Start for Carroll.—Delay at Bismarck.—Have some shooting.—Journey by steamer up Missouri.—Land to hunt every day.—Come upon an old hunter. His history and end.—The remaining Indians concerned in the Minnesota massacre.—Arrival at Buford.—Freak of a lieutenant.—Symonds joins me.—Start with Major Reed for Judith Basin.—The ways of Indian agents described.—Join Colonel P—— in camp.—Good news of game.—Adventure with a bear.—Description of the Judith Basin.—Hunting mountain-sheep.—Reed and Bowles at home.—Visit the Crows' camp. Go with them to meet the Bannocks.—Buy a horse from the Bannocks 287

CHAPTER XXIII.

A nice-tempered horse.—A large band of elk.—Putting out baits for bears. The first a failure. The second a success.—Buy a new pony.—A good bargain.—Fishel goes for letters.—Antelope-stalking.—A useless dog.—Fishel has his ponies stolen. He and I pay a visit to the Crow Indians.—A buffalo-run with the Crows.—The Indian game of "Hand."—A visit to the ranche.—Tendoi, the chief of the Bannocks. Stories of him.—Unpleasant quarters.—How Bowles got his wife 308

CHAPTER XXIV.

Reed shoots a grizzly bear.—A splendid hunting-ground.—Wholesale massacre of deer.—The Colonel shoots a grizzly. I get one the next night.—Another bear.—Tendoi pays us a visit. His appreciation of curry.—Suspicious tracks.—Horse-thieves.—Expedition to destroy them.—Horses stampeded. The cause.—Fishel and I go and see the Crow war-dance.—Crow sham fight.—Foolish freak of an Englishman.—The war-dance. Unpleasant reflections thereat 322

CHAPTER XXV.

Symonds leaves us.—I explore the Little Snowies.—Follow the trail of a grizzly.—Try to get back to camp.—A difficult road.—A fine view.—Plenty of game.—I enjoy a siesta.—An alarming awakening.—Peculiar rocks.—Mountain-sheep.—I bag a grizzly.—Good sport.—Meet a party of white men.—The Greenhorn.—Attempt to lasso the grey.—Indian attack defeated by Greenhorn.—Stories of grizzlies.—Sheep-ranches 332

CHAPTER XXVI.

Visit Crazy Woman Mountains.—Difficult ravine.—Park-like country.—Narrow escape from a grizzly.—We make for the trade-road.—The end of my grey horse.—Some bragging hunters.—I part

company from Colonel P—— and the men.—The stage waggon.
—Dangers of stage-drivers.—A companion joins us. Queer story
about him. I ride part of the way with him.—Arrival at Miles
City.—I am offered quarters. Which I decline.—Call on General
Miles.—Stories of General Miles.—I leave Fort Keogh with the
General.—Rough Journey.—Yellowstone Kelly.—Arrival at Fort
Abraham Lincoln.—Kindness of American officers.—Road agents.
—More anecdotes of General Miles.—Arrival at Chicago.—The
present state of my old hunting-grounds.—Conclusion 348

LIST OF ILLUSTRATIONS.

	PAGE
He stopped about six feet from me and shook his fist .. .. *Frontispiece*	
Our hut in the Thickwood Hills..	33
I drew my revolver and fired at him	91
He removed his blanket, in spite of the rain, and wrapping the musket in it laid it down	139
I was surprised to see a waggon on the bank ..	149
I fired at his chest	207
The Comanches made a rush at us ..	223
My pony spun round so quickly ..	299
I saw a row of shining copper-coloured faces ..	337

SPORT AND ADVENTURES

AMONG THE

NORTH-AMERICAN INDIANS.

CHAPTER I.

Leave England.—Voyage and arrival at Quebec.—Proceed to Toronto and then to St. Paul's.—Threatened rising of the Sioux. Its causes. The storm bursts.—We start for Fort Carlton.—Description of journey.—Arrival at Fort Abercrombie.—Hostile Indians.—Reach Georgetown.—Attack on Fort Abercrombie.—Barbarity of the Indians.—Retreat in canoes.—Awful storm.—Arrival at Pembina.—Arrival at Fort Garry.—Our Guide and preparations to start.—" The early bird catches the worm."—A Red-River cart.—Leave Fort Garry.—Crossing the Saskatchawan.—Arrival at Fort Carlton.—Fight between bloodhound and wolf.—I astonish the Indians.—A boxing-match. Its consequences.—Murder at council of Indians. Its results.

I LEFT Liverpool in June 1862, by the Allan line of steamers, for Quebec, choosing this route as it was the only one which would carry dogs, as I had a young bloodhound, a son of Grantley Berkeley's celebrated dog "Druid," which I wished to try against wolves on the prairies.

While in Liverpool I met two English gentlemen, also on their way to the West, and intending, like myself, to fit out at

Fort Garry, on Lake Winnepeg, so we agreed to join company for so long as it suited us, and I will call them M—— and C—— in the following pages.

The incidents of one passage are very much like another, so I will say very little of this one. We had the usual heterogeneous collection of passengers, and the usual sweepstakes each day as to the run of the ship, and also a rather unusual one, and that was, as to which foot the pilot would place on the deck first when he came on board, there being intense excitement when he stopped on the ladder to speak to the captain. The usual whales and icebergs were seen; but nothing of any interest occurred till we reached Quebec, where we landed, having done the run in eleven days.

We went to Russell's hotel and remained there two days, visiting the citadel, the heights of Abraham, &c., and left on the third day for Toronto, where we had some friends.

From Toronto we did not stop again till we reached St. Paul's, now a city of more than four hundred thousand inhabitants; but then it was only a straggling town of four or five thousand, most of the houses being built of wood, and many of logs only. Here the railway then ended, and we had to travel by Burbank's coach to Georgetown, on the Red River, a distance of four hundred and twenty miles, where we should find a small steamer bound for Fort Garry.

The scenery round St. Paul's is very fine, the city standing on the banks of the Mississippi River, which are here about two hundred feet high, and the country round being hilly and beautifully wooded, and containing some of the loveliest lakes in the world, surrounded by woods, and so clear that you can see the pebbles distinctly at a depth of twenty-five or thirty feet.

We found a good deal of excitement in the town, as it was threatened by the Sioux Indians, under "Little Crow," who thought themselves wronged by their agent, and had begun what ended in the Minnesota massacre. It seems that the Sioux had come in to get their yearly supplies of blankets, ammunition, &c., from the Government, and found that only a portion of these having come, the agent refused to serve out anything till the arrival of the remainder. The Indians had only brought food for so many days and were soon on the verge of starvation, when one day there drove up to the agent's house a waggon drawn by four span of very fine fat oxen. A number of half-starved Indians were standing round, and one of them felt the oxen with his finger, remarking to his companions what a grand feast they would make. On this the driver hit him with his whip, and was at once shot dead by the Indian, and within five minutes the agent and his family were all murdered. This was the last straw only, as the Indians had had a good deal to complain of before this happened. They all immediately disappeared to mature their plans, and there was a lull which preceded the awful storm which broke soon afterwards. This had happened before our arrival, and all who could do so had left St. Paul's, expecting it to be attacked at any moment.

It turned out afterwards that what had delayed the outbreak was the fact that "Hole-in-the-day," the great Chippewa chief, had not been able to join the Sioux, and his tribe refused to rise without him. He had come into the town to buy ammunition, and had been seized and put in jail, where he remained till the whole thing was over, and his tribe, living all round St. Paul's, had prevented the town being attacked.

We found here about thirty Englishmen, who, having been tempted by a bubble company to subscribe forty pounds apiece on the understanding that they should be transported to the gold mines of British Columbia, had been cast adrift here, most of them without money, and we found them sweeping the streets, chopping wood, and doing any work they could find, some of them being broken-down gentlemen, and none of them ever having done any manual labour before.

In spite of much good advice as to the danger of proceeding any further, we took our places in the express waggon—a four-horse coach—which made the journey between St. Paul's and Georgetown once a week, stopping for the night at small log stage stations, where the accommodation and food were both very rough, the latter being almost invariably pork and corn bread, with very bad coffee. The first portion of the drive was through a very pretty country, and, as the driver let us get out now and then to shoot grouse and ducks, the time passed very quickly. There was, however, the chance that the Indians might attack us at any moment; so that the front seat of the waggon was a complete armoury, the driver having a revolver and a rifle beside him, and the conductor, who sat behind, being armed in the same way. The conveyance itself was like a long waggon, with three cushioned seats across it, hung on leather straps, which were very long, and caused it to sway a good deal from side to side, the whole having a cover on "bows," which could be rolled up; the luggage being placed behind, where there was also a small seat for the conductor. The teams were very good indeed, but often quite new to the work, and unused to being driven four-in-hand, so that sometimes they would run away, and we flew along over the prairie, the driver whipping instead of trying to stop them; the ground being so level that they were invariably tired before we came to a bad bit of ground. After leaving the woods and getting on the prairies the journey became very monotonous, the only houses we came across being the one where we dined, and our night's halting-place.

At about one hundred and twenty miles from Georgetown we stopped for the night at Fort Abercrombie—a two-company post, where the soldiers were almost all of them Germans. Of course, the whole conversation here was about Indians, and they were expecting an attack, Indian scouts having been seen on the surrounding hills for some days. The officer in command was somewhat doubtful of the courage of his men, most of them being recruits; but he had strengthened the defences, and had placed two small guns in position.

On the second day from the Fort we reached Georgetown, a very small place, of some ten or twelve log houses and a large stage station, which we found almost deserted by all but the stage agent and his men, all the settlers having gone down the Red River in flat boats, as some Indians had been seen in the neighbourhood. The stage agent—a very plucky fellow—declared that he would remain alone, if necessary, and defend the company's property, and we offered to remain and help him, but circumstances rendered this unnecessary.

The day after our arrival came the news of the attack on Fort Abercrombie and of the massacre of a number of settlers throughout Minnesota. It seems that the commanding officer's fears about the courage of his men were justified; for when the Indians made a rush at the place, they retreated into a block-house, which stood in the middle of the fort, and was meant to be used only in the last extremity, and out of this they refused to come, till the officers and a few American soldiers drove them out with their revolvers; the place being saved by the two guns, which frightened the Indians by the noise they made. Some of the settlers had been murdered under circumstances of awful barbarity, and one poor woman crawled seven miles into Fort Abercrombie with her nose, ears, and both breasts cut off.

On the morning of the second day from our arrival at the station, orders came from the company at St. Paul's for the agent to close the station, and make his way to the nearest town with the horses, and we heard, just before leaving, that the coach immediately following the one by which we had come had been attacked by Indians, and the conductor killed, the mails being thrown into the Red River. This made our staying at the station any longer an impossibility; so finding that the steamboat which usually ran between this place and Fort Garry had ceased to do so, owing to the unsafe state of the country, we bought two bark canoes, and, laying in some provisions, we started for a four hundred mile paddle down one of the most crooked and, I should say, muddiest streams in the world; there being hardly a place on its banks where you could land without sinking to your knees in black mud.

Canoe travelling was a new experience to all of us, and we were very nearly upsetting a great many times, as the canoes were round-bottomed and very light. At the time I am speaking of, the banks of the Red River were entirely uninhabited, and the course of it is mostly through vast prairies, making it very monotonous, especially as we often paddled for an hour and more, only to find ourselves within a few hundred yards of where we started from, the river having wound in almost a complete circle. For some days nothing of any consequence happened. We saw a few antelope and might have stalked them, but we were afraid to fire; so we lived on pork and coffee: the weather was fine; but about the fifth day we had an awful thunder-storm, such as none of us had ever seen. It came on at night, just as we were going to camp, and the rain came down in such sheets that, having no tent, we sat where we were and baled out the water, or we should have sunk. The thunder seemed just overhead, and the lightning was all but incessant and lasted till nearly morning, when we landed and waded through the mud to higher ground, where we wrung the water from our blankets and went to sleep. In the morning the sun came out and nearly dried our clothes, when a second storm came on and soaked everything again, and we had another miserable night on the same spot. The second day was fine, so we started again, feeling very miserable. All our baggage was damp, and our guns one mass of rust; our hands, too, being unused to paddling, were very much blistered. We struggled on, however, and about the ninth day reached Pembina, a small settlement with a custom-house, it being on the frontier between Canada and the United States.

We found the place deserted by everyone but the United States' custom-house agent, who had sent away his family, and had fortified the upper storey of his house, destroying the staircase, and going up and down by means of a ladder at a window, drawing it up at night. He had a bed covered with weapons, with the ammunition for each lying beside it, and would, no doubt, have sold his life dearly; but I am glad to say that he was not attacked, and was still at his post when the place was visited by the troops, who left a garrison there.

Soon after leaving Pembina we were very glad to meet with the steamer, which had come as far as this and was waiting for news, and now, on hearing what had happened, the captain decided on turning back and remaining at the fort till all was quiet once more.

Fort Garry was then a long straggling settlement, of about three thousand inhabitants, extending some ten miles up the Red River and about the same distance up the Assineboine River, the fort being built at the junction of the two. Most of the inhabitants were half-breeds, many of whom were married to Indian wives; so that the place was a curious mixture of an Indian camp and a white settlement, the wives' relations being very often camped round the houses of half-breeds. There was no hotel of any kind; so we put up a tent, which we bought, in the garden of one of the principal half-breeds, who had been recommended to us as a guide. This man's name was Louis Laronde, and he was considered the best guide and snow-shoe walker, as well as the strongest man, in the settlement.

For several days we were very busy engaging men and in buying horses, there being a good deal of competition among us as to who should have the best; and I remember that I got up once in the middle of the night and rode nearly forty miles to buy a horse, which was said to be the fastest in the settlement. We had all heard of him, but kept it to ourselves, as each one meant to get up early the next morning and go and buy him; but by that time I had him tied close to the tent door.

In the evenings we went to some half-breed balls, and found many of the women were very handsome, chiefly those who were the children of half-breeds, with no more admixture of Indian blood. Anywhere else you would have taken them for Spaniards; the only thing which spoiled them was their hair, which was always very straight and coarse.

At last our outfit was ready. We had two ponies apiece and three small carts between us, each drawn by a single ox, as we had been told that they went better through mud than ponies. Each cart contained a thousand pounds' weight; and the way in which the loads were adjusted was somewhat unusual, Laronde getting under the axle on his hands and knees, and raising the whole thing off the ground. We soon found that we had made a mistake in taking oxen, as they only did a mile and a half an hour, and riding with the carts was simply purgatory; so we exchanged them for ponies before we got out of the settlement.

A Red-River cart is an extraordinary structure; it stands on two wheels, and is made without a single piece of iron in its whole composition; the wheels have no tyres, and the felloes are fastened on with wooden wedges. The axles are of wood, and two spare ones are carried by each cart, as they wear out quickly; and there being no boxes to the wheels, I leave my readers to imagine the noise they make, this pleasant music being audible for miles.

When once out of Fort Garry, we passed very few houses, and those only during the first thirty miles, when they ceased altogether, and an undulating prairie country was spread out on all sides of us. Scattered over this were an immense number of ponds, some of them almost deserving the name of lakes, and these were always covered with geese and ducks, while snipe could generally be found round their edges, and you now and then put up a few swans, affording splendid sport, and making a very pleasant change from everlasting ham, which was the only kind of preserved meat which we could get at Fort Garry.

Wolves were very common, one or more being generally in sight, and we had many chases after them with the bloodhound, but, as he was young, he never did anything. When after the wolves one day, I had a very nasty fall. I was going down a hill at full speed, when my pony put his foot in a hole, and over we went, describing, as it seemed to me, at least three summersaults, and, as I was carrying a heavy ten-bore gun by a strap on my back, each time I turned over the gun hit me on the back of the head, raising a bump as big as an egg, and obliging me to sit some minutes before I could take in the situation and find out which way to ride home again.

We saw no big game, except wolves, till near Fort Carlton, when we made out a band of antelope with a glass, and one elk, which was, however, on the other side of the Saskatchawan, at a place where we could not cross.

Our first trouble was crossing the south fork of this river, the stream being swift and deep and about eighty yards wide. The carts being constructed entirely of wood formed a good raft, and as they were loosely made, we had only to remove the bottom boards and arrange them as a platform on the sides, and towing this over with a long rope, everything was got over safely; but when it came to the horses, we had some trouble, most of them refusing to enter the water; so that we had to drag them down and push them in, keeping them from landing again by pelting them with stones, and in this manner we managed to get them over to the other side, swimming over ourselves. From where we crossed the river to Fort Carlton was twenty miles, and we reached it safely. We found it to be a square stockade, about twenty feet high, having a bastion at each corner, while all round the inside ran a platform, some five feet from the top, to enable the defenders to fire upon any assailants.

There were small guns in the fort, but more for show than use. Mr. L——, a Scotchman, was in charge, and received us very hospitably. He put us all up, and our animals were turned out with the fort herd. We had piles of buffalo robes as beds and found them very comfortable, spreading our own blankets on the top.

We remained here a few days to recruit ourselves after our long ride, which had been made more tedious by the slow pace at which we had been obliged to travel so as to keep with the carts, as there was always the chance of an attack by Indians.

My bloodhound had as yet been of no use, and I began to fear that he had no pluck, as he would not face the sleigh-dogs at the fort, always keeping close at my heels when we went out and never leaving the house by himself. These sleigh-dogs were large animals, many of them being as heavy as he was, and numbered about a hundred. They had nothing to do in the summer, but took the place of the horses when the snow had fallen. They were of every colour and size, and were chiefly bred from Indian dogs crossed with Esquimaux, and any looks they might have had were spoilt by cutting off their tails, which got in the way of their harness.

Hearing one day that the sleigh-dogs had a wolf at bay in a bush near the fort, I took my bloodhound out and, driving off the other dogs, I let him go, when he at once rushed in and closed with the wolf, and for some time it was doubtful which would get the best of it, till the hound getting a chance seized the wolf by the throat and very soon killed him.

While we were at Fort Carlton we frequently had shooting matches, some Indians who had come in to trade shooting with us; and when coming back to the fort one day, with a double rifle in my hand, which I wished to fire off, I saw a crow coming over my head and fired at it, and no one was more astonished than I was when it fell dead, and from that day, as I firmly refused to waste any more ammunition on crows, I found that I had gained a wonderful reputation as a shot among the Indians—hearing of what I had done many months afterwards in an Indian camp.

We found at the "Post"—as all forts are usually called—a Scotchman named Alexander, who having tried a great many things and failed at all of them, had ended by becoming a Hudson's Bay Company's clerk, at twenty-four pounds a year and his food. Having some relics of his departed greatness yet with him, he went about in an old velvet dressing-jacket, bound with gold cord, with a cap of the same material on his head, and being a fine man and very handsome, he looked quite imposing and was the admiration of all the squaws.

One day I heard a story of him, which is worth inserting here. It seems that the Sioux and Cree Indians wished to make peace, and it had been arranged that they should do so at the Post. Accordingly the Sioux chief "White Cloud" arrived with seventeen warriors and camped outside the stockade, the Crees having also sent a deputation to meet him, and while the preparations were being completed, "White Cloud"—who was a splendidly-made Indian, standing over six feet in his moccasins, with a really fine face—almost lived in the fort. He was one day in Alexander's room, when the latter took up some boxing-gloves and put them on, telling "White Cloud" that these were the things with which the white man learned to fight, asking the chief if he would like to put them on. "White Cloud" of course had no idea of what would happen; for Indians never hit with the hands, and to hit one of them is to insult him most grossly. "White Cloud" said he should like to try them; so Alexander first took away his knife and pistol and locked them up; then putting him in the middle of the room and telling him to stand on his guard, he knocked him to the other end of it, and on his rising and rushing at Alexander, he was again sent to the same place. His rage, I was told, more resembled madness, and, tearing off the gloves, he tried to get his knife from the drawer; but finding it locked, he suddenly calmed down, or seemed to do so, and demanded to be let out. Alexander asked him what he would do when outside, when "White Cloud" told him that he and his men would instantly attack the fort and kill everyone in it.

Seeing that only desperate measures would have a chance of succeeding here, Alexander took a revolver from a drawer, and told the chief that unless he promised, within five minutes, to give up his intention and make friends, he would shoot him and chance what came of it. For some minutes "White Cloud" was obstinate, and then seeing that Alexander meant what he said, and being somewhat tempted by some presents which were promised him, he shook hands and, receiving his pistol and knife, left the room, carrying with him two bottles of whiskey, for which an Indian will do anything, and which they have no means of getting in the Hudson's Bay territories, as they forbid its sale to the Indians. Though never friendly again with Alexander, the chief kept his word, and no harm resulted from this foolish joke.

This chief showed me sometime afterwards some fourteen or fifteen wounds which he had received in battle, most of them being from knives and arrows, leading his followers to believe that he could not be killed. In consequence of this and of his great courage and strength, his authority over them, even in time of peace, was something wonderful. On one occasion his men were in the Post and had been giving a good deal of trouble by quarrelling with the employés, when Mr. L—— went to "White Cloud" and asked him to order them out. He went at once out into the yard in front of the Post and blew his war whistle, and when his men came running out of the different houses, he simply pointed to the gate in an imperious way, and they were all out in a moment. Happening to go into the kitchen soon afterwards, he found one of his men eating a meal which the cook had given him, on which he picked up a log of wood and knocked him down senseless, remarking that he hoped he had killed him, and this man, when he recovered from the blow, seemed to owe him no grudge.

Mr. L—— told me that when the meeting took place at which peace was to be made, what was intended for a friendly meeting very nearly ended in a fight. It seems that a Cree warrior, who was not among the number admitted into the council lodge, owed one of the Sioux a grudge; so, first ascertaining whereabouts he sat, and finding that his back was only a few inches from the skin of the lodge, he stabbed him in the back from the outside. Of course, there was immediately an uproar, the Sioux thinking that they would at once be murdered, as the Crees outnumbered them ten to one; but the Cree chief rushed to the door of the lodge and stood in front of it, barring the way, and ordered the murderer to be brought to him at once, and on his appearance, and when he had owned to the deed, he brained him with his tomahawk on the spot.

Such acts as these occur very seldom among what are called "Wild Indians," though when semi-civilized they are heard of frequently.

CHAPTER II.

Leave Fort Carlton.—Swimming horses.—Our first buffalo.—Laronde's method of killing buffalo.—Our first meeting with wild Indians.—Attempt to stalk antelope.—Immense herds of buffalo.—A run with buffaloes.—I run down a wolf.—Sudden appearance of three Indians.—An unpleasant adventure.—A night in an Indian lodge.—Rejoin my companions.—The advantages of steel hobbles.—Studying a buffalo at close quarters.—Prairie-dogs.—Return to Fort Carlton.—Our Party breaks up.—I leave for Thickwood Hills.—Sleigh-dogs.

AFTER remaining at Fort Carlton five or six days, we started once more, going south, intending to cross the south branch of the Saskatchawan River, and hunt between that and the Missouri in the neighbourhood of the Milk River. Crossing was as troublesome as before, a new horse we had bought utterly refusing to swim at all, so that after we got him in, he was carried down by the stream, and had he not reached a sand-bar, he must have been drowned. As it was we had to make a small raft and tow him across, holding his head above water.

One of my horses was so fond of swimming that I had to watch him when I took him to drink, or he would jump in and swim, and more than once he wetted all I had on him by doing so.

The first buffalo we met with was a great excitement to us all, though he was a miserable old fellow whom we would not have touched a week later. All the large herds had been driven south that summer, and many solitary old bulls had been left behind as worthless, this being one of them.

We had started early in the morning, having found fresh buffalo sign, and were all of us mounted on our best horses, meaning to have a struggle for first blood. My horse was the fastest, but M—— had one nearly as fast, and an old hand at the work, knowing as much about it as any man. This horse, having been carefully trained by Laronde, knew exactly the position to take up when chasing a buffalo, ranging up close to him on the off side, with his head opposite to the buffalo's quarters, so that when the animal charged he passed behind him to the left, and the buffalo had to turn completely round to follow him, by which time the horse was safe. We came on this bull suddenly on riding over some rising ground, and were not more than 200 yards from him. We were none of us ready, our guns being slung on our backs, but away we went helter-skelter, each man doing his best and getting his gun ready for action. I had a double ten-bore shot-gun, a muzzle-loader, and I do not suppose I could have had a worse weapon for the purpose; but breech-loaders were only just then coming into use, and the only one I had was a new one, and I did not like to risk it over rough ground. M—— had a 16-bore breech-loading gun, carrying ball, and C—— a single breech-loading rifle.

For the first quarter of a mile we were nearly neck and neck, and then my horse began to forge ahead, and I saw that I should have the first shot. I was soon alongside (for a good horse can very soon overhaul a buffalo) and fired, aiming well forward as I had been told to do, missing him clean and cutting up the dust in front of him. I was now a little in front of the bull, which putting his tail up charged me, and for a few seconds seemed to be awfully near, I climbing on the front of the saddle, as all "tenderfeet" do under such circumstances, having the idea that I was getting faster out of the animal's reach. As I got away and tried to turn my horse for a second shot, I saw M—— range up and fire, hitting the buffalo, which stumbled and stood still for a moment, and then seeing C—— close to him he made a desperate rush at him, and the two disappeared over a rise in the prairie, it seemed to me within three feet of one another.

On regaining control of my horse, I rode after them and found M—— and C—— standing over the bull, which it seems M—— had killed, and we decided that as he was old and thin, we would only take the tongue, this being always good eating. We had not been shown how to do this, so we supposed it was done from the mouth, and with great trouble we prized the jaws open, putting a wooden stirrup to keep them so, and then pulled at the tongue, only succeeding in getting about three quarters of it, and even this very much hacked about; the proper way being to set the animal's head nose in the air, by sticking the horns in the ground, and then to cut the skin from the under side of the jaw and take the tongue out from below, and in this way it is very easily done.

We found no more buffalo that day, but we got Laronde to go with us on the morrow, and soon came across a small band of five cows and two calves. Laronde went on ahead of us, as we had slower horses than the day before, and he had his old horse, which M—— had ridden on the previous day, and before we could come up with him he had four buffaloes down, three cows and a calf, and yet he was using a single muzzle-loading flint-lock gun, called a trade gun, and costing in London seven and sixpence. His plan was as follows :—The powder was in a bag carried on his belt and the bullets were in his mouth. He would put in half a handful of powder, and then drop in a wet ball, giving the gun a slap, to drive the ball home and the powder into the enormous pan, when he would lower the gun and fire at once, the muzzle being within a foot of the buffalo; and aiming just under the spine at the small of the back, the animal was down at once and could not rise again. I got one of the calves and C—— another cow. M——'s horse behaved badly and would not stand fire.

We should not have killed so many had we not been close to a camp of Crees, to whom we gave the meat and they gave us in exchange two wolf-skins. These were the first Indians that I had a good opportunity of seeing close, and I came to the conclusion that they were much better when not seen too near. M—— and I slept in a lodge one night, and we had to work hard to rid ourselves of the consequences.

One morning a small band of antelopes came near camp, and while they were examining it very curiously, not having our wind, C—— and I crept out and tried to stalk them. It was a bare prairie, but there were hollows here and there, deep enough to hide us, and with infinite trouble and much loss of skin from our knees (the prairie having been burnt in the spring and consequently covered with sharp stubs) we got within about two hundred yards. Here we pulled up some grass which we stuck in our hat-bands, and held up some in our hands in the form of a fan, and in this way we made another fifty yards, when seeing the antelope were beginning to get suspicious, we both of us fired, the only result being that something seemed to fall from one of them, and on reaching the spot we found a straight line of white hair, the only explanation of which was that the antelope C—— fired at, having stood broadside to him, he must have made a very bad shot, and his bullet grazed the animal behind, where he is covered with white hair, and cut off a line of it. I had made a clean miss, I suppose from excitement.

For some days we saw only scattered buffaloes, but as we approached the Missouri they were in good sized bands, and towards evening one day, we saw an immense number of them in the distance. It being too late to do much that day, we camped, and busied ourselves all the evening in getting things ready for a run on the following morning.

Laronde gave us a great deal of advice as to how we ought to behave under all imaginable circumstances, but in the excitement of a run, who can think of all this? and it would not be half so much fun if you could remember all your instructions; the getting into scrapes and out of them in your own way being the best part of it.

Early the next morning we were off, M—— and C—— armed as they were before, but I carried my twelve-bore breech-loader, having found it impossible to load the other gun on horseback without pulling up. The herd was where we had seen it on the previous evening, and by reconnoitring from a high mound we found a small ravine, and riding down it we got within about four hundred yards of the "pickets," as we called the old fellows, who were on all the high ground and were evidently guarding the herd.

As there was no further cover we came out of the ravine, and made for the buffaloes at a sharp gallop; they allowed us to get a hundred yards nearer, and then went off at what looked like a clumsy canter, but was really a pretty good pace. A race of a mile laid us alongside of the hindermost, but we were riding that day to get into the herd and see how they looked at close quarters, so urging our horses to do their best, and shouting to clear a road, into the middle of the mass we went, it being rather nervous work, as they could not scatter much at once, the outside of the herd not knowing what the matter was on account of the dust, which was awful. After being among them for some minutes the panic seemed to spread, and the mass scattered right and left, going off in two bands, and we pulled up and let them go, as we had plenty of meat in camp and did not come out to kill. I think this was the most exciting gallop I ever had, being my first, and not knowing how the animals might behave. It is curious to watch the tail of a buffalo while you are running him. It hangs down when you start and remains so for perhaps half a mile, then it begins to rise in the air by a series of little jerks, and when it is erect and the end begins to shake the head will go down, and he is going to charge, in which case, after running from him for thirty or forty yards, if you turn off at right angles, he will almost invariably go straight on and leave you.

C—— was once chased for more than a mile by an infuriated bull, as his pony was slow and only just able to keep ahead of the bull.

As Laronde told me that my horse had run into a wolf on the open prairie, I determined to try and do it again; so I started alone one day and tried all the high grass I could find, but saw no wolves, but as I was going back to camp one came on to the top of a ridge close to me, not knowing that I was so near, so I put my horse to his best and raced after him; I did not gain a yard during the first mile, but went gradually up to him in the second, and after he had thrown me out twice by turning suddenly, I rode right over him, and fired as I passed, hitting him and wounding him slightly, but I caught him very easily the second time and killed him. This sort of thing does not answer, however, when your horses are doing hard work and have no food but grass, so I did not do it again.

I tried the bloodhound several times after wolves, but he only caught one, and then we were not with him, as he had worn us all out and run away from us. He came back, however, in the evening with his jaws covered with blood and with marks of bites on him, so altogether he was a failure, especially as he hated the very sight of an Indian, and had to be tied up when any were in camp or he would have attacked them at once.

One evening we were startled by the arrival of three Indians in camp. It was getting dark, but we had not yet put on our first guard, so they took us entirely by surprise, coming in on foot so quietly that no one saw them till they were standing by the fire. They were apparently Assineboines, but had Sioux moccasins; these have a raw hide sole, while the Crees and Assineboines make theirs without a separate sole, the same leather going all round. They told us that they had lost their way, and seeing the fire had come to it. This was an utterly impossible story, and no one looking at their villainous faces would have believed that they did not come for some bad purpose. Their being on foot, too, was a very suspicious circumstance, as an Indian never walks on the prairie, unless he is going to steal a horse.

After they had had some supper they said they would go, but this our guide would not permit, telling them that they must remain till morning, and if they tried to go before then they would be shot, so they remained very unwillingly and lay by the fire all night. Had we let them go, they would probably have visited us again before morning, and have tried to run off our horses.

I had one unpleasant adventure before the end of the summer; I had been running buffalo, and had killed two old bulls after a very long run, during which I had turned so many times, that when I had taken the tongues I found I did not know the way back to camp. It was beginning to get dark as I took the second tongue, and I at once started in the direction in which I thought the camp was, but I had not ridden far when a snowstorm came on, making my chance of finding camp very doubtful. However, I rode on for about an hour, when I was wet through, and so cold that I had to get off and lead my pony.

For some miles I trudged on, firing my gun every now and then and stopping to listen for an answering shot; but hearing nothing, and as my pony was tired, I thought I would light a fire and remain by it until the morning, so at the next willow bushes I came to, I cut some of the driest-looking of them, and striking a match tried to light a fire; but everything was very wet and would not burn, so after I had struck some twenty matches without avail, I gave it up, and started again, firing occasionally till the priming of my gun got wet and it would not go off, when I had to content myself with shouting. As I was passing under a small hill I fancied my shouts were answered, and on looking up, I could, very indistinctly, make out some white figures standing on the top of it, and I at first thought it might be my companions, but on getting near I saw it was a party of about ten Indians, who beckoned me to follow them to some tents, which I now saw on the opposite side of the hill. They might have been " hostiles " for all I knew, but it was too late to go back, so I walked down after them, and giving my pony to an Indian, I went into one of the tents, being so miserable that I did not much care who they were, so long as I could get near a fire and have something to eat.

About twenty more Indians came in to have a look at me, and all of them shook hands, which was a good sign. I was given a big plateful of boiled buffalo-meat and some tea, and soon felt much better. I then made signs that I wished to change my clothes, which were soaking wet, and put on a blanket, and that the women had better go out while I did so, on which they all laughed, and the women crowded round and helped me to undress, pinching and slapping me when they had done so. They gave me a buffalo robe and blanket, which latter I put on Indian fashion, and felt almost one of themselves.

I soon turned in, hoping to have a good night, or rather morning, for it was now nearly five A.M. But alas! for the plans of mice and men! I had not quite gone off to sleep when I began to feel something biting me, and this feeling spread till I fancied I must be on fire, so I jumped up and found that it was only the usual inhabitants of an Indian's buffalo robe feasting on something softer than they usually got. On my telling the Indians what the matter was they laughed, and said I should soon get used to it; but not believing this I got up and put on some of my half-dried garments, and lay down again thinking that now my troubles were over, instead of which they were only beginning.

There are some few peculiarities about an Indian camp which very much interfere with the repose of anyone who is not used to them. The first thing which woke me once more was the pressure of the feet of some animals passing over me; then came a number of others of the same kind, and these seemed to go round and round the tent. It struck me almost immediately that they were dogs hunting for scraps, so I pulled my robe closer round me and dosed off again. Presently, however, I heard a yell followed by a rush, and the dogs passed over me again, followed by a furious squaw, whose big flat feet were not at all particular where they trod; and this happened several times till I felt as if I was lying in the sawdust of a circus, with the whole performance going on on the top of me. I moved at once, getting as close to the side of the lodge as I could, or I should have been flattened out, squaws as a rule being very clumsy and heavy. What made the chase last so long was the difficulty of finding the door, which was small, and as it was dark outside, did not show at all.

On the departure of the dogs, I thought I should have peace, but I was mistaken; the noise had woke up an Indian, who fancied that he could, with an effort, eat a little more, so he proceeded to get up and cook some meat on the fire in the centre of the lodge, and thinking he had a fine voice which should be cultivated, he sang all the time. This roused a second Indian to do the same thing, and it was almost morning when I really got off to sleep.

Sometimes there are other pleasant surprises for the visitor to a lodge, such as a disconsolate widow, going round the camp bewailing her lost husband, which she is supposed to do for six months, unless she gets another in the meantime. He may have beaten her every day with a lodge-pole, and she may have been delighted to have got rid of him, but she must nevertheless go through this performance, and it is always done at night. Then, too, some Indian often gets up and sings for an hour or more, beating an accompaniment on a tom-tom, and no one thinks of sending for a policeman or of shooting him, as would seem natural.

In the morning five or six of the Indians mounted and rode with me, seeming to know where our camp must be, from being acquainted with all the water-holes in the country, most of the small streams being now dry, and within an hour we met three of our men coming to hunt for me.

The Indians accompanied us to camp, from which I had been distant only about four miles, where I made them a number of presents and they left apparently very contented; but I met some of them afterwards at Fort Carlton, where they calmly informed me that for several days after seeing me to camp they had followed us, meaning to steal our horses, and said that they would have had them if a snowstorm had not hidden our tracks, so that they lost us. They owned that we kept very good guard, as they had lain and watched us for hours hoping for a chance, but did not get one, as we brought the horses in before dark and tied them to the waggon.

I had brought steel hobbles with me from England to lock on

at night made of case-hardened iron, and these, on one occasion, gave me a great deal of trouble. Seeing great quantities of ducks in some ponds near camp, one of my companions and I had our horses left for us, the waggon going on, and remained to have a day's duck-shooting. We had capital sport and returned to camp loaded, to find that my horse had been left with the hobbles on, while the key had gone on with the waggon. We tried breaking them with a stone, but found it to be impossible, as we could not get a good blow at them; so I had to wait with the horse till far into the night, while my companion rode after the waggon, nearly twenty miles, and sent one of the men back with the key.

Soon after this we returned to Fort Carlton, only one incident worth relating occurring on the way. I had run an old bull some little distance, when we came to a narrow " groove " in the prairie, looking almost like an old watercourse, and when the buffalo went down this I remained on the bank above, keeping parallel with him. After going a few hundred yards, the hollow came to an abrupt end, forming a perfect *cul-de-sac*, the banks being about ten feet high and quite perpendicular. Here I got off my horse, and sitting on the edge pelted the bull with earth; and he kept rushing at the bank, bringing down at each charge showers of dust and stones. It was a splendid opportunity for watching a live buffalo at close quarters, and I remained there and ate my lunch, after which I rode off and left him.

In this part of the country there were immense numbers of prairie-dogs, whose towns extend sometimes for thirty or forty miles, and make the prairie very unsafe to ride over on account of their numerous burrows. They are very amusing little fellows, and barked at us and shook themselves as if in a furious rage at our trespassing on their territories; and dived down into their holes the instant we came too near. They are so quick that they can duck at the flash of a gun without being hit by the shot, and we only got one, though we often fired at them. A friend of mine, an officer in the American Army, drowned some out by pouring water into their holes, but then he had about a hundred soldiers to help him.

On reaching Fort Carlton our party broke up, my companions going forty miles north of the Fort, where they put up a cabin, while I engaged a half-breed, named Badger, and his wife, and started for the Thickwood Hills, about ninety miles North-west of Fort Carlton, where I intended to pass the winter. Mr. L—— kindly allowed us to buy winter supplies at the Fort, it being the rule that nothing but furs should be received in exchange for supplies. Everything is valued at so many skins per pound or yard, as the case may be; the skin referred to being that of a beaver, which is here valued at two shillings, all more valuable furs being worth so many beaver.

Before leaving the Post, I bought the best team of sleigh-dogs they had there, giving a double rifle in exchange for them, and I also got a second team, paying for them in money.

When winter has once set in in these regions, horses are useless, the snow falling to a depth of from two to three feet in the open, and from seven to eight feet in the woods, where it has no chance of melting, and all travelling must then be done with dogs. I also bought two sleighs, and some elk-skins and brass wire for making harness, the latter being used to stiffen the collars. Having completed all our arrangements, we wished everyone good-bye and started for our winter-quarters.

CHAPTER III.

Scenery in the Thickwood Hills.—Building huts.—Tom Boot. His size and strength.—Our nearest neighbour.—Visit the South Saskatchawan.—Large Camp of Crees.—A Sioux Indian prisoner. His trial and fate. Attempts to save him.—We leave the Camp.—Return journey.—Dreadful spectacle.—Setting in of winter. Severe cold.—Description of trapping in winter.—Unpleasant adventure with Indians. Tom Boot to the rescue. His prowess.—A-ta-ka-koup makes friends.—Snow-shoe travelling.—A visit from Driver.

We had sent all our carts but one back to Fort Garry, as they were useless to us in the winter, and on this one we piled our winter supplies—tent, clothing, bedding, &c.,—with the two sleighs on the top, and I had hired an ox at the Post to draw it, as no pony could have done so. It was ninety miles to where we intended wintering, and this took us four days to do, as our load was so heavy and the country very wet and muddy; my man's wife, too, who had intended to walk, gave in, and had to be put on the top of the cart with her child, which did not improve matters much.

As we got nearer the Thickwood Hills, the country improved in appearance. The first fifty miles was along the river, through prairie, but after that we got among trees, chiefly pine, with lovely little prairies scattered through them making charming camping-grounds. At last we reached a place where there was a small opening in the trees, with a fine spring on one side of it—a perfect place for a house, so here we decided to erect our cabin.

We first of all put up the tent and a house made of boughs for my man and his wife, and then marked off a space, twenty feet by sixteen, clearing off the brush and levelling it; and then came the hardest part of our work, that is, cutting the logs. My man Badger was a good hand with an axe, but I was new to that kind of work, and found it very hard. We had drawn a plan of the house, making it of rather too elaborate a pattern, having gable ends, which are a great deal of trouble to build; and a house thus built is not any more comfortable than the common form of log house, which is made as follows:—You first put up a frame of logs, notched where they cross one another so as to let them lie close, and of the required dimensions, making the back of the house higher by two logs than the front. Out of this you cut what doors and windows you require. You then make the roof by sloping small straight poles from the lower to the higher side, and cover them with grass and a foot of earth, putting cross poles to keep it all on; and after making your doors and windows your house is finished on the outside, the only things remaining to be done being the chimney and floor, the former of these being always a difficulty.

We got on very slowly with our house, and were wondering how we were going to raise the higher logs, when an immense half-breed called Tom Boot happened to come along, and we engaged him to help us. This man being six feet seven inches high, and the biggest man in every way I ever saw, could lift a log by himself which Badger and I staggered under, and our house was soon built.

We made a door of a portion of our cart, and put in a parchment window made of deer-hide, inserting one small pane of glass, the only one they could spare me at the Fort, in the middle of it; then we made some very rough stools and a table out of more of the cart, and put down a floor of pine-logs, each log making one board, as we had no saw—a plan I cannot recommend, as being on economical principles.

Then came the chimney. Oh! that chimney! I think it took as long to build as the whole house. We would get it up about halfway, and in the morning find that it had fallen down again in the night. There were no stones about and no proper clay, so we had to work grass into the mud to make it stand. We made it across a corner, as being easier to build there, and left a large space for a fire, five feet square, in which we had some splendid ones during the winter. Why it did not take fire I cannot imagine, as we had put in any number of sticks to keep it up, and there was as much grass as mud in its composition.

We did not make any bunks such as are usual in log cabins, preferring beds on the floor made of the buffalo-skins which we had got during the summer, with our blankets on the top.

Our next task was to cut a lot of wood for the winter; and Tom Boot was splendid at this, a seven-pound axe being a mere hatchet in his hands, and we also put up a meat-stage and a small store-house. This done we began to look about us and see what neighbours we had, and found that we had only one within calling distance, and that he was a Cree called A-ta-ka-koup, which means the "spirit of the blanket;" he was very much married, having three wives and no end of children.

We made a call, Badger going with me as interpreter, but found them all away on their autumn buffalo-hunt, to lay in meat and tallow for the winter: however, they came back a few days afterwards and returned our call, coming a party of twenty or more, and stayed an unfashionably long time, being with us nearly all day and eating two meals, making an awful hole in our supplies, especially in the sugar-bag, out of which I could not keep the children's fingers.

Having made things fairly comfortable, we determined to pay another visit to the South Saskatchawan to get a supply of meat, as the weather was now cold, and the meat would keep until spring, freezing so hard that you could kill a man with a strip of it. We took two ponies for packing, hired from A-ta-ka-koup, and we each rode another; and on the third day we arrived at the camp of Badger's father-in-law, a Cree Indian, whose name was Mis-ta-wa-sis, or "the buffalo," where we remained two days.

Old Mis-ta-wa-sis was also well supplied with wives, having three of them, and lived in an immense buffalo-skin lodge, in which, besides his own family, there was room for two of his sons-in-law and their families, and still there was plenty of room for us; it was one of the few clean lodges I was ever in. He and I got to be very friendly, by the help of signs, and I promised to visit him again as we came back.

Two days' more travelling brought us to the South Saskatchawan, both this and the main river being solidly frozen over, so that we had no difficulty in crossing, and here we found a

Page 30.—Our hut in the Thickwood Hills.

large camp of Crees who were much excited about the capture of a Sioux Indian by some members of the tribe; the Sioux and Crees being once more at war, as the peace which had been made at Fort Carlton had lasted only one summer.

On our arrival we were given a small lodge by an Indian, who turned one of his wives out of it, and when we had put our saddles, packs, &c. in it and placed a boy to watch them, we went to pay a visit to " Big Bear " the head chief. We found him in his lodge, holding a council as to what should be done with the Sioux, and he hardly noticed us till this was over, when he informed me through Badger, on my inquiring as to the man's fate, that he was to be tortured on the next day but one. I remonstrated and offered to buy him of them, giving everything I had with me, but to no purpose, and I left vowing vengeance which I had no means of executing.

On the following morning I got leave to see the prisoner, whom I found to be almost a boy, very small and weak-looking but perfectly calm, though he had been told what his fate was to be. Badger managed to make him understand that I was trying to save him, on which he shook hands with me, but seemed to think he must die.

I went to see the chief again in the afternoon, and had a long talk with him, adding to my previous offers if he would let me have the Sioux, but he assured me he had really no power in the matter. During the night I went near the lodge several times in which the Sioux was confined, hoping to get him out in the dark, but always found it guarded, and was ordered back.

In the morning we left the camp, as we did not wish to see the torturing done, and late at night we reached a small band of Chippewas who were out on a hunt, and remained with them three days—seeing a good many buffaloes, but finding the running very bad, as there had been a light fall of snow, so all holes were covered, and I got one very bad fall in consequence. We loaded all the ponies with meat, and started on our return journey leading them, and on the morning of the third day we reached the Cree camp once more and found it deserted; but in the middle of it stood a big stake to which was bound all that remained of the Sioux prisoner, and a horrible sight it was. They had cut off his hands and feet with Indian hatchets, taking perhaps ten or twelve blows for each limb; then he was scalped, his tongue was cut out, and one of his feet was forced into his mouth, which had been slit to admit it, and he was stuck full of small spikes of wood, most of these horrible tortures, I was afterwards told, being done by the women. We buried him as well as we could with our hunting-knives, and proceeding on our journey reached home safely, stopping a few minutes with old Mis-ta-wa-sis on the way. Everything was just as we had left it, A-ta-ka-koup having been in charge, and I do not think that anyone had been in the house.

The winter set in soon after this, and we had furious snow-storms and the wind howled in the tops of the trees, though where we were we did not feel it. This time we passed in making dog-harness and mending our clothes, the former being slow work, as it is made of three thicknesses of elk-skin. I found that stockings were of no use, one's feet freezing in them. All the Hudson's Bay men use long strips of a very thick flannel called duffle, which is wrapped round the foot up to the ankle. Of this you carry a fresh supply, and the strips you have on must be taken off and dried when they become the least damp, or you will have frozen feet.

After the snow was down we had delightful weather, as bright as in summer, and there being no wind the cold was not unpleasant, though the thermometer sometimes fell to over 50° below zero. Big game was scarce, as it was unusually cold, and most of the deer and elk had moved south; but we managed to kill several early in the winter, and had fair luck when trapping, getting a good many marten, mink, foxes, and wolves. As this mode of trapping is peculiar to North America, I will describe it here. Having arranged which direction you will each of you take, you start off on snow-shoes, carrying some meat for food and for baits, coffee and salt, a knife, fork, and spoon, a plate, and a big tin cup which answers the purpose of both coffee-pot and cup, as you cool it in the snow, a small axe, and two wolf-traps, with two blankets rolled up and put on soldier fashion; all this is not a bad load when on snow-shoes and in deep snow. You keep as straight a course as you can, stopping when you come across "sign" to erect a fall-trap, which is made as follows:—

You first choose two young fir-trees growing about fifteen inches apart, and enclose a semicircle behind them with stout stakes driven firmly into the snow. Then you cut a small log, which you lay on the ground against the front of the trees, fastening it in its place by two uprights two feet high, opposite to the trees. You then cut a fall-log about twenty feet long, and place it between the uprights and the trees, filling up the space above it with short logs. You then prepare your trigger, which is about a foot long, and sharp at one end, on which you put your bait; then cut a short piece of wood, sharp at both ends, and raising the fall-log, support it on one end of this while the other holds the end of the trigger, and your trap is ready and will kill anything smaller than a fox—wolves and foxes requiring steel traps, which, instead of fastening to the ground, you simply tie to a rough log, so that the animal soon gets hung up, for if you pegged the trap down, he would bite the foot off and get away. On your way back in the morning, you take out what you have caught and rearrange your baits, generally going down your line twice a week; some professionals, however, go three times.

Your trouble is in keeping warm at night, two blankets being all that you can carry; but I got over this difficulty by leaving a deer-skin bag at the further end of the line of traps, taking it there on a dog-sleigh; and it is curious that no Indian will ever touch anything left on another man's line, or set a trap near one of his.

I had one very unpleasant adventure, which happened to me shortly before Christmas, and which very nearly ended badly for me.

We had with us a small keg of what the Hudson's Bay men call "shrub"—a kind of liqueur made with rum—which we were keeping for Christmas day; but one evening, having come home very tired and cold, I thought I would have a glass, and I had just finished it when A-ta-ka-koup came in, accompanied by six other Indians, who happened to be camped near his house—one of them being his son-in-law, and whom I had already met.

Now an Indian has a nose for spirit like that of a hound for a fox; so they at once smelt the "shrub" and asked for some, but, as I knew they would finish it and that then there would probably be a fight, I refused, telling them that I had very little of it, and was keeping it for medicine.

This did not satisfy them, however; and seeing that we had only one place in the room where it could be kept—a box which stood under the window—A-ta-ka-koup opened this and took out the keg. I was standing near him, and at once snatched it from him and threw it into a corner, and catching up an axe I stood in front of it. We had one candle burning in the room, as it was nearly dark and we were on the point of going to bed when the Indians came in. A-ta-ka-koup's son-in-law seized this, and throwing it down put his foot on it. I saw that this meant a fight, in which knives would be used, and that I had better get outside as soon as possible; so I went down on my hands and knees, taking the keg under one arm, and keeping close to the logs, as being the safest place, I made for the door, which was on the opposite side of the room.

I got on very well till I reached this, hearing the Indians searching for me and now and then touching them; but here I crawled between the outspread legs of one of them, who had set his back against the door, and who at once struck down with his knife, cutting me badly in the back. I seized him by the legs and upset him behind me, caught up a double gun which was close at hand, and opening the door I went out and closed it after me, drawing out the latch-string—the latch being on the outside.

Immediately on getting out of the house, I beat in the head of the keg with the butt of my gun and spilt the contents on the snow; the Indians bursting open the door as I did so made a rush at me, A-ta-ka-koup leading; but seeing that I took aim at him, he stopped about six feet from me and shook his fist in my face. I told him that I would shoot the first man who tried to touch me, at the same time backing away, to give myself more room in case of a rush. I had only two barrels, after which I meant to use the butt-end of my gun— a very poor weapon, as it would break at the first blow.

The Indians had a short talk, and then A-ta-ka-koup came towards me and told me that, as I had thrown away the rum and had threatened to shoot him, they would kill me, hinting, however, that I might buy them off; the whole thing being done to get all they could out of me. Poor Badger, being very little more than a boy, was frightened to death; he had not attempted to help me, and now advised me to give the Indians big presents, or I might be killed. This I, of course, refused to do, and they all sat down on some logs near the door of the house, occasionally shaking their fists at me.

I had come out in my socks, having removed my boots before they arrived, and as I was standing in the snow, I soon lost all feeling in my feet and knew that they were frozen; my only clothing, too, was a flannel shirt and a pair of drawers— rather light clothing for a night with the thermometer far below zero.

How it would have ended I cannot think; but just at the right moment up came Tom Boot, returning from a hunt. Now, fortunately for me, there had always been a rivalry between him and A-ta-ka-koup as to their relative strength and hunting capabilities; so, on seeing who the leader of the Indians was, Tom Boot asked him what the matter was, and on being told what I had done and that they intended to kill me, he ordered A-ta-ka-koup to stand out of the way and let me go into the house, and when he refused to do this, Tom seized him round the waist, picking him up like a child, and threw him against the logs of the house, stunning him, and causing the others to draw back hastily. Tom Boot then carried me into the house, as I was by this time too stiff to walk—shutting the door, and taking no notice of the other Indians.

I asked him if he thought we were safe, on which he smiled, and said that there was not a man on the Saskatchawan who dare come into a house where he was if he did not wish him to do so. This I found to be true; and there was a tradition that he had only once hit a man, and had then killed him.

Tom Boot had been for years in the employ of the Hudson's Bay Company, at the time of the rivalry between that company and the North-West Fur Company, and had seen a great deal of fighting which went on between their employés when they met in an Indian camp. Both companies used to hire fighting men to drive their rivals out of any camp to which they had gone to trade, and I was told at Fort Carlton that two French-Canadian prize-fighters had come on purpose to look at Tom Boot, having heard a great deal about him, and that they had walked round him and declared him to be too big to be any good, on which he picked up one of them and threw him at his companion, both of them coming down, when the Frenchmen walked off, not wanting any more.

On the present occasion he was very good to me, rubbing my frozen feet with snow, making me some tea, and doing all he could for me, and remained with me till morning. Just then A-ta-ka-koup put in an appearance, looking very dilapidated—his face having been much cut by the logs, and one of his arms was in a sling.

He seemed to be as friendly as usual with Tom Boot, till the latter happened to leave the cabin, when he showed me a lock of Tom Boot's hair, which he said he had pulled out during the struggle, and by means of which he assured me he could make him "heap-a-sick." It seems that Indians—who are very superstitious—believe that if an enemy can get hold of a bit of their hair, he can, by throwing a little now and then into the fire, cause them to have a very serious illness.

A-ta-ka-koup had come to make peace with me, as I was much too valuable a friend to quarrel with, and he had brought me a pair of moccasins as a peace offering.

For a long time I would not look at him or his offering, though the latter lay just in front of me, and when he called my attention to it I pushed it towards him, when he would wait a few moments and then put it in front of me again. This went on for fully an hour, as I was employed in making some dog-harness. When I had finished what I had been doing, I called Badger and gave the old fellow a good talking to, ending by saying that if I had any more trouble I should leave that part of the country, and he would then lose all I had intended giving him before I went away in the spring. He was very penitent, and we eventually shook hands, and I had no reason to find fault with him again. After this I often went hunting with him, and found him to be a first-rate tracker and a wonderful man on snow-shoes in deep snow.

I had come to America believing that a man could do eight or even ten miles an hour on snow-shoes, and that you went along on the surface; but all this I found to be a mistake—the fact being that when the snow is soft you frequently go in to your knees, and have at each step to shake off the snow before making another, and when there is a crust and you do go on the surface, the jar is so great that you are even sooner tired—five miles an hour being fast travelling.

The snow-shoes we used in the North were very different from those used in Canada, as ours had the ends much more turned up and ended in a point, while in Canada they turn up very little and are rounded in front. Ours, too, were very much longer, many of them being over five feet in length.

It is very amusing to see a beginner, who has fallen with his snow-shoes on, trying to get up; his hands find no firm resting-place in the deep snow, and his face is buried in it, while the points of his snow-shoes stick in, so that he cannot turn himself over; and it is only after he has pounded so long at the snow that he has made it solid, that he can manage to raise himself far enough to remove the snow-shoes and get up.

I had a visit from an old Indian trader called "Driver" about this time. I had seen him in Fort Garry and had told him of my intention to winter somewhere near Carlton; so hearing of me from some Indians, he had come out of his way to pay me a visit. He had been an Indian trader all his life, and had done well at it, in spite of the Hudson's Bay Company, who had tried to starve him out many times.

He told me that no man could oppose them in the North, being too far from his base of supplies, but that down here he did as he liked. He had once sold the forbidden whiskey just outside the gates of Carlton, but then he had a number of rough men with him, and could not be meddled with.

On another occasion he had penetrated into the heart of Athabasca with a trading outfit worth about eight hundred pounds, and would have made it pay well if he had been let alone; but the Company heard of it, and sent north at once to tell the Indians that if they would not go near him or sell him anything, they would give away as presents an outfit equal to his; and this they did—poor "Driver" selling nothing and being nearly starved.

I thought I would give him a really good dinner; so having some buffalo-hump ribs, I roasted them myself, and expected to hear him enthusiastic in their praise; but no, not a word did he say; so I asked him what he thought of the meat, which was as tender as a well-kept chicken, on which he said that he preferred something that he could get hold of, which he could not do with what he had just eaten.

He left me, after remaining two days, inviting me to visit him at his camp on Red Deer River; but I did not do so, though his account of the quantity of game there was most tempting.

CHAPTER IV.

A moose-hunt.—Description of my tent.—A-ta-ka-koup in camp.—Hunting moose on snow-shoes. Deaths of a bull and a cow. Lynx-hunting.—Tom Boot a nuisance.—F——'s history. His miserable condition. I take him with me.—Beautifying the hut.—F—— and I visit my late companions. Our journey.—The wolverine.—Getting F—— home.—Badger neglects the traps.—Narrow escape of being murdered. My precautions for the future.—An invitation to a stealing-party.

A-TA-KA-KOUP having found some moose sign not far from the hut, we arranged to have a hunt together, remaining out several nights, and Badger was to look after my traps in the meanwhile; and a few days later we started, taking two of my dogs, and a light sleigh, so as to camp comfortably.

We did not attempt to hunt till we were ten or twelve miles from the cabin, and then we put up a comfortable camp, in a hollow surrounded by bushes. This particular kind of camp was an idea of my own, so I will describe it.

I got a squaw to make me an A-tent, closed at both ends, and used this on the dog-sleigh instead of the usual big sheet; when going on such a hunt as this, and when we had chosen a spot and shovelled away the snow, after laying down a foot of either willows or small fir branches, we put up my tent on its side, the other side forming a slant, and the two ends keeping out all draughts, making us very comfortable. A-ta-ka-koup rather laughed at it when he saw it unpacked, but he laughed no more when he was lying in it, and said that his squaw should make him one.

In a dry country such as that was, where a storm was a rarity after the snow was once down, such a shelter as this was far better than a tent, being much more easily warmed, as a fire could be lighted so much nearer to it; and many a night I have lain in my bag, chatting with whomever formed the party, and felt as if I would not change my quarters for the finest room in the world.

On this occasion the amount of chatting was necessarily very limited, as A-ta-ka-koup knew only about twenty or thirty words of English; but he was a grand companion in other ways, being always ready to get up, however cold it was, and make up the fire, besides cutting all the wood, and bringing most of it into camp.

Sometimes he seemed to forget that I did not understand him, and would go on talking, evidently, from the signs he made, telling me of battles he had fought and of men he had killed, and I would give a grunt now and then—Indian fashion—as if I understood it all.

Having made a very snug camp, we started at once, and soon came on moose-tracks of that morning. A-ta-ka-koup said that they were those of three cows and a bull, and we followed them for more than an hour, by which time we were evidently close to them. The snow was here very deep, as we sank in nearly to our knees with snow-shoes on, and the moose evidently had to jump to get along at all.

As we were going round a small thicket we heard them start, and almost immediately they broke cover about two hundred yards ahead, going pretty fast. A-ta-ka-koup seemed to be confident of coming up with them, and started on the run after them, going at the rate of perhaps six miles an hour, which he could not have kept up for long, and I followed at about the rate of five miles. I had had so much snow-shoe travelling that I was in good condition, but I was not such an old hand at it as he was, so that he continued to gain on me, and in half an hour was two hundred yards ahead and gaining still, in spite of all I could do.

I then heard a shot, followed by another, and came up to him standing over a cow, where I left him, as he told me the bull was not far in front, and in a few minutes I saw him, evidently labouring, about a hundred yards off; so I fired, missing with the first barrel and hitting him too far back with the second, on which he increased his speed for a few hundred yards, and then stood at bay. Thinking him weaker than he really was, I went up to within ten yards of him, when down went his head, and in about three tremendous jumps he was almost on me. I fired at his head, and, fortunately perhaps, missing that struck him in the neck, dropping him at once—not three feet from me. He was a splendid fellow, and had a good head, which A-ta-ka-koup carried to camp for me, where we hung it high up on some boughs, intending to fetch it in the spring.

On returning to camp, A-ta-ka-koup took the sleigh and dogs and went to fetch some of the cow meat, the bull being too tough to eat.

As there were a good many lynx-tracks about, A-ta-ka-koup

went home the next morning to fetch some dogs which he had, and which were good at treeing lynxes; so I took my shot gun and hunted for grouse round camp. There were a good many ruffed grouse and a few willow-grouse, both being capital eating; and I had six of them broiled by the time A-ta-ka-koup returned. He appreciated them thoroughly, and declared that for the future he would always have them cooked in that way, the usual Indian manner of cooking them being to throw them into a pot after skinning them.

The next day we started after lynx, taking my sleigh-dogs with us, as they made so much noise if tied up in camp, and might attract some passing Indian.

A-ta-ka-koup's dogs soon found a fresh trail, and away they all went—my dogs leading, as they were in better wind, and we followed as fast as we could. As we went along, A-ta-ka-koup explained the tracks to me, seeming to know what turns they had made and which dogs were leading at the time, and as his dogs were very much smaller than mine, they made a track about half the size.

We had not gone far when we heard them all giving tongue, and knew that the lynx was treed, and soon came to where he had gone up a low fir tree. A-ta-ka-koup came up first, and fired, on which the lynx dropped wounded among the dogs. Mine immediately bolted, sleigh-dogs seldom having much pluck; but the two smaller ones went in and killed him in good style. We found two more during the day—losing one and killing the other. I had the luck to get the shot, as I happened to take the right-hand side of a thicket, whilst A-ta-ka-koup had to go some way round.

We had one day at white-tailed deer, but had had luck, as

we only got one, the reason being that A-ta-ka-koup's dogs behaved badly, by rushing on in front and putting up the deer long before we got near enough to shoot, for which conduct they got an "Indian beating," which was much worse than that given by an English keeper.

On the fifth day we returned home, having had a most enjoyable hunt.

On our return we found Tom Boot camped near the hut, having come to live on us, as he was too lazy to hunt for himself, and was very insolent if you refused him anything; and here he remained nearly the whole winter, begging and stealing, and altogether he was an awful nuisance.

Late in December I paid another visit to the fort to get supplies, and found there a Scotchman named F——, who had had rather an eventful career.

He was the son of a clergyman in Edinburgh, and had run away from school when he was sixteen, and turned actor. As he did not make much money at this, he had gone out to St. John's, New Brunswick, just after the greater portion of that city had been burned down. Here he had hired himself to a house-painter, and had developed a decided talent for that kind of work, being particularly good at imitating different woods; but after a time he got tired of this, and had gone to George Town, Demerara, where he had set up for himself as a house-painter and decorator, and had done well. He then returned to Scotland and married, and had two daughters.

Then came the British Columbian gold boom, and, bitten with the mining mania, he had sent his wife and daughters to Iowa to some friends, and had paid forty pounds to a bubble company, which had contracted to take him to the mines for that sum—being one of the men whom we had heard of in St. Paul's when the company broke up. Having a little money still left, he bought an ox and a cart, and travelled alone to Fort Garry, and worked there to make some money to buy a fresh outfit, and with this he started for British Columbia—a journey of twelve hundred miles; but on reaching Carlton his ox died, and when I found him he was living in a miserable lodge with some old Indians, who were given scraps from the fort, which he shared with them, as it was against the policy of the Company to help any white man coming into their territories, wishing to discourage immigration, as it interfered with their monopoly.

He was so miserable when I found him that I think he would have died that winter, not being used to cold or able to eat much of the food, which was only such as the sleigh-dogs got.

I found him to be a very pleasant and amusing man, who had seen a great deal of life of most kinds, and we soon became friends; so when I was about to leave the Post I proposed that he should come and pass the winter with me, an offer which he accepted.

The journey back to my cabin was a dreadful trial for him, as he would not use snow-shoes, so that the track we made would not bear him and he had to struggle along in two feet of snow. Where the going was fairly good he could ride on the sleigh, but then he immediately froze, so that several times we had to stop and light a fire to warm him.

We were three days doing the ninety miles, and I think that Badger and I were quite as thankful to see the house as he was, though the roughness of it struck him at once, and his spare time during the winter was spent in beautifying the inside.

He had some paints with him and began first of all on the fire-place, which he painted all over, and then ornamented by representing a marble mantlepiece with vases on it; and he did it so well that all the Indians who came in would go up and touch it, and then look at it sideways to see why it appeared to stand out. He restopped the house inside too, and painted the stopping blue, I, however, had my doubts as to its being an improvement.

When making his bed, instead of sleeping on the top of a number of buffalo-robes and bear-skins which we had bought of the Indians, he would get under them, retaining two only to lie on, and would even then say he was cold.

For some days he thought he would cook instead of Badger's wife, but we found that what he prepared had such an extraordinary flavour that we reinstated our old cook. He had the remains of some West-Indian sauces with him, and he would put these in, adding a quantity of cayenne pepper, which he could eat as we did salt, as he had lived fifteen years in South America.

About a week after F——'s arrival, I made up my mind to go and pay a visit to my late companions, whose house was only about forty miles from mine, making them near neighbours for that part of the world; and I at last persuaded F—— to go with me, as I intended taking four dogs and a sleigh, and he could ride most of the way.

I engaged a Cree Indian called Ki-chi-mo-ko-man, or "Big knife," to act as guide, as Badger knew nothing of the country north of the Saskatchawan.

It took us two days, and I thought that F—— would have given out more than once, as the snow was soft and he was forced to walk occasionally, but we arrived at last, and found M—— and C—— living in a much less pretending house than ours, it being made on the principle which I have described.

They had put up bunks for beds, using fir boughs for mattresses; and as the bunks were one above the other, you could not sit up in comfort, nor had you light enough for writing or reading, which we often did in bed when it was very cold.

They had had fair sport, and Laronde being a much better trapper than Badger had done better in that way, but had been very much troubled by a wolverine, an animal which is the trapper's worst enemy, as it goes along his line of traps and takes out anything which may have been caught, and tears up all that it cannot eat, apparently out of pure mischief. One of these animals had destroyed a number of good skins for them, and it did not seem possible to catch him, though they had tried poison and many kinds of traps.

I heard of some being killed with spring guns, and it was in this way that they eventually got him. Indians and trappers nearly always torture a wolverine when caught, very often roasting him alive over the fire.

We remained only one night with my friends, as Christmas was near and I had a good deal to do before then. Unfortunately there was a snowstorm on the night of our arrival, which made the travelling very bad, burying our tracks so deeply that they were of no use to us on the return journey, and we were obliged to walk most of the way.

Ki-chi-mo-ko-man, too, was not nearly so good a man in camp as A-ta-ka-koup, as he shirked his work, and being more used to cold than ourselves, we were obliged to get up in the night to replenish the fire.

I have already described my leather A-tent, which was invaluable when such a man as F—— was with us, who would have frozen if he had slept in the open. He had made himself a buffalo-bag too, and watching him getting into it was very amusing. The process is simple, being merely to open the mouth of the bag and step into it, then giving a jump and pulling the bag up at the same time, continuing this until far enough in to sit down, when you slide yourself in, turn the end in under your head, and you soon get warm if lying by a fire: your breath contributing a good deal towards the warming of the inside air, though I fear the ventilation is bad. Now with F—— the jumping was the difficulty, his attempts much resembling those of a young elephant, making even Ki-chi-mo-ko-man laugh.

I found during this trip that a man with a heavy beard and moustache labours under great disadvantages in a very cold country, as his breath freezes it all into one solid mass. This was the case with F——, and we had great fun by making him laugh, as this necessitated his opening his mouth so that he felt as if all the hair was being torn out by the roots.

Very soon after starting F—— had to get out and walk, and in less than an hour he was in difficulties. I cheered him up as well as I could, and Ki-chi-mo-ko-man frightened him by telling him of Indians who had been partially frozen and then eaten by wolves (an instance of which I saw myself on another occasion); but it was all of no use, and about four o'clock on the first afternoon he sat down and declared he would go no further. We put him on the sleigh and managed to get him to a good camping place, where we remained till morning.

We started quite briskly the next morning, and there was no trouble till after dinner, as we only stopped once for him to warm himself, but very soon afterwards he gave out again, and sitting down he wished us both good-bye, saying that he meant to remain where he was and die. We lit a fire and warmed him thoroughly, and got him on another mile or so, but beyond that he would not go, and it was only by pretending to quarrel with him and by hitting him, when he got furious and chased me, that I got him home at last. It took several days to appease his wrath, and to prove that I only did what I had done to save his life.

When I got home I found that Badger had been neglecting the traps, spending most of his time in A-ta-ka-koup's house; and on going along my line I found that a wolverine had paid the traps a visit, and had eaten two martens and left nothing but the tail of what must have been a fine fisher, a skin which is worth fully two martens. I got one fine wolf, and I fear that the poor animal had been several days in the trap, as he had eaten everything in the shape of a twig within reach, and had gnawed the bark from the log to which the trap was fastened.

On my way home I was crossing a small ridge when I saw A-ta-ka-koup's son-in-law, the man whom I had thrown over my head in the struggle for the "shrub," and who had never forgiven me, go quickly into a clump of small fir trees, which were on my way to the hut, and I also noticed that he had a gun in his hand, and seemed to move in a stealthy way as if he had seen me coming, and did not wish me to know of his being there. Now I had been told by Badger that he had vowed to be revenged on me for what I had done to him, so that he probably meant to waylay me and shoot me as I passed. I was about an hour's journey from the cabin, but the snow was in good order, so I turned aside from the direct road home, and I do not think I ever made better time on snow-shoes in my life.

Going straight to A-ta-ka-koup's house, where I found him at home, I told him what I had seen, and assured him that I should always in future carry a gun, and that if I ever met his son-in-law I should shoot him. A-ta-ka-koup left the house at once, and on his coming to see me in the evening, he told me that he had sent his son-in-law south, to his father's camp on the Saskatchawan, and that I should not see him again; but to be on the safe side, in case the man had not really gone away, from that day I always carried a revolver, and took with me a favourite dog, so that he might not get a chance, or I feel convinced he would have taken it.

The dog I refer to was a huge white Esquimaux exactly like a wolf, which I had made very fond of me, and which always slept against my back, adding greatly to my comfort.

That day two strange Crees whom no one knew arrived and stopped with me, saying nothing of their errand on the first day, but they asked me the next morning whether I would join them in a horse-stealing expedition, which they and some of their companions were going to undertake in the Blackfoot country, south-east of where we then were.

Of course I refused, much to their surprise, but A-ta-ka-koup's son joined them, and I heard from him the result of the attempt.

It seems that they reached a large Blackfoot camp, and found out where the horses were herded, but were discovered by a horse-guard and had to fly, losing one of their number, and my informant was also wounded. They only escaped through their being much better on snow-shoes than the Blackfeet.

Such expeditions as these are looked upon as being strictly honourable, and are not regarded as stealing; though an Indian's ideas on this subject are not very orthodox, as with them it is only wrong to be found out.

CHAPTER V.

How to make a plum-pudding.—Our Christmas party.—Nocturnal visits of F—— and myself to the plum-pudding.—Our daily routine.—F—— does not enjoy winter.—I am summoned to a Cree council.—A night apparition.—The Cree camp. Accusations against me. Enmity of some of the Indians. Rescued from a dangerous position by " White Hawk."—A new religion.—Impunity of lunatics.—Leave Cree camp.—Mis-ta-wa-sis corrects his wife with an axe.—Attempt to marry me.—A-ta-ka-koup propitiates the hunting god.—Camping in the snow.—A dog-sleigh described.—Behaviour of dogs.

We were now within three days of Christmas, and began to look up our materials for the festivities of that day. We had reserved some buffalo-hump ribs, which having been frozen for more than two months would be tender; we had, too, a bottle of whiskey, obtained at the Fort, and the materials for a plum-pudding, and this last was our only difficulty, none of us knowing anything about the manufacture of that article.

F—— having lived in South America for fifteen years had not seen one all that time, so I constituted myself chief cook and F—— was appointed kitchen-maid, and we commenced operations by F——'s sewing two towels together for a pudding-cloth and my washing out our best wooden bucket for a basin. The ingredients—currants, raisins, and citron, which we had carefully saved—were then inspected, and the first thing we noticed was a most lamentable deficiency in the quantity, not more than half of what we had brought being found; but of course no one had touched them. F—— said he had found a stray raisin or currant now and then, and I had done the same, and had thought it was of no use leaving it to be spoiled; however, this could not account for so large a deficiency. Then we found a good many percussion caps, shot, powder, and other trifles among the fruit, but we agreed that none of these were poisonous, so we picked out as many as we could and left the remainder. Our chief doubt was the eggs, of which we had brought four dozen packed in bran; but these were all unmistakably bad except four, which were doubtful, so we gave them the benefit of the doubt and put them into the bucket with 7 or 8 lb. of flour, about $\frac{1}{2}$ lb. of currants, $\frac{1}{2}$ lb. of raisins, and some citron-peel. It struck me that the proportions might not be correct, but it was the best I could do. I then added about 2 lb. of suet, cut fine, and a small tin of baking-powder; it was our last, and I had my doubts about its strength, so I put it all in and poured in a lot of water and stirred it for about an hour, F—— taking a turn now and then. We then put the pudding into the bag, sewed it up, and deposited it in the camp kettle, which we placed by the fire so that it should not boil too rapidly.

All this had been done two days before Christmas day, so as to have plenty of time, and the event showed that we had not begun too soon. When we went to bed we left the kettle beside the fire all night and recommenced boiling the pudding in the morning; but the cooking only seemed to harden it, so that in the evening we sent for A-ta-ka-koup's wife and paid her to boil it all night, telling her that it was White man's medicine and sudden death to an Indian (which in its then state it well might be), lest she might be tempted to try it; of course she said she had done what we had paid her for, but it seemed just as hard in the morning.

There were some five or six Indians encamped in the neighbourhood, whose chief amusement consisted in sitting for hours against the wall of our house, not uttering a word the whole time, and we invited all these and the A-ta-ka-koup family to dinner, and on their arrival we ranged them all round the room, we ourselves sitting at the table, and Badger served the dainties to us.

First we all had a glass of grog and drank to the health of the Queen, the Indians wondering why we stood up as we did it. Then slices of buffalo were handed on the ends of sticks to all the Indians, these being the fasionable substitutes for forks in those regions, and saving a great deal of breakage and consequent loss of temper; and then came the pudding, which had been left in the towels till the last moment so as to give it every chance. On sticking a knife into it, it was hard work to get it out again, and when it was extracted it brought with it more of the pudding than is usual.

A portion was at last cut for everyone and handed round, but though on most of the slices a plum or a currant, and in some cases two or three, were visible, there was not that enthusiasm about it which we had hoped for, everyone eating his or her portion in silence. My piece reminded me of what schoolboys call "turnpike pudding," plums occurring about as often as turnpikes do in travelling.

After dinner we had a talk about game with the Indians, and then turned in, having dined fashionably late to give the pudding an opportunity of becoming soft; but before we went to bed we marked what remained of it showing how much we were to eat each day, and finding that we had some 5 lb. left, enough with care to last us five days.

On trying to sleep I could think of nothing but pudding, till at last I thought I must have one small piece more; so I got out of my buffalo-robes, crawled to the box, and raised the lid; but that sly man F—— had piled some things on it after putting out the light, and down they all came with a great noise. F——, it seems, was awake and also thinking of pudding, and he immediately shouted out asking who was at the box: I told him that I only wanted the smallest possible piece, which I took and retired to bed, replacing such of the fallen articles as I could find on the box, a thing which evidently F—— did not expect, for presently down they all came again and there was the man who had abused me for taking the pudding doing the same thing himself, and I am sorry to say that we each of us made two more visits to the box during the night, and when we came to look at it in the morning we found one of us must have taken more of the pudding than he should, as it had dwindled down to about 1 lb., so not liking to be reminded of our misdeeds we ate that for breakfast.

After the dissipations of Christmas, we settled down once more to our weekly routine, which was as follows:—

On Monday I went along my line of traps and took up what had been caught, and had happened to be left by the wolverines. On Tuesday I returned home, doing the same thing. On Wednesday I generally went deer hunting with A-ta-ka-koup or Ki-chi-mo-ko-man; and on Thursday I did what was necessary round the house, shot rabbits, which, by the way, turn white in winter, and on Friday and Saturday I again visited my line of traps. Sunday being a day of rest we employed ourselves mending our clothes, dog-harness, &c., and read once more one of our very few books and newspapers.

F—— was very miserable during the whole winter, almost living in bed with all the spare skins and rugs heaped upon him. I have come home sometimes and have missed him, and on calling to him have been answered by a small voice coming from under an immense heap of deer- and buffalo-skins; when it appeared that, the wood giving out, he had dreaded the cold too much to go outside and cut some, and Badger being also away hunting he had crept under the skins and had been there for hours shivering in spite of their weight.

I found game becoming very scarce, and by the end of January we were very nearly out of meat, and the flour was getting low, so it was determined that Badger and I should pay another visit to his father-in-law's camp, and we were waiting for good weather for our start when a runner arrived to summon me to a big council of the Crees, which was to be held on the north fork of the Saskatchawan.

He did not know why I was wanted, or said he did not, and returned at once. The day after he left we started, taking a sleigh and four dogs, a little flour, and some presents in the form of beads, brass wire, sham jewellery, and powder and lead for the Indians. The snow was deep and the travelling bad, but by following the tracks of the runner, who was on snow-shoes, we got on fairly and did some twenty miles a day—a good day's journey with dogs being from forty to sixty, according to the state of the snow.

Our second night out was on the open prairie, and we had had to carry wood with us and to sleep without any bushes or fir-boughs under our buffalo-skins. The fire being very small and likely to go out soon, we had turned in early, and in the middle of the night, feeling very cold, I put my head out of my buffalo-bag to see what sort of a night it was, when to my extreme surprise I saw two Indians seated smoking their pipes on the opposite side of the embers. I thought at first that I must be dreaming, but on my moving they both raised their heads, and I saw that they were men and not the fancies of a dream.

I at once woke Badger, and on his questioning them, we found that they were Crees and on their way to the big council to which we were also bound, and who, having seen our fire, had come to warm themselves.

The next evening we reached the Cree camp, which we found to consist of nearly two thousand Indians, no women or children being present. I was given a lodge and was told that the next meeting would be held at sunset that evening.

After making our lodge as comfortable as possible and lighting a fire in the centre of it, I sent Badger out to discover, if possible, why we had been summoned. He returned in about an hour with the information that the Crees, hearing that I had been killing a good many buffaloes, had been most indignant, and had sent for me to say that I must leave the country at once.

The main object of the council was to discuss certain wrongs which they thought they had suffered at the hands of the Hudson's Bay Company in allowing their enemies, the Sioux, to trade at Fort Carlton.

I attended the meeting in the evening, which was held round a circle of fires, the chiefs and soldier Indians sitting two and three deep round the circle, the younger men being in the middle keeping up the fires.

The first speeches were all about their differences with the Company, till one of the Indians pointing to me reminded them of their having sent for me; and then one of the younger chiefs rose and began what Badger told me was a speech against white men not belonging to the Company killing game, especially buffalo, in their territory; he was very moderate and calm about it, but he was followed by an old Assineboine chief, whose name I remember was "Big Vulture," who was by no means calm; in fact he worked himself up into such a rage that he several times shook his fist at me, and slapped his knife meaningly. His speech had a bad effect, Indians being very easily roused by a man who is eloquent. On his sitting down I rose, Badger putting what I said into the Cree language. I began by saying, That I was a stranger from a very distant land across the big water; that I had there heard of the noble Red Man and had come to visit him, bringing him many presents, some of which I had now with me. That I had only shot what game I had wanted for food; and that during the summer I had only killed thirteen buffaloes, several of which were old bulls, and therefore useless. I then said that the "Great White Mother" (as they always call the Queen) took a great interest in her Red children; and that I should go back and say how kind they had always been to me. Here I was interrupted very rudely by a young Indian sitting near me, who wanted to know whether I had brought presents for all of them. Of course I was obliged to say that I had not, on which he worked himself up into a fury, ending by saying "that if I were allowed to go back, many more white men would come," on which an old Indian, who had seated himself beside me, touched me on the arm and pointed towards the tents, evidently meaning me to go with him, which I did, taking Badger with me.

When we reached his tent, which was a very large one and evidently belonged to a chief, he motioned me to a seat and told me, through Badger, that if I had remained at the council I should certainly have been killed; but that with him I was safe.

He said that he was chief of a large band of the Crees then present, and being a friend of the white men would protect me; but I must remain in his tent till the council broke up, which it would probably do in two or three days. Not a very pleasant prospect as I had no books or newspapers with me.

Badger was sent for our things and reported that the talk at the council was still about me; and that a good many Indians were opposed to injuring me, as it would do them so much harm with the Company.

Late in the evening I was surprised by five of them coming in and a sort of service being held, during which something wrapped in a beautifully dressed buffalo-calf skin was laid in front of the chief and treated with great veneration; and after the service was ended and the Indians gone, I asked him what this was, and what the service meant.

He very carefully unfolded the skin and produced a book, evidently made of sheets torn from a large ledger, the paper being lined foolscap; and this he very reverently held up to the light of the fire, when I could see some watermarks in the paper; and these, he told me, were the beginnings of a new religion, which was being revealed to him by degrees. He assured me that there was more of it on the paper then than there had been a short time before; and that soon the whole of it would be there, when he would be the greatest chief in North America.

Of course I did not attempt to put him right, as he would not have believed me and might have turned me out, which would have been very awkward just then. It seems that the service had been a series of prayers to the new God, and that the five Indians were the only converts he had made so far.

One great reason for my safety while with him was that most of the Indians looked upon him as a madman; and, as such, under the special protection of the "Great Spirit." I have seen a good many lunatics in Indian camps, and they were always well cared for, and perfectly safe from everyone, no matter what they might do. One of them has taken a chief's gun from a lodge in which I was sitting and walked away with it; and the chief has only followed him on the chance of his laying it down, and never dreamt of taking it from him.

The camp broke up on the morning of the second day, much to my delight as I had had to remain the whole time in the tent, and had been constantly stared at by hundreds of Indians, who were coming in and going out all day long, evidently hoping to get presents; but my host advised me not to give any, as I had not enough for all and should consequently only make enemies; but I found out afterwards that he hoped I would give the whole of them to him for having saved my life.

I remained another day with my old friend, who was called "White Hawk" (a most inappropriate name, as he was one of

F

the darkest Indians I ever saw), and before I left he asked me whether I would give him a testimonial, showing me some which he had from various members of the Hudson's Bay Company.

I gave him one, mentioning in it what he had done for me, and we parted.

I reached Mis-ta-wa-sis' camp on the evening of the day I left "White Hawk," and fancied he did not greet me as warmly as usual; and on inquiry I found that he had almost killed one of his wives the day before with an axe, and was afraid of what I might say to him.

I immediately left his lodge and said I would never enter it again, at which he was very much hurt, though he said nothing, and I moved into one of the neighbouring lodges, where I found an old Indian with four daughters, one of whom he very much wanted me to marry, bringing the young lady for me to look at; and on my refusing as politely as I could, she rushed out of the lodge in a great rage and did not again appear.

On my return home I found F——, as usual, very miserable, since, having had no one to chop wood for him, he had nearly starved and was almost frozen. I remained two days to cut a good supply, and then started for a last hunt with A-ta-ka-koup, as there were signs of a herd of deer having come south lately.

We remained out four days, and got seven deer, a wild cat, three wolves, and a fox; and I had a good opportunity of seeing the way in which the Indians try to propitiate the hunting God when on the trail of game.

We had followed three deer nearly all day, jumping them once but not getting a shot, when we ascertained that they were in a large thicket about three or four hundred yards ahead of us. A-ta-ka-koup stopped me and lit a small fire, at which he sat down, and lighting his pipe he blew a whiff to the north, south, east, and west, and one upwards. He remained solemnly looking at the fire for nearly an hour, evidently praying, and then declared himself ready, and approached the bushes on one side, placing me on the other; and very soon the deer came out close to me. Having remained so long by such a little fire my fingers were almost frozen and I missed the first; but broke the hind leg of the second, and A-ta-ka-koup ran it down, bounding through the deep snow like a deer. He seemed to think that my hitting the deer was in answer to his prayers, and was very pleased.

I have before mentioned what a good companion A-ta-ka-koup was when out hunting, and how he was always ready to make up the fire at night, and in this he was a great contrast to most Indians, who will try and shirk work in camp, leaving you to do everything.

It is amusing, when camping in the snow, to observe the little artifices put in practice to make your neighbour get up and renew the fire instead of doing it yourself. I have seen men pretend to have nightmare, screaming and kicking in furious style; then they have coughing fits or roll against their neighbour. Anything is better than getting up yourself, as it means wading through the snow to fetch more wood, and sometimes going far into the timber to get it, and taking a good deal of snow into your bag when you turn in again.

Sleeping out in a snowstorm is a curious experience, till you are used to it. Snow falls so rapidly in that country that you very soon have from six to eighteen inches of snow on you; and I shall never forget my feelings when waking up one morning and putting my head out of my bag, I found myself, as I thought, deserted. The whole prairie for miles was perfectly level; the dogs, sleigh, and my companions were all gone, and it was most curious, when the real state of the case occurred to me and I had shouted several times, to see the snow open in one spot and reveal a man's head, and in another a dog's. On this occasion enough snow had fallen to cover the sleigh and everything on it, the latter being some fifteen inches high.

When speaking of a sleigh as used with dogs, of course one does not mean such a one as is used in Canada for horses, even on a small scale. A dog-sleigh is simply a board of birch-wood fourteen inches wide and one inch thick, and about ten feet long, having one end turned up and tied back. Along the sides of this board are arranged loops of raw hide for lashing, and the way it is packed is as follows:—

A large sheet of buffalo-leather is laid on the board so that perhaps four feet of it projects all round. Your baggage is then arranged along the sleigh, care being taken that it shall not be quite as broad as the board. When the load is high enough (and it must not exceed sixteen inches) you wrap the spare leather over it, tuck in the ends, and lash with raw hide rope, made of elk-skin. When travelling with plenty of dogs, you often have what is called a carriole with you, in which you can sit and go to sleep while your driver manages the dogs. The carriole is made of a board of the same size as the sleigh; but three feet from the hind end is placed a piece of board as a back, two feet high, which is kept in its place by cords going from end to end and passing over the top of it, and the space between the back board and the front of the sleigh is filled up with parchment sides, making a very snug place to take a nap in, the motion of the sleigh being very smooth and noiseless.

Sometimes on a steep slope the driver has to hold a cord in his hand to prevent the sleigh going down too rapidly, and should he slip or let go his hold the result is disastrous. On one occasion we were passing along the side of a hill, and Badger was holding a line attached to the end of the sleigh, when from some unknown cause he let go, and as I was on the sleigh at the time away I went down the hill, winding the dogs (who are harnessed singly, one in front of another) round the sleigh, thus tying me up and preventing my getting out when we reached the bottom. The dogs used for sleighing are always savage animals, one remove from wolves, and very few of them will allow anyone but their driver to touch them; so on reaching level ground they all began to fight on the top of me, and my chances of being bitten were very good indeed, and the situation not at all pleasant. The unwinding took some time, and was accompanied by a great deal of beating.

When nearing a fort you generally strike a firmly pressed snow road, made by hauling in firewood; and the dogs knowing where they are, always start off at a furious rate, which is kept up to the fort, perhaps some eight or ten miles or even more; and should there be any sudden turn in the road, round some stump or tree, the sleigh is upset, and then you must walk the rest of the distance, as nothing will stop them but the sleigh becoming jammed between two trees, and the chances of this happening are very small.

CHAPTER VI.

A bear-hunt.—Curious story of a bear.—A wolf-hunt.—Indian dogs.—Visit Fort Carlton.—Recipe for Rubbiboo.—A ball at Fort Carlton.—Ponies wintering in the snow.—Intelligence of sleigh-dogs.—Ingratitude of Ki-chi-mo-ko-man.—Tom Boot a thief. Determine to punish him. A-ta-ka-koup joins me in the enterprise. Surprise Tom Boot. Tremendous struggle. Tom Boot receives a thrashing.—Leave our hut for Fort Carlton.—Serious difficulty at the river. Nearly starved. Rescued by boat. My feet frozen.—The manufacture of pemmican.—Frozen fish.—A professional bear-hunter.—F—— and I part.—Effect of eloquence on Indians.

I HAD always told the Indians who came to see us that if they brought us word when they chanced to find a bear's wintering-hole we would reward them liberally; so, shortly after my return from visiting my friends, an Indian boy came to me from Ki-chi-mo-ko-man to tell me that a bear's hole had been found, and that I must come at once, as it being now the month of March, the bear was likely to come out any time. Badger and I therefore started the next morning, taking with us two dogs and a small sleigh for our bedding. The crust on the snow was good, and we were in excellent training, so that we reached Ki-chi-mo-ko-man's house late that night, having travelled nearly forty miles.

We found a number of Indians camped round Ki-chi-mo-ko-man's house, many of them having been at the big Cree council to which I had been summoned. These men told me that they did not think I should have been killed, even if old "White Hawk" had not taken me under his protection, but that I should most certainly have been robbed of all I had with me, and have been warned out of the country.

The following morning Ki-chi-mo-ko-man, Badger, and I started for the bear-hole, which was about four miles from the cabin, and found that it was in a small thicket of willows, and that the only aperture was a breathing-hole, some three inches in diameter. An Indian had taken shelter in the bushes during a snow-storm, and had discovered the hole by accident. It was arranged that Ki-chi-mo-ko-man should stir up the bear, and that Badger and I should stand ready—I with a double sixteen-bore rifle and Badger with a single Indian trade gun. It took a good deal of stirring to make the bear move, and then, with a loud grunt, out he came—a half-grown, cinnamon-coloured bear—and he was at once rolled over by a shot from the double rifle. I was stepping forward to take a nearer view of him, when out came another huge bear, which turned out to be the mother, who, taking in the state of affairs at a glance, came straight at me. I had snow-shoes on, so I could not run away; I therefore took careful aim at her chest, at about ten feet distance, with my remaining barrel, and fired. She fell, but I think would have been up again in a moment, had not Badger, who usually did not display much courage, stepped forward and, putting his gun to her head, finished her. Her skin measured 7 feet 10 inches by 6 feet 4 inches, and I think she weighed 600 lb.

While at Ki-chi-mo-ko-man's, an Indian told me a very curious story of a bear, which I believe to be true, as all the Indians there said it was so. It seems that almost all the Plains Indians desert their old people when they are poor and cannot pay to be taken care of, and that in the early part of that winter some Assineboines, on their way south to kill buffalo, had deserted an old woman, giving her, as usual, a little food and water, a small axe, and a worn-out lodge, which last they put up for her. Soon after the Indians had left her, she lighted a fire, and was cooking some food when she fancied she saw the snow under the fire heaving up; and a few minutes afterwards the head of a bear came out, evidently only half awake. Now the nose of a bear is its most vulnerable point, and the old woman knew this; so she hit it several times with the axe, using all her strength, and killed it. She then dragged it out and skinned it, and cut up the meat and dried it, and lived on this for some weeks, till some Hudson's Bay men, who happened to pass, took her into Fort Pitt, where my informant told me she then was.

When with Ki-chi-mo-ko-man I saw one of the very few pretty Indian women whom I have ever come across. She was the daughter of an old Cree, and had been married to a member of the same tribe; but he was too lazy to provide for her, and she had left him and returned to her father. I remained two days with Ki-chi-mo-ko-man, going on the second on a wolf-hunt, as a great many had been seen round the house; but we only killed two. Our mode of proceeding was to form line and beat all the thickets, a number of curs of all kinds assisting, and when a wolf was started all the dogs were put on his trail and we did our best to keep up. Wolves are thin at that time of year, and consequently weak, so that we only lost one of those which we started. On our way home in the evening we came on a lynx, and if there had been sufficient daylight, I think we should have killed it, as they generally go up a tree after a short chase, and can then be very easily shot; but it got so dark that the dogs ran away from us, and only returned in the middle of the night.

These Indian dogs are very like wolves, and look as if they must have some wolf blood in them. When going into an Indian camp in the night, it is advisable to carry a thick stick, and to call for some Indian to come out and act as guide, or you might very easily be killed by them. They collect in packs, and though cowards when alone, their number gives them courage, and they will attack a man in a moment. If I was in an Indian camp and wished to leave it, meaning to return, I used always to borrow an Indian's blanket, and cover myself entirely with it, when the dogs would come and smell me and let me pass.

On the third day Badger and I returned to our house, and after resting the dogs for a day, we started again for the fort to arrange for having our horses, which had been herded with the fort band, brought out to the house. Travelling was fairly good, and we reached the Saskatchawan on the evening of the second day, crossing to the fort in the morning. The river is here about a hundred yards wide, and runs between banks fully two hundred feet high, and on the opposite side stands Fort Carlton.

Mr. L—— was very glad to see us, but could not give us anything but pemmican, as all game had gone south, and no fresh meat had been brought into the place for a long time;

but he had some potatoes, and with these and some pemmican a dish was manufactured called "rubbiboo." The recipe is simple; and I will give it here for the benefit of housekeepers. You take as much pemmican as you think will be eaten, and having thawed it at the fire, you beat it up into fibres and put it into a frying-pan with some grease. You then take some boiled potatoes, and mash them up with a fork, and stir them in, adding salt and pepper to taste, and the result is "rubbiboo." Eaten hot, and taking care to be very hungry, it is not bad, and the hungrier you are the better it will be.

On the evening of our arrival Mr. L—— got up a ball for us, the company consisting of about twelve or fourteen half-breed women, and about twice that number of men—half-breeds and Indians—and his wife and himself, Mrs. L—— being the only white woman present. The ball began at 7 P.M., the illuminations being sundry saucers of fish-oil with wicks in them, and the refreshments consisting of a glass of whiskey and water all round and tea. I have certainly seen more beauty and more elaborate dresses, but I never saw a dance kept up with more spirit. I began rather diffidently, but soon warmed up, and I think I jumped as high and made as much noise as the others, which seemed to be all that was required. The dancing was kept up till midnight, by which time I was utterly worn out, and very glad to turn into my buffalo-bag. I have forgotten to say that the event of the evening was having a dance with Mrs. L——, who kindly gave each of us one turn round the room, and as there were nearly thirty of us, this was no small undertaking. The steps were extraordinary; Mrs. L—— valsed, and her partners ran round her, or jumped round, as the fancy took them. A good many Indians were present who had come from Fort Garry, and might be called partially civilized; but a number of Crees, who were in the neighbourhood, came and flattened their noses against the windows, and anything more horrible than they looked under these circumstances can hardly be imagined.

In the morning I borrowed a pony and rode down the river some twelve miles to where the fort band of horses was, an Indian boy going with me to show me the way; and I do not think I ever saw anything more curious than the appearance the prairies, where they had been feeding, presented. The ponies are turned out late in the autumn, and have to shift for themselves until the following April, and, if judiciously herded, they will come up quite fat, though this fat is soft and will not last if they are at once worked hard. When the snow becomes deep, they scrape a hole and get into it, pawing away the snow till they get at the grass, when they will enlarge the hole at the bottom, to get as much grass as possible, and when they can reach no more they plunge out and make another hole, the sides of these holes serving as a protection against the cold winds of winter. A prairie after they have left it presents much the appearance of a dilapidated piece of honey-comb. After arranging that the horses—of which I had three—should be brought to my house during the following week, I went back to Fort Carlton, and the next morning returned home, taking three days to do the journey, a snow-storm having made the going soft and hidden our tracks.

I had while going back an opportunity of watching the wonderful intelligence displayed by these sleigh-dogs. I had my best train with me, and the trail being bad had put a big black dog called "Papillon" in front. This dog's strong point was the finding of difficult trails, and now, though the snow had covered the trail we had made in coming and had made the whole prairie level, yet this dog kept to our old road the whole way, rendering it unnecessary to beat a track for him. The old trail was only some three inches underneath, and when he got off it he was in deep snow at once, but this I never saw him do with more than his fore feet during the whole ninety miles, and yet our trail was very winding, going round clumps of bushes, trees, &c. continually. If I had been racing I should have put my favourite dog "Jumper" in front, as he was much the most active dog I had, and thoroughly knew what he had to do. My man took as much pride in this team as coachmen do in their horses, and considered them the fastest team on the river, which they probably were.

Hearing that we were leaving the country, all the Indians within twenty miles came in, hoping to get presents, and amongst others came Ki-chi-mo-ko-man. Now this Indian had hunted with me on several occasions, and though he seemed to think that I went to cut wood &c. for him, still we had always got on well together, and I had made up my mind to give him a good many presents; so I called him in one morning and, telling him that I was much obliged to him for all he had done for me, and that I hoped I might meet him again on some future occasion, I gave him a splendidly-coloured blanket, with brilliant stripes at the ends, an axe, two hunting-knives, and a number of small things. He thanked me very earnestly, and said that he should always remember his white brother, and a great deal more to the same effect, and then gathered up his presents, which were a large armful, and was leaving the house, when I missed a small broken penknife, which was valuable to me as being the only one I had. It was broken all to pieces, and had only one sound blade remaining; but Ki-chi-mo-ko-man had taken a fancy to it, and had been handling it for some time. On my asking him if he had it, he said he had not; but I saw him close his hand on something, and catching hold of his hand, I took the knife from it. He got in a great rage, and asked me whether I was going to take it away from my red brother, and on my saying that I was, he called me mean and everything bad he could think of, and said I was no better than all white men, who only came for what they could take from the Indians. On this I made him put everything down, and turned him out of the house, and the whole of that day he remained with his back against a tree, looking at the door of the house, hoping I would relent; but finding I took no notice of him, he returned to his cabin.

When I came to look over my things to see what I had to give away, I missed a number of articles, and could not find them anywhere. Now when your house consists of only one room, 16 feet by 13 feet, it is not very easy to lose anything, and I concluded that they must have been stolen. Badger was away at the time, but on his return I asked him if he knew anything about them, on which he told me, with great reluctance, that while I was on my last hunt with A-ta-ka-koup, Tom Boot had come and had taken a number of things, telling Badger that I was going away and would never need them, and threatening to beat Badger if he told me: he also said that if I followed him to try to get the things back he would shoot me; and yet this man would have starved during that winter if I had not given him food. I at once went to see A-ta-ka-koup, and asked him if he would go with me to try and recover my property. Now A-ta-ka-koup had never forgiven Tom Boot for having thrown him against the logs of the house, and this looked like a good chance of being even with him. I made A-ta-ka-koup promise not to carry any weapon, though I had a revolver hidden away myself, and finding from some Indians, who were camped by my house, that Tom Boot was encamped about twenty miles due south of us, we started one morning, and reached the small prairie on which his lodge stood before evening. A-ta-ka-koup went ahead to reconnoitre, and remained in hiding till he saw Tom Boot go into his lodge, when he returned to me. Our plan was as follows: we were to creep up to the lodge after the fire was out, and we might suppose that Tom was in bed, when we were to enter quietly—A-ta-ka-koup jumping on his shoulders and I on his legs, and then we were to tie him, if possible, and recover my property.

We remained on the edge of the prairie for two hours after sundown, and until I thought I should be frozen, when we crept up to the lodge and peeped in. Everything was quiet, and we could hear Tom's heavy breathing; so we went in. A-ta-ka-koup sprang on one end of Tom and I on the other, and then began an awful struggle. I know I was thrown about like a ball, and got some terrible blows, but fortunately from bare feet.

After what seemed an hour, and might have been only five minutes, of this, we managed to tie him with buckskin thongs, and were able to get up. In the meantime his wife, who had at first taken us for hostile Indians killing her husband and had bolted, was screaming in the distance; so I sent A-ta-ka-koup to tell her what it was all about, on which she returned and tried to untie Tom, and when we prevented her she attacked us with an axe; and it was only when A-ta-ka-koup threatened to kill her that she desisted, and sat down and cried. Tom Boot refused to speak, so we gave him a good beating with a raw hide rope, took such things of mine that we could find, and left, telling him that if he came near my house again he would be shot at once.

We camped about two miles from the scene of our struggle, both of us being worn out; and I know that I felt as if I had had a severe beating myself. On reaching home the next day, I found the horses had arrived and were looking very well and fat; though of course very rough in their coats. They were the three best I had bought for buffalo running the year before, and the one I intended to ride to Fort Garry was the fastest horse in the Red River settlement, the other two being nearly as good. Not one of them was more than $14\frac{1}{2}$ hands, but they were very strongly built.

On the 7th of April we started for Carlton for the last time, Badger driving a sleigh whilst I rode one horse and led the other two. The spring had not yet set in; but the sun was very warm and the snow was melting fast, so travelling was very bad indeed. Badger had left his wife and child with A-ta-ka-koup.

We had given away so much that the sleigh was very lightly loaded, there being nothing on it but our bedding and guns, with F—— sitting on the top. On the evening of the third day we reached the north bank of the Saskatchawan, to find that the ice was just breaking up, and that we were too late to cross. Now this was serious, as we had very little to eat and had given away most of our blankets, intending to get new ones at the Fort; however, there was no help for it, and we had to camp, and by lying very close together we managed to get through the night fairly comfortably, or at least Badger and I did so; but F—— declared that he was frozen stiff when daylight appeared, and we only thawed him by lighting a fire on both sides of him.

Mr. L—— and a number of the men from the Fort came down to the opposite bank during the next day; but they could do nothing for us, as the ice was now coming down in immense masses, and from the way in which the smaller pieces were ground up by the larger ones, we saw what our fate would be should we attempt to cross. Our only chance was to find some game, so Badger and I took a horse each and hunted up and down the banks for miles, getting only three grouse and a few squirrels; we also saw a band of antelope in the distance, but were not able to stalk them on account of the ground being covered with half-melted snow and water.

On the afternoon of the third day F—— was so miserable that I shouted across, offering ten pounds if they would bring a boat over, and I saw them go away to fetch one. Towards evening, a heavy flat-bottomed boat was in the water, and three strong half-breeds were poling her across, keeping off the masses of ice with great difficulty, and in ten minutes they were in our camp. Of course the horses had to be left, so we turned them loose, and getting into the boat we were soon in the Fort. Here I found that my feet had been partially frozen, and they had to be put into iced water to thaw them; as the circulation slowly returned it was curious to see small icicles form on them, which adhered quite firmly, while the pain was very great. It is quite common for men to lose fingers or toes, and in some cases one half of the foot. As it was, I only lost some of the nails and a small portion of one toe. This laid me up for some days, during which nothing could exceed the kindness of Mr. L—— to both F—— and myself. There was no food but pemmican; but we were always hungry, and soon got to like it when in the form of "rubbiboo" and used to eat an enormous amount of it.

I have said nothing about the manufacture of pemmican, so I may as well do so here, as it is a lost art now that the buffalo has disappeared. The buffalo-meat is first cut up into thin slices and dried in the sun or over smoke until it is as hard as leather; then the skin is taken raw, cut square, and sewn into a bag about three feet long by eighteen inches wide, with the hair outside. The meat is then taken and beaten with a flail until it is all fibres, and the fat is melted in large kettles and about three inches of the bag is filled with boiling fat; an equal quantity of fibre is then put into it and is beaten down with a heavy stick used as a rammer, then more fat is poured in and more fibre; and so on till the bag is full. It is then sewn up with raw hide or sinew and beaten flat, and is ready for use. Thus prepared it will keep for three years, only becoming dry with age, unless it is kept in a damp place, when it becomes mouldy. Sometimes it is made with buffalo-marrow instead of fat, in which case it is rather nice, as the marrow always remains soft; and again I have eaten it with sweet berries in it, which is also an improvement. Its appearance is against it, as it very much resembles what we call dog-greaves in England, and it is cut up in the same way, with an axe. It is said that on no food but this can a man do so much work or go so far, which seems likely, as it is one half fat. In the Hudson's Bay Company it is the regular winter food for all the employés, or I should say was till the buffalo was exterminated, which is now practically the case.

Further north, a great many white fish are caught in nets set through holes in the ice, and these are nearly as nourishing as pemmican. A man gets 2 lb. of pemmican or 6 fish a day, and a dog when in work the same. When not working, these last are supposed to require no food, or at all events they do not get it. In cooking two fish, which is generally done by standing a frying-pan with them in it in front of the fire at a considerable angle, the men get generally about a quarter of a pint of oil, these fish being very fat, and this they burn in their lamps. It is a curious sight to see the frozen fish stacked in the yards of the northern forts, each being as hard as a stone, and in this state they are kept five or six months.

On this occasion I met at the Fort the first Indian I ever knew who was a professional bear-hunter, and this he continued to be in spite of the dreadful manner in which one bear had torn him. His only weapon was what is called a trade gun. This man was following the trail of a large grizzly, and coming on him very suddenly the bear charged him; he at once fired steadily at the horse-shoe on the chest but failed to stop him, and knowing that he could not escape by running, and that a bear will very seldom touch any portion of a living man but his face, he threw himself down and held his face firmly to the ground; the bear came up and tried to turn him over, but failing in this bit one of his legs and then sat down and looked at him for a minute; he then got up and walked off slowly, thinking, I presume, that the man had died very suddenly. Now if the Indian had remained quietly where he was until the bear had left the place all would have been well, but he got up before it was out of sight, and the bear hearing him chased him. The Indian threw himself down in the same position, but the bear was not to be taken in a second time and tried hard to turn him over, tearing off the whole scalp in his efforts, when the man fainted, and on coming to himself found that he had been bitten in three or four places, and that the whole of the skin was gone from the top of his head. When I saw him he had a bandana handkerchief bound round his forehead, and on taking this off, I saw that he had been entirely scalped, the skin being gone nearly to the eyes. In spite of this he was the best bear-hunter on the Saskatchawan, and made a fair living by selling the skins.

The time had now come for F—— and I to part, as he wished to continue his journey to the mines in British Columbia, and I found that he would not have much difficulty in getting to Fort Edmonton, near the head waters of the river, whence parties of Hudson's Bay men often crossed the mountains to the Fraser River, where the mines were. It was arranged that he should remain at Carlton till the spring had set in, and then join the first party going up the river.

I had been able to buy a little corn at the Fort, so that my horses, which had been brought across, were now in very fair condition, and by riding them gently at first we hoped to do the six hundred miles to Fort Garry in about twenty days. I laid in a few provisions, such as tea and sugar, flour, salt, and pemmican, these being all I could get, and one of the half-breeds made me a very good pack-saddle for our third horse, so that we were ready to start.

I arranged to leave the bloodhound at the Fort, as the journey would have been too much for him, Mr. L—— promising to send him down at the first opportunity. A farewell supper was given in my honour, at which the only dish was "rubbiboo," and we wound up the evening with a dance, not getting to bed till after midnight. At the end of the evening F—— gave a recitation from "Julius Cæsar," which impressed the Indians very much. He had been an actor for some years, and remembered portions of a great many plays, and these he would recite with a blanket round him "à la toga." Some of his performances at our cabin before a large and select audience of Indians had been most successful, though they did not understand one word of what he said. No people admire eloquence more than Indians do, and a man who can speak well can do what he likes with them. This was shown very clearly in the case of "Sitting Bull," the supposed murderer of General Custer in 1876. He was chief of a very small band of Sioux, and he raised himself by his eloquence to be chief of the whole nation.

CHAPTER VII.

An Indian swims the Saskatchawan.—Start from Fort Carlton.—Prairie fire and narrow escape.—Unpleasant surprise.—A Sioux camp. Interview with the chief. Suspicious circumstances. A parley with the chief.—A fight and a race for life.—Our mode of travelling.—Arrival at Fort Garry. Our miserable appearance.—The composition of galette. —The Sioux outbreak and cause.—Threat to sack Fort Garry.—Enmity between English and French half-breeds.—My new guide, and his character.—Kindness of the citizens.—Start from Fort Garry and method of travelling.—Desolation of the country.—My first night in a bed and consequences.—Taken for a half-breed scout.—Expedition against the Indians. Its utter failure.—Death of Little Crow.—Execution of Indians.—Start for England.

On the morning of the 17th of April, Badger and I got everything ready for our start; but we were delayed for some hours by the arrival of an Indian, with a waggon and a pair of ponies, on the opposite side of the river. I heard a great deal of shouting going on, and went down to see what it meant. It seemed that the Carlton ferry-boat had not yet been put into the river, there being still a good deal of ice going down, and the Indian was urging them to put it in at once. This they refused to do, nor would it have been of much use to this man if they had consented, as stretching the rope across the river and arranging the apparatus would have taken an entire day.

Finding that they would not do as he wished, the Indian shouted to us, to say that he should swim the river—waggon and all; and this he prepared to do, driving down to the edge of the water, and fastening all he had with him on the seat, which was a board placed across the waggon, and this he secured with a rope. Everything was done to prevent his trying to cross, but to no purpose, and we saw him drive into the river—the ponies seeming rather to like it. As soon as he was clear of the bank the current carried him rapidly down, and we had to walk fast to keep abreast of him. The ponies' heads showed plainly, and they seemed to be swimming strongly and to be gaining ground—their driver standing on the seat, and urging them on with wild shouts. Once they struck a sand-bar when more than half over, but they plunged off again, and reached the bank more than half a mile below the fort, at an angle of the river where it was shallow. It was impossible to drive up at this point; but the ponies were brought up, and the waggon was left to be carried up in sections.

All this prevented our getting off till the afternoon, and we only made some ten or twelve miles that night, camping on a small stream running into the Saskatchawan, having crossed the south branch of that river. A great number of wolves came to serenade us that night, seeming to know that we were leaving the country. We fired at several of them, as it was a beautiful moonlight night, but we did not get any.

The next day we were up at dawn, and as our breakfast was not a very tempting one, we were soon off, and made, I should think, about thirty miles by sunset. The country was uninteresting, being what is called a rolling prairie, covered with small ponds, on which were a few ducks, and of these we managed to shoot three, and when they were split open and broiled they made us a capital supper.

The first eleven days of our journey were very uneventful, the only incident being the unsuccessful stalk of a white-tailed deer and the shooting of two wolves; but on the night of the twelfth day we were awoke by feeling our feet burning, and on jumping up we found the whole prairie on one side of us on fire, and three sides of a large blanket on which we were sleeping quite black. We at once rushed to the horses, pulled up the picket-pins, and rode them into a swamp, by the side of which we had camped in order to get willows for our beds. We then rescued our bedding, or what remained of it, and our rifles, which, lying in the middle of the blanket, had escaped damage, and joined the horses in the swamp. The fire soon passed us, leaving the whole country a black desert, the ponds and a little marshy ground round them being the only green spots—not a pleasant prospect for us, as we had to follow the fire, our journey lying in the same direction. There was no use in going to bed again; so we had breakfast and started at once, making a long day's journey. We hoped to find that the fire had been stopped by some large stream, but all those which we passed during the day had been too small for the purpose, and the fire had leaped over them. We had therefore to camp by a swamp, and picket our horses in it, their only food being the wet rushes, which were very bad for them, as such food is very likely to give them colic.

I noticed that Badger had been in very bad spirits all day,

and I found on questioning him that he felt sure that hostile Indians were near us, and that the fire of the past night was an attempt by some small party of them to stampede our horses. Knowing that we were in friendly Indian country, I did not agree with him, and in any case there was nothing for it but to push on. The following day we got into an unburnt prairie again, the fire having taken a turn to the south, as there was a good deal of wind blowing in that direction, and a small stream, which sufficed to turn it.

On the fourteenth day of our ride, we were off late, having made another unsuccessful attempt to stalk some antelopes; but these had been so much frightened by the fire, and the ground was so bare, that we could get no nearer than three hundred yards—too far for a round-ball rifle.

Some time afterwards we fancied we saw a mounted man disappear behind a hill ahead of us; but as we saw nothing more of him, we concluded it must have been an elk, and we were riding along carelessly, when, on mounting a ridge, we found ourselves close to a small Indian camp of nine lodges. They were so elaborately painted and so large that Badger at once said they must be Sioux; but it was too late to retreat, and the man we had seen was in the middle of the camp talking to some sixty or seventy Indians, who were evidently expecting us, as there was no surprise expressed at our appearance. As we rode up the Indians retired into their lodges, only some boys remaining to look at us, and we noticed that there seemed to be no women with them.

The proper thing to do on arriving at an Indian camp is to enter the chief's tent, so we looked round, and seeing a spear and a number of scalps hanging over the door of the largest of them, we entered, and found three Indians seated round the fire. A very tall, black-looking Indian seemed to be the chief, so I motioned to Badger to sit on one side of him, while I seated myself on the other. All three Indians stared straight at the fire, and I was sure that something was wrong; so I determined to put the matter beyond doubt, and lighting my pipe, I passed it round. Now no greater insult can be offered to a man by an Indian than to refuse to smoke with him, and yet all these men passed my pipe back to me—not one taking a single whiff.

Badger recommended our starting at once, but I was very hungry, and helped myself to some boiled buffalo-meat from a pot on the fire, Badger doing the same. It gave me a curious feeling, sitting by those three silent Indians, who were probably our deadly enemies, and old stories of Indian atrocities came back to me in a very unpleasant manner. I had a large Tranter revolver and Badger had a Colt; but what could we do against seventy men? It was a bad sign that no other Indians came into the lodge, and the camp was unnaturally quiet—a few low, muttered sounds being all we could hear. They had no dogs with them, which I could not understand then, though I did so afterwards, and there being boys, and yet no women, was another unusual circumstance.

As soon as we had eaten all we wanted of the meat, I told Badger to go outside and tighten up girths, and mount, and that I would join him on hearing that he was ready. This he did, and in a few minutes called to me, on which I rose and backed to the door, not caring to give them a chance of stabbing me behind. On getting outside I found Badger mounted, and holding my horse with one hand and the pack-horse with the other, so I took mine, and put my foot in the stirrup to mount, when the saddle—which was only an Indian one, and fastened on with a surcingle—turned partially round, and I had to undo it and put it straight, and this I was proceeding to do when the chief and his two friends came out, and at the same time the other Indians—who Badger said had been watching him from the doors of their tents—also appeared. The chief came up to me and, pushing me on one side, asked, in very bad Cree, how I dared to come hunting on his territory. He then said he was a big chief, and owned all the country round, and that he hated the white men, who had never done him anything but harm. I answered through Badger, who had translated most of this, that he was not a Cree at all (for we had found out from his dress, and especially from his moccasins, that he was a Sioux) and had no right to be where we found him; that I had seen one man of his tribe tortured by the Crees for being where he then was, and that a similar fate awaited him if he did not at once leave and go south; but that, so far as I was concerned, I was an Englishman and friendly with all Indians. He answered that he could not be my friend, but that if I would give him my horses and rifles, I was free to go where I wished. I of course said that this was impossible, as I was a long way from home, and in a country where game was very scarce and hard to get even when one was armed, but that if I gave up my rifle I must die; I was willing, I said, to exchange horses with him, he giving me two for one, as mine were so much better than his. On this he took my horse by the bridle and was leading him away, and when I stopped him he opened his blanket and hit at my head with a long club which he had concealed under it. I had

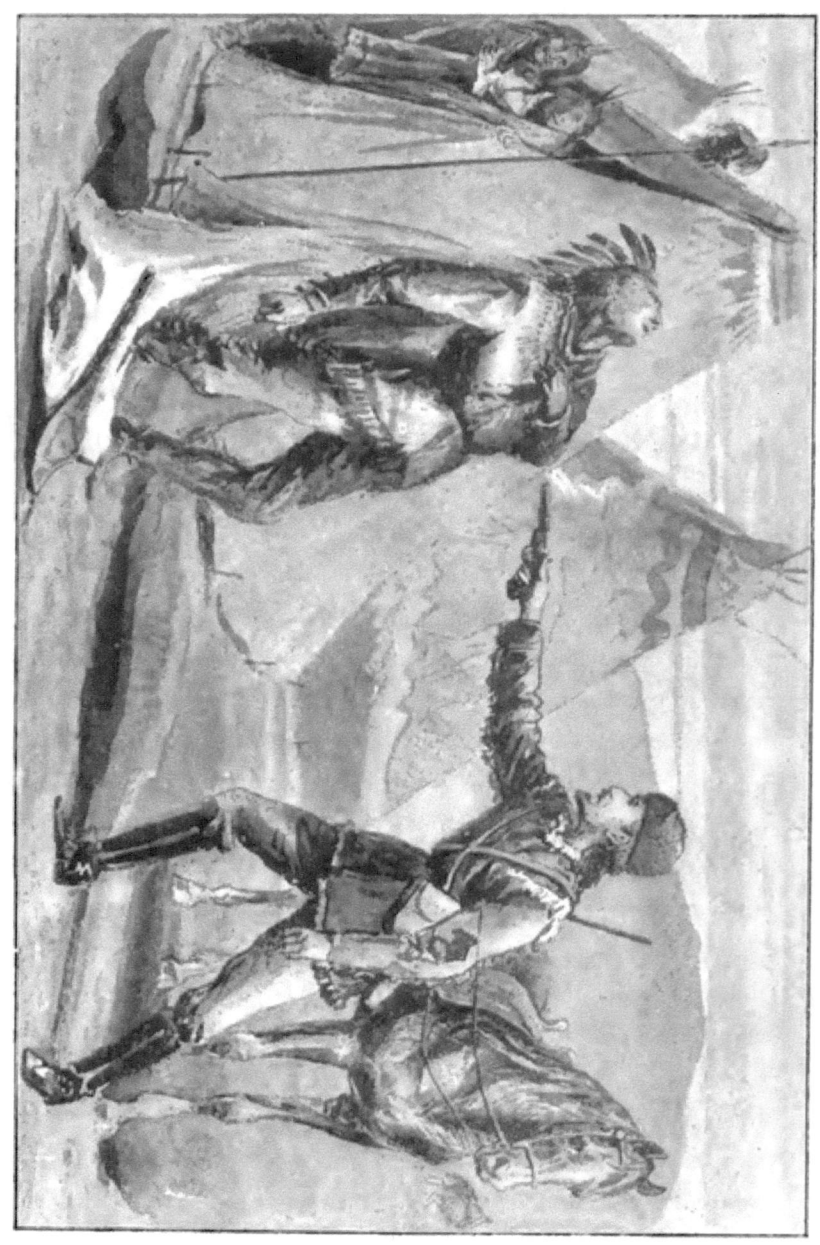

Page 23.—I drew my revolver and fired at him.

unbuttoned my holster, but I was too late in drawing my revolver, so I threw up my left arm to ward off the blow, which broke the arm above the elbow and cut my head open. I drew my revolver and fired at him, hitting him in the chest, and thinking that I could not possibly get away, I fired at him a second time, the ball taking him in the throat just as he staggered back. I then put my back against my horse, which being used to firing had stood quite still, and faced the other Indians. These, on seeing their chief fall rushed into their tents, and I knew they had gone for their guns, so making a desperate effort, I scrambled on to my horse and rode off, Badger having already started and being some distance in advance. A good many shots were fired at me during the first few hundred yards, but I lay forward on my horse, and they all missed me, though some of them seemed to come pretty close. I soon caught up Badger and told him that he had to stick to me or I would shoot him, and being little more than a boy, only twenty-one, he was so frightened that I do not think he wished to leave me.

The Indians' horses were several hundred yards from their camp, and it took them fully ten minutes to get them and saddle up, but at the end of that time we saw them coming strung out in a long line. We were fully two miles ahead by this time, and we kept our horses at three-quarters speed, which we found prevented their gaining on us. As we rode along Badger and I consulted as to our best route, as he knew the country well, and so far as I could judge from what he said, for an Indian or an half-breed has a very poor idea of miles, we were nearly three hundred miles from Fort Garry, the first settlement being some twenty miles nearer—a fearfully long ride for one's life on grass-fed horses. Ours were certainly much faster than those of the Indians, but these last, though small, are used to hard work and poor fare, and to being ridden long distances without resting, and we knew that the Indians would not hesitate to use the points of their knives to drive them along. We were going from two o'clock in the afternoon till nearly seven in the evening, when we were able to take a rest, as the moon rose late and it was very dark.

The Indians, though wonderful trackers, could not follow us until morning, as the moon did not give sufficient light for tracking, so we determined to throw them off the scent if possible, and after Badger had bound my arm across my chest with strips cut from my leather hunting-shirt, we started again at midnight and rode about two miles due north, choosing a hard rocky ridge, as it would not leave much trail, and then we again rode in the proper direction, which was due east.

Up to this time my arm had not been very painful, having been apparently numbed by the blow; but it had been swinging about for five hours, and when we came to examine it we found that the bone had come through the skin in one place. Badger bound it up very well and fastened it firmly; but the pain was now very great, and nothing but the certainty of being tortured if caught kept me going. Up to about nine o'clock the next morning we thought that our ruse had been a success, but then the Indians appeared again, running the trail like bloodhounds. We had, however, fully three miles start and managed to keep it all day, though we had to make frequent halts to breathe our horses. That night we passed in some heavy timber, where I remember that the noise made by insects was so great as to resemble that made by a threshing-machine a hundred yards away. Here we seriously discussed the possibility of making some kind of a shelter with trunks of trees, and keeping the Indians off, in the hopes that some friendly Indians might come up and drive them away; but the state of my arm finally decided us to give up the idea, as it was very much swollen and looked as if it might mortify. I kept cold water on it continually, and as we passed ponds at frequent intervals, I could keep the bandages cool.

Our plan of travelling was to halt soon after sunset, when Badger rubbed down the horses and staked them out, watering them when cool; we then slept, or tried to do so, for about three or four hours, when we mounted and rode at a canter till nearly daylight. The horses had then two hours more rest and were rubbed down again, working the sinews of the legs well with the hands, after which we mounted and rode all day, getting off now and then for a few minutes. By these means, we had gained a good many miles on the Indians, who sometimes did not come in sight till nearly twelve o'clock, when the fast riding began.

Badger behaved splendidly during the ride, and was very hopeful of our escaping. The horses were getting very thin, and we had to throw away nearly all our pack, including a rifle and a lot of ammunition, breaking the former so that it might be of no use to our pursuers. On the morning of the fourth day, our ride having lasted three days and three nights, we came to the first house, which was inhabited by a man with his wife and one child. When they heard that the Sioux were only a few miles behind us, they got in two horses, and leaving everything, joined us.

We saw the Indians once during the morning from a high

mound, but soon afterwards we came to five or six more houses, the inhabitants of which turned out armed and rode out to meet the Indians, a body of nearly twenty men, and we were safe.

I do not suppose that two more miserable-looking wretches ever rode into a settlement than ourselves. For four days we had not used water, and our clothes were dirty and a mass of rags; then, too, my hair had not been cut for nearly a year, and I was the colour of light mahogany. We stopped at the first house, and one of the women dressed my arm for me, after which we went to bed and stayed there for nearly twenty hours; then we had a good meal of pork and potatoes, and in the afternoon rode on to Fort Garry, where we attracted a good deal of attention, our horses being mere bags of bones.

Riding through the settlement, for there was no town there at that time, I met a good many people whom I had known the previous year, and all of them were very anxious to know where I had turned up from, and why I was in my present condition; but I only answered them by asking for the baker's shop, as some new bread seemed to me the one thing of all others that I most desired, for no one who has not gone without it for months can imagine what the craving for it is. I had eaten nothing but "galette" in camp or in my log cabin during the winter, and at Fort Carlton had only got rolls made with soda.

I may as well mention that "galette" is made of flour, water, and "saleratus," mixed as dough and formed into flat cakes, one of which is then put into the frying-pan, and this is placed in front of the fire; when the cake gets stiff it is taken out and put by the fire with a stick to keep it up, another is then put in the frying-pan, and so on till you have cooked enough for the party. It is not bad when hot, but only fit for making bullets when cold.

When I reached the baker's, and was given a new loaf and a pound of butter, I ate them in about equal proportions, and do not think I ever enjoyed anything so much in my life.

At that time there was no hotel of any kind in the settlement, so that one of the settlers kindly put me up, and I soon recovered from my fatigue, while a half-breed doctor set my arm after a fashion.

I found the place in a state of great excitement, and it seemed that the outbreak of the Sioux Indians, to which I have before referred, and which took place the previous year while we were on our way to the settlement, had culminated in an awful massacre, nearly 1400 men, women, and children having been murdered in one night, under circumstances of dreadful barbarity. These Indians had plundered the whole of Minnesota with the exception of three or four towns, had burned all the settlers' houses, and had carried off a number of women and a great many cattle. The United States' troops had been sent to the spot and had scattered "Little Crow's" band for a time, but could not catch any of them, and it was some of the members of this band who had chased me.

It appears that when "Little Crow" was driven from Minnesota he took refuge in British territory, collecting his scattered men, till he was said to have more than 1200 warriors under him, and with these he now marched on Fort Garry, sending a runner to say that unless he was given so much money and so many horses, &c., he would sack the settlement. There really was no danger if the half-breeds would only work together; but this they never would do, being always divided into two parties, English and French, very jealous of one another and frequently coming to blows. The settlement in addition was so scattered that it was impossible to defend it all, and many of the settlers were for bribing " Little Crow " to go away, though fortunately these were outvoted, and a body of rangers was raised, but this was not until I had left.

Being anxious to reach a town and have my arm properly attended to, I made enquiries as to the best way of going to St. Paul's. The distance was about six hundred miles, and no houses would be found on the way, everything having been burned by the Sioux, who were scattered all over the first half of that distance.

None of the half-breeds to whom I spoke seemed willing to act as guide, and I began to think of trying it without a guide, taking Badger with me, when I heard of a French half-breed called Isidore Maronde, who lived some ten or twelve miles north of the Fort, who, everyone said, would face anything for money. He bore a bad character, being rather too ready to use his knife in a quarrel; but this was a small matter, so I sent for him. His appearance was not in his favour, his face being a bad one; but he was a very fine man physically, and was said to have been in many fights with the Indians. He at once said that it was only a question of money, as he was quite ready to face the " Devil " himself if properly paid for it; and it was at last arranged that for guiding me to St. Paul's and getting back the best way he could, he was to have £50 in money, a fine double gun of mine, and the three horses which we should use on the road.

The next thing to do was to find the horses, for although I

should have liked to have taken on the three horses which I had brought from the Saskatchawan, they were so utterly worn out that it was doubtful whether they would ever be worth anything again, and in any case it would be months before they could be ridden on such a journey as that which I was about to undertake. I let it be known therefore that I wanted three fast horses, strong enough to carry heavy loads for six hundred miles in fourteen or fifteen days, and I very soon had several hundreds brought to me.

In those days the half-breeds lived almost entirely on buffalo meat, going twice a year for a big hunt on the prairie to get it, and bringing home dried meat and pemmican in the spring and fresh meat in the early winter. These hunts necessitated their owning a great many horses, and these from the hard life they led, and the amount of galloping they got after buffalo, could go almost any distance on nothing but grass, and over all kinds of ground without falling. We selected three of the best of these, and had them well fed and exercised for several days; we also bought a new outfit, provisions, &c., taking nothing but what was absolutely necessary, and our weapons consisted of a shot gun and two revolvers. It was of no use our taking rifles with any idea of making a fight of it, in case we should meet Indians, but a shot gun might be of use in procuring us food, as grouse and ducks abounded. Nothing could exceed the kindness of the inhabitants of Fort Garry, the Bishop, Dr. Anderson, kindly offering me a carriage and pair to take me down to St. Paul's, saying that he did not care if he never saw it again; but this would have been a novel way of travelling through a dangerous Indian country, especially as we were going where there were no roads.

On the 2nd of May we said good-bye to everyone, and got off about five o'clock in the afternoon, a good many settlers coming a short distance with us, and bidding us adieu as if they never expected to see us again. Our idea was to ride at night, hiding away in the daytime, and this we did throughout the journey.

The whereabouts of "Little Crow" and his band was known, so that we could avoid him, but there were small parties of his warriors wandering about all over northern Minnesota and southern Dacotah, through which territories our road lay, and we had to be constantly on the watch. Maronde used to ride ahead at a canter, and I followed, leading the pack-horse, which was fastened to my sound arm. Now and then we saw fires, and had to make a detour to avoid them, and several times we heard shots fired, but this was during the day, when we were well hidden in some thicket or under the bank of a river. Our horses, though not so good as those I had ridden from Carlton, were very fair and in capital condition, and we frequently went at a canter for hours. We passed several burnt farmhouses, and in front of some of these there was a row of graves, showing where the soldiers had buried the dead.

The first inhabited house which we reached was near a small settlement called St. Cloud, and here we had our first good sleep, for it takes a long time to get used to turning day into night. There were only two small rooms and a "lean-to" used as a kitchen, one of the two rooms being a bedroom and the other the living-room. I found a number of lumberers staying there, and as I said I had not slept in a bed for ten nights I was given the only bed, and thought I was most lucky, though I had afterwards reason to change my mind.

We had arrived about eleven o'clock in the morning, and having passed the dangerous portion of our journey, we determined to take a day's rest, so remained until the following morning. When night came I took possession of my small room, the lumberers and my guide sleeping on the floor of the living-room, and my host and his wife in the stable. The first feeling was delightful, and I was just luxuriating in it when I felt something at my neck, and a little later it felt as if I had a blister on. I got up and lighted the candle, and found the pillow alive with B flats; they swarmed everywhere and the walls, or rather logs, were also covered with them. It was out of the question trying to sleep there, so I put on some of my things and went into the outer room, stumbling over a man as I did so. He asked me what was the matter, and on my telling him he laughed at me, and said I was a pretty frontiersman to care for such trifles, and that if I was not going to use the bed he would do so, and he proceeded to move his things into my room, while I took his place on the floor. I had just got off to sleep when out he came again, using most unparliamentary language, and declaring that he had been very nearly lifted out of bed.

Of course I had a good laugh at him, when he and I adjourned to the stable, where we finished the night very comfortably on some hay.

The next day we rode into St. Paul's, and after putting our horses into a livery stable, we went to the principal hotel in the place. Here they were at first disposed to refuse us admission, till I reminded the landlord of my having been there the year before, and of my having left some things in his charge.

Dinner was just beginning, so I washed my hands and went

in, my dress consisting of a leather shirt, leather trousers and moccasins, and a fur cap, all of them being very much the worse for wear. Maronde, after looking into the dining-room and seeing some ladies, refused to go in, and was accommodated elsewhere. My appearance caused quite a sensation in the room, and there was a great deal of whispering among the guests, and a waiter was sent to find out who I was. Among those present was a general officer of the United States' Army and his staff, many of the latter having their wives with them, and I had not been long at table when an aide-de-camp came to tell me to go to the General at once, he evidently taking me for a half-breed scout. I sent to say that I would come when I had finished my dinner, and on my going to him, the General apologized for his apparent discourtesy, although he did not tell me what he had taken me for, nor could I blame him much for the mistake he had made, when I looked at myself in a full-length glass.

I found that he had been sent to take command of some twelve hundred men who were about to march against the Indians, and was therefore anxious to get any information he could as to their whereabouts, the nature of the country, and of the best route to take.

I told him that the men he was taking with him would be of very little service against such enemies, being almost entirely infantry, and I advised him to raise a body of rangers from the half-breeds of the Red River, any one of whom was equal to two Indians; but I could not get him to agree with me, as he was quite new to this kind of fighting. I told him that the Indians would hang round his line of march, cutting off stragglers and shooting his sentries, they themselves being always invisible.

Events turned out as I had predicted: the expedition started, saw a few Indians in the distance whom they failed to catch, remained out about three months, harassed in every way by the Indians, and returned having done nothing.

In the meantime, " Little Crow's " band, finding themselves cut off from their hunting-grounds, rose against their leader, who fled to Fort Garry and was shot by a Scotch settler, for the price put on his head by the U.S. Government. His men came in and gave themselves up, and were tried by court-martial, some three hundred of them being condemned to be hung. This wholesale sentence was, however, not carried out, orders being sent from Washington that all the Indians should be retried, and eventually only thirty-two or three were hung at Mankato, a square platform being erected, round the sides of which they were executed.

Curiously enough, while walking one day in the streets of St. Paul's, I found among a number of photographs of Indians a portrait of the man who had broken my arm, whose name was Ki-chi-ma-ka-ses, " the Little Fox," and who was chief of one section of the Sioux. He had come frequently into St. Paul's before the massacre, and had been photographed, as had also " Little Crow " and many other Sioux. I found there was a reward of a thousand dollars on his head; but it would not have been advisable to have stopped in St. Paul's on the chance of getting it, as there was no one, except Badger, to prove that I had killed him.

I went to a surgeon about my arm, and found that the half-breed doctor had merely tied some splints round it, and that now it was too late to do anything, the bones having set themselves, giving me a stiff arm for life, but not interfering much with its use for shooting, riding, &c. He said nothing but the healthy life I had been leading had prevented mortification from setting in.

I left St. Paul's for England soon after this, and thus ended my first trip to America.

CHAPTER VIII.

Return to America.—Start for Kansas.—Warning against obliging strangers.
—The town of Troy.—Horse-racing. A soft thing.—A breakdown.—
A wrestling-match.—My new man Fox. His objection to sheriffs.—
The settlement of White Rock. Its history.—A happy hunting-ground.
—A Tenderfoot's first run with buffalo. He prefers walking.—A
wonderful mare. I buy her.—Trying Brown's courage.—Appearance
of Indians near camp.

I RETAINED such pleasant memories of my visit to the prairies in 1862 that I determined to go again; so I left England in June 1866, intending to hunt during the summer on the prairies of Kansas, and to winter wherever I could hear of there being plenty of game.

I started alone, but came across a young Englishman on the steamer who had a great desire to see the West, so we arranged to go together. After a short stay in Canada, we reached St. Joseph's, Missouri, where we intended to fit out. And here let me warn anyone who may think of doing as I did to beware of specious men who offer to buy horses, mules, and outfit for them, on the plea that they know the people and their ways, and can save them a lot of money. I am of course speaking of total strangers, who come up and introduce themselves to you, and whose appearance is often in their favour. Such a man, whom I will call "the Colonel," which was the name he generally went by, was most anxious "to save me all trouble," so after thanking him profusely I commissioned him to buy me a good span of mules, and four horses suited to the West, the result being as follows:—There were a span of fine-looking mules of which one was lame and had been so for months, one horse which had been sold because he was a confirmed bolter, another because he ate up his bridle, reins, or anything else with which he might be fastened, and a third because he was touched in the wind, the fourth was a "race-mare," who could do a mile in some wonderfully short time, and of whom more hereafter.

Fortunately I got my men myself, taking them on the recommendation of an old freighter, and very good they both were—Ivor going as cook and Ben as driver, the only necessary qualification for the former berth being the knowledge of how to make a fire and to put on water to boil, all the rest being supposed to come.

It took ten days to get everything together, and about the beginning of July we started, our outfit being carried in a light waggon, in which we had nearly twenty-five hundredweight, much too great a load over such roads. M—— and I had two horses each, riding one and leading the other, and the two men travelled on the box of the waggon.

I must not forget to say that I had on this trip a number of patent compendiums, than which nothing could have worked better or seemed more convenient in the shops, but all of which we gradually threw away, as they became dinted and no longer fitted one inside another.

On leaving "St. Joe," as it is always called, we were told that a good place to camp the first night would be at the town of Troy, as it was not so far but that we could easily send back for anything which had been forgotten, as it was only thirteen miles from St. Joe. We kept a good look out as we rode along so as not to pass the place, and when we arrived at a house and barn, thinking we must have done thirteen miles, we asked a man, who was sitting in front of the house, where Troy was, on which he laughed and said that we could see all there was of it, the place having been planned and pegged out but never built, one house, a barn, and the pegs representing the town. There used to be many places of this kind in the West, represented by grand pictures at agents' offices and railway-stations as flourishing towns, and when credulous people had bought corner lots, and came to visit their property, they found much such a town as Troy.

The first four or five days of our journey, through a number of small settlements, were very uninteresting, the only game being a few grouse, and the only incident, my losing ten pounds in a cleverly managed horse-race of three hundred yards. A settler came into camp one morning on a poor-looking horse, and offered to run it against anything we had for ten pounds (fifty dollars), the distance to be three hundred yards. I took him up and saddled the race-mare, thinking I had a "soft thing." The race was to be on the sandy road, which here ran along the side of the hill, having a ridge on the outside of it, and turning just beyond camp round a sharp corner. We started from a point a short distance on our side of the corner, my opponent taking the inside, and when he came to the turn, he crowded me out of the road on to the ridge, so that my mare nearly came down, and he won easily. Knowing all I do now, I should not have paid the money; but I was green then, and did so, and it was a good lesson to me.

We had a piece of bad luck just before reaching the last settlement, a place called Lake Sibley. We were going along very well, and were thinking of camping for lunch, when the mules shied at a dead ox, which was lying on the road-side, when the front axle broke and the waggon rolled over. Fortunately, the mules behaved well and broke nothing; but we had to camp where we were, away from wood and water, and unpack the waggon into the tent, the weather being stormy, and we made a shelter for ourselves out of the waggon-cover. I rode to the settlement the next morning to try and find a smith to put on a new axle, but found that one must be sent for from St. Joe, involving a delay of a week; so rather than remain where we were, I exchanged the waggon for another, giving money into the bargain, though mine was a new one, whereas the one I got was several years old.

During the evening we had a good many visitors to the tent, and among others the man of whom I had got the waggon, and another man called Brown, who wanted to go with us as guide, as he said he knew all the country we wished to hunt over and was not afraid of Indians. The waggon man, whose name was Belknap, began bragging of his wrestling, telling us that he had never been thrown, on which Brown said it was quite time that he should be, and challenged him to come outside. Of course we all went out to see the fun, and the two men stripped and clinched, when Brown, first making a feint, threw Belknap over his shoulder, giving him a bad shaking;

a second struggle ended in the same way, after which Belknap said very little. I heard in the course of the evening of another man, whom everyone said I ought to have, whose name was Fox, and who seemed from all accounts to fear nothing, having been out by himself on the Solomon River hunting for a lost mule, when no other ten men in the settlement would have done it, as the Indians were very bad just then; so I determined to go and see him in the morning, having already engaged Brown. I found him digging a well for a new settler, at a small place a few miles lower down the Republican River, and after a short talk engaged him. Seeing that he was barefooted, I said that he had better go into the settlement and buy himself some boots, and that I would advance him the money, on which he replied that he had rather not do so, as the sheriff wanted him, and would perhaps detain him, as he had killed two Germans in a gambling row; and it came out, too, that if our journey led us in the direction of Texas, he could not accompany us, as the sheriff of Houston also wanted him, though he would not say why. He was evidently a first-class desperado, but as our trip was a dangerous one, his pluck more than counterbalanced everything else. I tried to get boots for him, but the few they had at Sibley were all too small, and he had to go barefooted, and make himself moccasins from the first buffalo we killed.

The following day we left Sibley, and two days' travelling took us to the north of a creek called "White Rock," on which we expected to remain some time. This place had a curious history, having already been settled nine times, each set of settlers having remained only a part of a summer, and being then scared away by Indians. One lot had just left, and it lowered Brown very much in our estimation when we found that he had been one of them.

I could not discover that a single man, woman, or child had been actually killed during the whole nine summers, but one man had been wounded this last summer, and the rest of them seemed always to have run as soon as they either saw an Indian or the track of one. For some miles up the creek we came across houses, in many of which everything heavy, such as beds and stoves, had been left; and we also found a number of small corn-fields, just coming into ear, which we determined to visit later on. We kept on for about thirty miles until we had passed all houses, and then made a comfortable camp, not only putting up two tents, but erecting a bough shelter from the sun, which we called the "dining-room," and also cutting a smoke-house out of the bank of the stream for buffalo-tongues, of which we had promised to bring back a supply.

We had not seen much game so far, and nothing bigger than a turkey, but above our camp found it very plentiful, including white- and black-tailed deer, any number of turkeys, and a good many elk, while by going south we found plenty of buffalo. It certainly was a "happy hunting-ground," and we had it, and were likely to have it, to ourselves, so far as white men were concerned. The Indians were our only trouble, and as they knew that the creek was deserted, there was not much to tempt them to come near us.

My friend M——, having lived all his life in a town, knew nothing of riding, though I did not know this till afterwards; and a few days after we reached this camp I proposed to have a run at buffalo, so we started, I riding the bolter, and M—— the omnivorous animal. The country was rolling prairie, with very often a dry watercourse in the hollows, and as these were overgrown with sunflowers, we could not see where they began, the sunflowers being higher than our heads.

A ride of about two hours took us to a high ridge, from which we had an extensive view, and we could see many small bands of buffalo, of from three or four to fifty; and choosing one of these, as they were on good riding ground, we made for them, keeping in a hollow which hid us till we were within a quarter of a mile of them. We then tightened our girths and loaded. I was using a sixteen-bore double gun, and M—— a double rifle of the same calibre, which I had lent him. I noticed that he held his reins very awkwardly and had some trouble in managing his horse and holding his rifle at the same time, but I was too excited to think of anything but the run before us, so leaving the hollow, we rode on to the level, and were at once seen by the buffaloes, which commenced going off.

Giving a shout and telling M—— to put the spurs in, away I went, leaving him a little behind me, and we were going down a steep hill, when I heard strange sounds in my rear, and turning round in my saddle, I saw M—— holding on both before and behind, and flying about in an extraordinary way, his hat and gun gone, and he evidently being on the point of coming to grief himself; and just as I turned my head to see what was in front of me and to pull up, I heard a thud, followed by a loud groan, and saw M—— on his back, heels in the air. I caught his horse as he passed me, and then rode back, finding M—— unhurt and unable to account for what had happened; the rifle was not broken as I feared it would be, so he remounted and we started again, taking a new direction, as our buffalo would have alarmed all on that side. On going round a point of timber we came on an old bull, and immediately gave chase, and after many turns and two furious charges, I killed him, having to give him seven bullets before he dropped. M—— came up as I was taking out the tongue, and owned that he could not manage a horse and a gun at the same time, and that for the future he would content himself with stalking. We tried a good deal more ground, looking for cows and calves; but the country was disturbed, and we had to go back to camp with one tongue only.

On reaching camp, we were surprised to find a young fellow from Sibley who had come, hoping to sell us a very nice little bay mare, but he wanted a hundred and fifty dollars for her, and I thought this too much. He asked if he might remain a few days and hunt with us, wishing to have a run at buffalo; and I of course said yes, as there was plenty of room in the men's tent. On the following morning Brown, the stranger, and I saddled up for a run, I taking my race-mare, and Brown M——'s second steed, who made noise enough for a locomotive, and we started south, keeping to the east of the ground we went over the day before. A solitary bull was soon met with, and not knowing whether we should find any more, we got ready for a run. I supposed that I was going to have it all to myself, as my mare was nearly sixteen hands, while the bay, whom her owner called "Polly," was not more than fourteen; she was, however, made like a race-horse, having a good shoulder and good muscle behind.

We started together and remained so for a short distance, when the locomotive dropped behind, and I put on a spurt to leave the mare, who, however, remained at my knee, though I was doing my best; a minute later she passed me easily, going over the rough ground like a cat, and the stranger got the first shot, and in the end killed the bull, I being simply nowhere, as my mare tried to run away on hearing the firing, and being very bad when the ground was rough.

I need not say how disgusted I was, though the mare's owner behaved very well and refrained from chaffing me. We took the bull's tongue, and Brown having joined us, with his horse entirely pumped, we started once more, but found no buffaloes till late in the afternoon, when we came on a small band of cows and calves, which scattered on our chasing them; and I managed to get one after firing nearly twenty shots, as my mare jumped many feet every time I raised my gun, so that it was impossible to take any sort of aim.

On the way to camp I exchanged the race-mare for the pony, giving fifty dollars to boot, though she had cost me two hundred dollars (£40). This was by far the best animal that I ever sat on in America, and though so small she seemed to make nothing of my fifteen stone, going over awful ground without a stumble, even at full speed, and standing fire like an old shooting pony. Although I gave a long price for her I did not regret it, as she was the means of saving my life more than once, as will be seen further on. I owned her for three years, and then sold her to a companion on my leaving for home.

The mare's owner left us the next day, and we moved south to the Solomon River, the large herd of buffalo being on the other side of it, so that it took us nearly half a day to reach them from where we had been camped. We established our-

I

selves on the forks of the Solomon, which was, although we did not then know it, a favourite rendezvous of the Sioux, their usual camp being not quite two miles from where we then were.

Brown and I went out a few days after our arrival, and as the grass was bad and our horses thin we went on foot. After walking some miles, and seeing nothing but some very wild antelope, we suddenly noticed what I took at first to be smoke among some trees ahead of us, but which I recollected soon afterwards was nothing but some dead cottonwood trees standing among green ones, as I had remarked the same appearance a few days previously and had gone to see what it was. I thought this a good opportunity to test Brown's courage, about which I had my doubts, as he was always boasting of the number of Indians he had killed; so I pretended to think it was smoke, and told Brown that I should go and see what it meant, on which he refused to accompany me, and started off in the direction of camp, saying that he did not call that courage, but fool-hardiness. After walking a short distance, however, I turned and overtook him, and had a good laugh at him, telling him what it really was, when he assured me that he knew it all the time and merely wanted to try me.

On our return to camp we found that we might very easily have come across some Indians, as eight or ten of them had during our absence ridden on to the bluffs which overhung the camp, and had shaken their spears at those in it.

We had a consultation that evening, and all the men, with the exception of Fox, wished to give up the trip and return home; but as the latter assured me that he would go on with me alone if necessary, they were at last shamed into remaining.

CHAPTER IX.

Find a Sioux camp-ground.—The omnivorous horse.—A Rocky-Mountain moose.—A large turkey-roost.—A deserted settlement.—Fox thinks he is going to die.—Crossing the river under difficulties.—A fast buffalo-calf.—Adventure with a buffalo.—Camp deserted. Another made. Row with the men. Brown discharged. Remove to old camp.—More buffalo-hunting.—Surprised by Indians. Cut off from camp. Plan of getting through. Its success and safety.—Neighbourhood getting too warm.—Fox declines going near a sheriff.—Return eastwards.

As we found a great deal of Indian sign about, and came one morning on the big Sioux camp-ground, which was so close to us and which had evidently been lately occupied, we thought it wise to move some miles up the Solomon River, where we camped on a small stream which ran into it, and found capital grass and a spring of ice-cold water.

Here the horse whose peculiarity it was to eat his reins gave us a specimen of his skill. M——, to whom he belonged, had been out for a ride, and on coming home had taken off the saddle and bridle, and had tied him to the waggon-wheel by his picket-rope, meaning to put him out later; but this he forgot to do, and there he remained all night. In the morning we found he had torn off all he could reach of the waggon-cover, and had then pulled out a bag containing sixty pounds of sugar, of which he had eaten all he could, trampling the remainder into the ground—a great loss, as we were so far from any place where we could get any more.

A day or two after this, M——, Fox, and I were out after buffalo, when we came across a fine badger, which, finding he could not get away, flattened himself out on the prairie, thinking, I suppose, that we should not then see him, and sank so low that he did not seem to be more than two inches thick. M——, who had never seen one, asked what it was, on which we told him that it was a " Rocky-Mountain moose," and as such it was described in his journal and in his letters home.

Hearing from Brown that there was a good-sized settlement, where we could probably buy sugar, about sixty miles down the river, Fox and I determined to go there, making a circuit to avoid the Sioux camp. We calculated on doing it in three days, and took our best horses and weapons, as it was very likely we might be chased by Indians. The first day we camped a few miles below the forks of the river, seeing no fresh Indian sign, and we killed two turkeys from a roost close to where we camped. There were at least two hundred in it, and only a few of the nearest flew away when we fired, so that we could easily have killed many more. We had gathered a number of mushrooms during the ride, and with these and broiled turkey we had a splendid supper.

On the following day we reached the settlement, which lay on the opposite bank of the river, and found it deserted. There were some twenty houses, and they seemed to have been left very suddenly, as many small things were lying about round the doors, which in most cases were open. We went into some of the houses, finding, as on White Rock, that everything heavy had been left behind; and in one—a very small house, of one room only—we were surprised to see short red hair lying about all over the floor, the explanation of which we heard some months later. It appears that a few days before our arrival there had been an Indian scare, and all the settlers had run away, the man who lived in this house first cutting off his hair close to his head to avoid being scalped should the Indians get him. On our way back, Fox had an attack of ague, and, plucky man as he was in other ways, he entirely broke down under it, and we had to camp where we were, almost without provisions, as we had shot nothing that day. For some hours he thought he was dying, and he would pray one minute and use the most awful language the next. In the morning he was well again, and we reached camp that evening, only to find M—— and all the men down with the same complaint, the camp being on very low ground. We therefore determined to move, crossing the river so as to be nearer the buffalo. The banks were high at this point, the one on the opposite side being about eighty feet from the water to where we could rest the mules, and that eighty must be done with a rush.

The proper way would have been to empty the waggon and to have carried the contents over; but everyone was so miserable that we determined to chance it, as the mules, having done nothing lately, were fresh and in good order. Going down was comparatively easy, as we tied the wheels, Fox and I managing the waggon, the others lying in it, as they felt too weak to help. The water was shallow, but the bottom was muddy, and we had a struggle to reach the opposite side: however, we sent the mules at the bank and got up halfway, when they stopped and the waggon began to come back. Now we were on a slope which was at an angle of 45°, and going back meant a total smash and a very bad time for those inside; so, shouting to them to get out and help us, Fox and I each seized a wheel, and held on as I think I never held on to anything in my life, so much depending on it. The others recovered with marvellous rapidity from their illness, and to see them jumping about you would never have believed that there was anything the matter with them. The mules were staunch and tried again, and this time we reached the resting-place, from which the slope was more gradual. We camped about three miles further up the river, in a small bend of it—a capital place if we were attacked, as the water was deep all round the bend. The only timber was near the tent, and the men made quite a little settlement, putting up a large dining-room, covered with a spare tent-fly, and making benches and a table: we had also a smoke-stage, hitching-bar for the horses, and the two tents.

Here the buffalo were all round us, and a large band crossed the river just above the camp on the evening of our arrival; so M—— and I crept up under the bank, so that fully a hundred must have passed within three yards and never scented us, the wind being from them to us. It was great fun to watch some of the young ones, who hesitated about going down the steep bank, being butted down by the old fellows. One of these, by the way, missed his blow, and nearly came on the top of us.

I had a run on the following day after the fastest calf I ever chased. I was mounted on my bolter, and though I ran the horse to a standstill, I had to give it up, so I returned to camp and changed the saddle to the mare, and again went after the calf; and in five minutes it was dead, the mare going up to it at once.

Meat being plentiful, we gave up hunting for a day or two, and let the men go out and kill some old bulls, their tongues being as good as any others; so M—— and I remained in camp mending our clothes, cleaning our guns, &c., and making experiments in cookery, though we were very seldom able to eat what we had cooked.

One evening we heard turkeys flying up to roost, and on going to the spot after dark found the trees full of them, and we brought back five fine ones. This is a very tame way of getting them, however, as they are shot sitting, and you cannot well miss, using a shot gun and no. 6 shot, which, by the way, is much more deadly than a larger size, if you fire at the head and neck. A better way was to run them into the bushes on horseback when you found them out feeding, and by following them at once, they would rise all round you and give you some very pretty shots.

One of our amusements in camp was to find a red-ants' nest, and then one of the white ant, and to lay a train of sugar or syrup from one to the other, and lie down about halfway between the two and watch the result. Before long you would see a mass of them coming from both sides, and when they met the fun began. They would first form up into a solid body on each side, and seem to hold a palaver, after which they would separate and, rushing across the intervening space, would seize an adversary; they would throw him on their backs, and carry him off to the ant-hill, where, of course, he was stowed away for food. It was wonderful to see with what ease they could carry an ant as big as themselves, and in half an hour the destruction must have been awful. They drew off after a time, most of them being away already with captives, and we felt we were even with them for all the sugar they had carried off from us, the only thing which would keep them out of the tent being a line of coal-oil.

A few days later M—— and I had an amusing adventure with a buffalo, which we had wounded and were following through a country intersected by a number of small streams, when we came to one of these with a very steep bank, about fifteen feet high, and at the bottom of this the buffalo—an old bull—was waiting for us. He came up with a rush, very nearly catching us, as we had not been expecting him. We both fired, and bolted in opposite directions, and he took after M——, who, instead of going down the bank into the timber in the bottom, ran along it, and had a very close shave for it, just doubling in time. On seeing him disappear, the bull stopped for a moment, giving me time to get in a shot, which struck him well forward; on which he slowly descended the bank, close to where M—— had gone, and walking into the stream lay down and rolled over.

Thinking that he was dead, we both went up to him, leaving our rifles against a tree a few yards away, and before taking out the tongue we sat down on his body and began to discuss the affair, when the buffalo gave a violent heave, nearly throwing us off, and then tried to get up, causing us to go up the bank faster than we had come down, forgetting our rifles in our hurry. It was, however, a last effort, and he was soon dead. It is astonishing how much lead a buffalo can carry away if not hit in the right place. I remember on one occasion putting sixteen no. 12 balls from a shot gun into one, and then having to wait a long time for him to die, as my ammunition was exhausted.

I had been out one day with Fox after antelope, and had had good sport, having killed three, when on returning to camp we found it deserted, everything having disappeared. It was too late to hunt for it that night, as it was very dark; so having nothing but simple saddle-blankets by way of bedding, we made a large fire, and sat by it nearly all night, and started on the waggon-trail very early in the morning, and found our camp pitched on a hill, about four miles away, the top of which was fortified with boxes and sacks of flour, &c.

On inquiring what it meant, the men told us that a large band of Indians had passed by the day before, going along a ridge not more than a mile from camp, fortunately without seeing it, and that, as the band came from the direction in which we had gone in the morning, they gave us up as lost, and packed up everything, moving to where we found them, and meaning, if we did not return early in the morning, to go back to the settlement. There was a stormy scene, which ended in my discharging Brown, of whom everyone was heartily tired, giving him the broken-winded horse to ride into Sibley, where he was to leave him for us. He was always talking of what he would do when there was no danger, and did nothing but counsel flight when it came. We returned to our last camp as soon as Brown was gone, and the following morning the buffalo were close to us, a small band coming almost up to the tent. They were not more than thirty yards from it, when one of us happened to go out, which frightened them.

Fox and I had some very exciting gallops after them, getting into the middle of a big herd, and having them so close all round us that sometimes we could have touched them with our hands. A false step on the part of one's horse, and our buffalo-hunting would have been at an end, as we should have been trampled to death by those behind; the only drawback was the dust, which hid everything outside the radius of a few yards.

I had gone out by myself one morning on the mare, and had ridden about five miles due south, when I saw two white-tailed deer feeding on the other side of some timber, on the edge of a small stream. They were about two hundred yards out on the prairie—much further from cover than they are usually seen. I tied up the mare on the near side of the timber, loosened the girths, and taking off the bit hung it on the saddle, leaving the head-stall on, and fastening the saddle-rope to a bush. I then crawled out towards a small rise, from which I could see the deer, and on reaching it raised my head, and as I did so I saw two Indians raise theirs. I jumped up at once, and ran to where I had left the mare, making capital time, slung my rifle on my back as I ran, and drew my knife, with which I cut the rope, jumped on the loose saddle, and, guiding the mare with my hands, galloped out of the timber and on to a ridge.

Here I looked round and saw that the Indians were not coming, but that they had gone some way down the timber to where their horses were, and were now mounting. I got off, put on the bit, fastened my girths, and remounting, galloped off the prairie as I thought for camp, wondering very much that I was not pursued; but on reaching a high point the apparent mystery was explained—as I was going straight away from camp, and the Indians knew it, as was proved by their derisive shouts as I turned and came back. I saw now that I was in a fix, the Indians, to the number of seventeen, having spread out in a line between me and camp. I knew of no place for which I could make on this side; but how I was to get through them was the question.

So far as I could see with a glass, they had no big horses, and I did not think that any Indian pony could catch Polly; still five miles was a long gallop, and the ponies would be driven by every means known to Indian cruelty, so that I was far from safe, even if I did get through the line.

At last I thought of a plan, and proceeded to put it into execution. I rode along the line of Indians at a hand gallop, they keeping parallel with me, gradually increasing the pace till I had dropped the slow ponies, and had about eight of the fastest opposite to me, and this I kept up for about two miles, by which time there was a gap of quite three hundred yards between the first lot of Indians and the second. I had been edging in gradually, and was now not more than a hundred yards from them, when I suddenly turned, and keeping the butt of my gun going against the mare's ribs, I rode through the gap, lying as flat as I could on my horse. I passed within sixty or seventy yards of those behind; but though they fired, it was while galloping over rough ground, and no aim could be taken, so that neither I nor the mare was hit, and I was soon out of shot and gaining fast, and it now all depended on whether the mare could hold out. She had done two miles before I got through the line, making it a long gallop; so I eased her a little up the hills, which fortunately were not very steep, and the only place where the Indians gained on me was at two old watercourses, at which I had to hunt for a crossing, whereas they crossed wherever they came to them. On mounting the ridge above camp I emptied my revolver rapidly—a signal we had agreed upon—and three of the men ran out to meet me and fired at my pursuers, who turned and rode off, making insulting gestures at us.

It had been a very close thing; for although the mare held out nobly, she was nearly done when I jumped off and loosened the girths.

The Indians had no doubt calculated on capturing me alive, or they would have used their rifles when I first saw them, and had I been mounted on any other horse in camp, they would most likely have succeeded. As this was only my second trip on the plains, I may be excused for having made the mistake I did in galloping away from camp thinking I was going towards it; the whole thing, too, was so sudden that there had been no time to think.

As this neighbourhood was getting too warm for us, we hitched up at once, crossed the river, and, carrying water with us, camped on a high ridge, cutting grass for the animals, all of which we tied to the waggon; M——'s rein-eater being fastened with a trace-chain to the end of the pole.

The Indians could only have been a small party, as we saw nothing more of them; and on the second evening we reached our old camp on White Rock.

Fortunately the buffalo had come north again and there were thousands on the creek, making it easy to supply camp, as we dare not now hunt at any distance from it, and always went in couples, as in those days very few Indians had rifles, and two men could keep off a number of them. This being obliged to remain in or near camp was very slow work, and we made up our minds to return to St. Joe, being confirmed in our intention by the arrival of two Pawnee scouts from Fort Kearney, who reported that the country was full of small bands of Sioux. They had been travelling at night, and during the previous one had passed several camp-fires.

Fox left us at Sibley, not caring to go any nearer to the sheriff; and our only incident on the return journey was my winning my fifty dollars back, with twenty-five added to them, from the man who had cheated me going out. Our animals were so thin that he was deceived, and my mare won very easily.

On reaching St. Joe I went east with M——, giving up my intention of wintering in the mountains, and I sold off the outfit except Polly, whom I left to be taken care of for me till the spring.

CHAPTER X.

Another expedition to White Rock.—A fighting butcher.—The fate of Fox.—Excitement about Indians.—Advised to turn back.—Settlement No. 10 at White Rock.—Bold settlers.—Examine buffaloes at close quarters.—The bold settlers demoralized.—A large herd of elk.—Desperate struggle with a horse. Laid up from a kick.—The fate of our buffalo-tongues.—Settlers about to avenge themselves. Their indifferent armament. A serious consultation. The expedition given up.—I intend going alone to Fort Kearney.

I RETURNED to St. Joe in the spring to meet a friend from England, whom I will call F——, and we arranged to make another expedition to the White Rock country, going further west than we had done the year before. We determined to buy everything ourselves this time, and to have no more roarers or bridle-eaters; so we let it be known that we wanted horses, and they soon poured in, and we selected from them three very fast ones, whose names were "Jeff," "Rob," and "Bally," also a very good white pony and a pair of horses for the waggon. We secured Ivor, my cook of last year, and were some time in getting a second man. At last, however, we heard of a butcher called Douglass, who had fought seven others in the market, and had strewn them all over the place; so we thought he would be just the man to suit us if we came across any Indians, and getting him out of jail, we engaged him.

Shortly before starting, we had bought a half-bred bulldog, taking a fancy to him in the market; but after having him a day or two he was stolen, or else strayed away, and we offered a reward of ten dollars for him, and a man brought him back the day we started, declaring, of course, that he had found him one day in his yard. After crossing the Missouri, we drove through a struggling suburb of St. Joe, and were passing a whiskey-saloon, when one of a number of rough men standing in front of it claimed our dog, saying that he had found him a few days before, and that he had been stolen from him that morning. We told him we had paid one reward for him and should pay no more, on which the man advanced to take the dog, his companions seeming to be inclined to back him up, when Douglass got off the box of the waggon, and asked them if they had heard of a disturbance there had been in the market a few days before. They replied that a big butcher had, they had heard, scattered a good many of his companions, on which Douglass told them that he was the man referred to, and that he was ready to do the same thing again if necessary, on which they cooled down again wonderfully, saying that they only wanted what was right, so we drove on.

We camped again at Troy, which had not grown a bit since my last visit, and reached Lake Sibley without anything happening worth mentioning. Here I inquired for Fox, on which the man to whom I spoke took me a short distance, and pointing to a mound under a tree, told me that Fox lay under it. It seemed that after I left, Fox and Belknap (the man from whom I had bought a waggon) had started together on a hunt, taking with them, among other things, a lot of sham jewellery, which I had brought out for the Indians, and not wanting it, had given to Fox, and that about a week afterwards Belknap had come back, riding one of the two small mules which they had driven in their waggon, and said that they had been attacked by Indians and that Fox had been killed, and that he himself had escaped by cutting a mule out of harness and riding off.

As this story was highly improbable, a party started for the place where Belknap said that the waggon was, to inquire into the matter and get at the facts, and on arriving there they found Fox lying in the bottom of the waggon, with his head on his arm, as if asleep—the ball which had killed him having entered under the arm and passed upwards, so that he must have been shot while asleep. His money was gone, but the waggon was not plundered, and all the sham jewellery was left, which was the first thing Indians would have taken. The party returned at once to Sibley to hang Belknap, but found him gone, and he had not been heard of since. There was a good deal of excitement in the settlement about Indians, a woman having been killed at a house on its outskirts, and two men had been shot at when herding horses about a mile away, and the horses had been driven off.

We were advised to turn back, but we had got away safely the year before, and we believed we should this time, so we determined to go on. On coming in sight of the mouth of the White Rock, F—— and I, who were riding ahead, saw a number of tents there, and of course our first idea was, Indians; but on using a glass we made them out to be white men, so we rode on and were soon in the camp, and it turned out to be a tenth lot of settlers, who had come to reoccupy the houses on the creek. We camped near them, and had a long talk with them that night, giving them our experience of the place, and saying that we hoped they meant to remain longer than their predecessors. On this they were very indignant, asking us if they looked like the sort of men who would run away; and they certainly did not, if that went for anything, which, however, was not our experience. They were putting up a large block-house on the Republican River, just opposite to the mouth of the creek, to which they said they should retreat if hard pressed, not with any idea of running away afterwards, but to make a good stand and give the Indians a lesson. They also said that they hoped we would fall back on them if attacked. We bought some milk and eggs from them and crossed the river, promising to let them know if we found Indians up the creek. There were about thirty men in the party, beside women and children, and they looked as if they ought to give a pretty good account of a hundred Indians; but in this case appearances proved to be deceptive.

We found the houses on the creek much as we had left them the previous year, excepting that the buffalo had broken down many of the fences to get at the corn, which they must have enjoyed immensely. Game seemed to be more plentiful than ever, buffalo being everywhere, and we saw plenty of fresh sign of elk and deer.

I did not go in so much for running buffalo, as I had killed so many in that way, but F——, who was new to it, had some capital runs. The new horses were a decided failure, for having been trained to run short distances, three and four hundred yards, at top speed, we could not break them of it; so that you went up very rapidly at first, and just as you were getting near the buffalo, up would go their tails and they stopped, urging them after that meaning the breaking of a blood-vessel and bleeding at the nose. I crept up a ravine one day, at the head of which three old bulls lay asleep, and watched them for some time, lying not more than nine feet from the nearest, every now and then throwing a small piece of mud at his nose, making him bellow with rage, thinking, I suppose, it was the flies that worried him. After I had examined them sufficiently, I jumped up and gave a yell, on which they sprang to their feet, tumbling over each other in their haste, and made off.

One night we were awoke by an unearthly scream, coming from the other side of the creek, and on going in the morning to see what it had been made by, we found it was a puma, which had scented us, and expressed in this way his displeasure at finding us in his hunting-grounds.

After about three weeks on White Rock, F—— and I determined to go into Sibley to get some butter, eggs, &c., taking a straight cut across country, as being nearer than going by the mouth of the creek. We remained one day, finding some letters for us, so we stopped to answer them, and then returned to camp by our old road, and on reaching the block-house we found the whole party living in it and in a great state of excitement. The Indians had paid them a visit within a few days of our leaving them, just as they were getting ready to go up the creek, and had speared a man within a hundred yards of the block-house; and although there were more than a dozen men in it at the time, there had not been a single shot fired at the Indians to try and save him, though there were only seven of them.

I am afraid we spoke our minds very freely as to what we thought of them, and we cannot be said to have parted friends. A few shots would have been quite enough to have saved the poor fellow, and there was not the slightest fear of the blockhouse being attacked.

On arriving in camp we found all well, and no Indian had been seen, though the men had done a great deal of hunting. A few days after our return, F—— came across a band of about five hundred elk. He was riding along and had seen no sign of game, when there was a noise as if several companies of cavalry were dashing out of a ravine to his right, and this enormous band of elk appeared on the opposite side, and the bulls tossing their great heads in the air, stood for a moment to see what had disturbed them. F—— had time for one long shot, and dropped a fine bull, which was in such good order that he had more than three inches of fat on the brisket, and kept us in lard for some weeks.

One of the horses I had bought at St. Joe was so much given to running away, that he could not be safely ridden at any pace but a walk when in a town; but this he had given up on finding that every time he tried to bolt he was whipped instead of being stopped, so that it did not pay, there being practically no end to the galloping ground. He was a very handsome animal and had wonderful bottom, but never having been fired off he was very hard to manage when running buffalo. He would spring on one side when I fired and would bolt, and the buffalo would be out of sight by the time I had stopped him and turned him in the right direction. I had, however, got him much quieter, and one day had killed a cow and tied most of the meat on his back. It was the first time I had made him carry it home, as I had generally sent some one for it, but this time I thought I would try it, and apparently he did not object. I was standing in front of him, putting on my coat, when he turned his head round and smelt the meat, seeming to take in for the first time what it was, and then began as desperate a struggle as I ever had with a horse. He kicked and reared and jumped. I was holding on to the bit, and was often taken off my feet, the meat flying about and hitting him and driving him nearly mad. I knew that if I let him go he would join the first herd of buffalo he met with, and I should probably never see him again; so I hung on, skinning my hands and being pounded by his knees till, thank goodness, the buckskin strap gave way, and the meat fell, and I managed to lead him back to where the buffalo lay. Here I secured him to the cow's head and blindfolded him with my coat; I tied on some more meat, mounted and got ready before I removed the coat for the second act of the performance. He saw the meat at once, and started across the prairie, jumping and bucking. I managed to turn him in the direction of camp, which was about three miles off, past which we flew, nearly stampeding the picketed horses, and making the men think I was pursued by Indians. I described a circle on the prairie and returned to camp, the horse being now as quiet as a lamb, and by tying him up near where the meat hung, and making him constantly carry a little, I soon got him quite used to it—the only trouble with him being that he would sometimes kick as you passed behind him with the lash-ropes, once hitting me on the thigh and bolting; and if it had not been for the cook's passing near me, returning from a hunt, I should have starved, as my leg swelled up so much that I had to cut my trowsers open, and I was six miles from camp and unable to move.

I do not think I was ever in a more perfect hunting-ground than this was in those days—the danger from Indians giving it that dash of excitement which is always needed to make any life really perfect.

Our cook had improved very much under F——'s tuition, the following being a common bill of fare:—Soup, curry of turkey-breast, antelope steaks, rice-pudding with syrup, and good strong coffee—not a bad bill of fare when seasoned with hunger sauce.

We had a number of buffalo-tongues salted and smoked, but these were for our friends at home, and were taken every care of, to be eaten eventually by the servants at an hotel in St. Joe, where I left them for some months forgetting all about them; and when I wrote directing them to be forwarded, I was informed that the rats had eaten them all, which, as they were fastened up in a barrel, was impossible.

One day, after I had recovered from my kick, we were startled just as we were going to dinner by seeing a considerable number of men coming up the valley, who at first we supposed to be Indians, as they were several miles distant, and some of those who were riding in front had yellow bandana handkerchiefs round their heads, and wore old blue soldier overcoats, a dress much affected by the Sioux. A glass showed, however, that they were white men, and they proved to be sixteen of the men whom we had left at the mouth of the creek. We asked them what was the matter, on which they told us that they had fully expected to find us all killed, as the Indians had again visited Lake Sibley and had carried off a woman and a child, and had fired into several of the houses. They were now, they said, on their way to the Sioux camp, to demand the surrender of the woman and child, or to take them by force, if necessary. They spoke so confidently, that we really believed they meant business this time, and told them that if they would stay to dinner, three of us would join them, and could guide them to the Indian camp, as it was most likely the large one we had found the previous year at the forks of the Solomon River, to which the Sioux came every year. They agreed to this and picketed their horses. Dinner for nineteen people was a serious affair, but we managed it at last, cutting up almost the whole of a small deer to make a stew, as their appetite was enormous. When dinner was over, we thought that perhaps it might be as well to ascertain what amount of ammunition the party had brought with them. They were armed with a most miscellaneous collection of firearms, no two being alike; some had long muzzle-loading Kentucky rifles, others old Tower muskets, and a few had muzzle-loading shot guns, not exactly the weapons to face Indians with. When we inquired as to ammunition, a lamentable state of things was disclosed, many having no more than the loads which were in their guns, and very few had more than six rounds. We offered, however, to make up deficiencies and lend rifles to those who had shot guns, as we happened to have a good number of the former in camp.

The men asked for time to talk the matter over, and went aside for that purpose, returning to us in a few minutes, to say that it would after all be very foolish to go any further, as they were only a small party, and knew nothing about the number of the Indians. The fact was that the Lake Sibley people had succeeded in exciting them for a time, by an account of the outrage, but that their courage had now all oozed away at their finger ends. Nothing we could say was of any use, and they ended by mounting and returning the way they had come.

My horse "Jeff" was by this time so thin, being unused to doing without corn, that I determined to start the next morning, and to take him to a ranche which we knew of, about ninety miles north-west of our present camp, and about thirty miles from Fort Kearney, to which place we had directed letters to be sent, so that I could kill two birds with one stone. I meant to leave the horse at this ranche till the end of our hunt, when I could fetch him, buying a pony at Kearney to replace him and to ride back on. The ranche was owned by an Englishman, whose name was Martin, who we knew would feed the horse up and keep him till I came for him. F—— and the men were to remain in the present camp, unless game became scarce, when they were to leave a paper at a certain spot, telling me in which direction they had gone, as I expected to be back again in eight days at latest.

CHAPTER XI.

Start on my journey.—Miserable weather.—Appearance of three Indians I compel them to breakfast with me. An uncomfortable breakfast-party. I bid them adieu.—Reach the ranche.—Report of our having been murdered.—Mr. Martin. His history.—Visit to Fort Kearney.—Interview with Major North. His recent fight with Sioux.—Start on my return journey.—Uncanny sight.—Dense fog.—Camp on Little Blue River.—Horse missing. Vain efforts to track him.—Weary journey back to ranche. Quite done up. Kindness of the Martins.—Return journey to camp.—A pleasant surprise.—Narrow escape from Indians.—A horrible sight.

I STARTED the next morning with as light a load as possible, only taking my blankets and a small waterproof sheet, coffee, two days' bread, a tin cup and plate, knife and fork, and enough meat for one day, trusting to kill game on the way. I carried a repeating rifle holding nine cartridges, a knife and small belt axe, and a hundred rounds of ammunition.

I only knew the first twenty miles of the road, but had studied it on a map; and as the house I was bound for was on the great Californian stage road, I could not well miss it, as by going north I was bound to strike this road. I calculated on doing the ninety miles in two days, camping on a stream called the "Little Blue" the first night, when I should have done two thirds of my journey.

It was a fine morning when I left camp, and I had a very pleasant ride through a pretty country, chiefly rolling prairie, till I reached the Republican River, which I crossed without any trouble, jumping a fine elk as I landed on the opposite bank; but very soon afterwards it began to rain heavily. About midday I halted to dine, making my small fire among some bushes, in case of Indians being about. Having rested two hours I started again, being by this time wet through. I fortunately had brought a compass with me, as I could not see more than a few hundred yards ahead; and late in the evening I struck the Little Blue River, and camped in as sheltered a spot as I could find, putting up my sheet as a tent.

Indians dislike bad weather quite as much as we do, and on such a night as this would be under the shelter of their lodges; then, too, the fog was so thick that a fire could not be seen far, so I made up a good one and risked it.

It was a very rough night, and the rain blew under my shelter, making me very wet and miserable, so I was glad to get up at daybreak to make a fire. It was still raining, and I had very hard work getting it to burn up, and was obliged to go down on my knees and blow at it, when, happening to look towards the hills on my side of the river, I saw what I took to be three buffaloes, but knowing that they were everywhere just now, I thought no more of them.

Having made the fire burn, I got in my horse and saddled him, tying him close to my sleeping-place; I then put on my tin cup full of water to boil, and cutting my meat into "kabobs," I peeled a dry stick, and threading them on it, sloped them over the fire to roast, this being one of the quickest ways of cooking meat. Everything being now in trim, I looked to see what had become of the buffaloes, as it was much lighter by this time, when I was very much startled to see that they were three Indians, who had come nearer and were watching me. I beckoned to them, making the peace sign, to come into my camp, but they replied by pointing over the hill, and beckoning me to go with them, and as I shook my head they turned and were walking away.

It was, of course, of the utmost importance to know whether they were friendly or not, so I walked out towards them, on which they turned and came back towards me. I had my rifle in my left hand, and was holding my right in the air, with the open palm to the front, the universal peace sign among Indians. They answered my signal in the same way, and we met and shook hands, when I again pointed to my fire, and intimated that I wished them to come and have breakfast with me; but again they refused, and started to leave me. Now, of course, this would never do, as they would soon be back again with a number of their companions, and if they were Sioux, as I strongly suspected from their moccasins, my hair was not worth an hour's purchase. I called to them, therefore, and made signs, that if they would not go with me, I should shoot them, taking aim at one of them as I finished my signs.

The party consisted of an old man, who had a musket with the barrel cut short, and two young men, one of whom had a bow and arrows, and the other a cavalry sabre; and thinking I meant what I threatened, they slowly followed me to the fire, I going backwards, and keeping my rifle ready, till we all stood by it. I then sat down on one side of the fire and they on the other, and with my rifle in my left hand, I gave them the kabobs with my right, and then passed the coffee, first

Page 141.—He removed his blanket, in spite of the rain, and wrapping the musket in it laid it down.

putting in some sugar, of which all Indians are very fond. The only thing which made me feel uncomfortable was the old man's musket, the muzzle of which pointed my way, so I told the old fellow to lay it down on the grass, but he refused to do this, making signs that the grass was wet and would hurt it; so I took aim at him again with my rifle, on which he removed his blanket, in spite of the rain, and wrapping the musket in it laid it down. We now became quite friendly, so much so, that they finished all my coffee before I had had any, and it was necessary to get water to make some more, and this involved going to the stream, which I managed to do walking backwards, still holding my rifle. The Indians made up the fire, and we soon had a second brew and some more kabobs, which they made better than I did, it being a favourite Indian way of cooking meat when on a hunt.

It was now about time for me to go, and fortunately I had already saddled the horse, and had only to make up my small pack, put on the bridle, and mount, when they rose, evidently expecting me to go with them, and were very much surprised and gesticulated violently as I rode off, waving my hand to them and feeling rather uncomfortable, till out of gunshot, lest they might shoot me in the back. The last thing I saw of them as I topped the next ridge was all three running in the direction in which I supposed their camp to be, on which I put my horse into a hand gallop, and kept him at it for more than an hour, so as to get clear of the neighbourhood of the Indians as soon as possible.

I arrived about three o'clock at Martin's ranche, and noticed that they seemed surprised to see me, Martin telling me afterwards that a report had been brought into Fort Kearney that we had all been murdered by the Sioux on the Republican River.

I remained two days at the ranche luxuriating in new bread, butter and cream, and a comfortable bed. And here I may as well say something of my host, as he was a good specimen of what can be done by perseverance and pluck.

He had come out from England about twenty-five years before, having been a groom in a racing-stable, and his love of fighting was always getting him into trouble. He had worked for wages in the Eastern States till he had saved enough to start with on his own account, when he had moved west, and had put up a house on the stage line between Nebraska city, on the Missouri River, and California. Here he had kept a station, where the overland stage changed horses and the passengers passed the night. This he had gradually added to, and had enclosed fields, till he had a good ranche, which he worked with the help of one man and his wife and sons, finding a ready sale for all he raised to the freighters who were continually passing. The life had been a very hard one at first, and they had to be constantly on their guard against Indians, who on several occasions ran off animals and fired into the ranche, but had never ventured to attack it. He told me that two of his sons, the eldest being only nine, were one evening bringing in the cows, both of them riding one horse barebacked, and that when about a mile from the ranche, some Sioux, who had no doubt been lying in wait for them, suddenly appeared and chased them, yelling as only Indians can. The boys, though frightened, stuck to the cattle, and brought them in safely, closely followed by the Indians, who were driven off by Martin and his eldest son, as they happened to see them coming; and it was then found that an arrow had passed through the hinder boy, and had stuck into the one in front, pinning them together. I saw the marks of the wound on one of them, the arrow having passed through on the left side of the spine and low down.

When I asked Mrs. Martin if she had not been very much frightened, she answered that she had lived too long in the West for that, and her husband added that once when some Indians, supposed to be friendly, had come into the house and had been very insolent, finding only a woman at home, and taking whatever they fancied, she had, as he said, gone for them with an axe-handle, and had driven them out of the house in no time. Martin had, he told me, come out with only enough to keep himself and his wife for a few weeks, and he owned to being worth thirty thousand pounds, all of it being made without speculation or mining.

I left the ranche on the third day for Fort Kearney, a ride of thirty miles, to get letters and a few supplies, and arrived the same evening. The Commandant kindly put me up, and made me remain the next day, as he wanted me to meet a Major North, who was in command of about six hundred Pawnee Indian scouts, and who was away at a ranche on the Platte River. Major North was an Englishman who had come out to America when very young, going eventually into the army during the war, and was appointed to the command of the scouts about two years before my visit to Kearney. These were picked men from the tribe, and, now that they were well disciplined, did good service against any hostile Indians, being mounted and armed as soldiers.

Major North came in the following morning, and told me

that he had only returned from a scout on the Republican River a few days before, and that he had been driven in by the Sioux, the following being his account of the affair:—

It seems that he was out with about a hundred and fifty of his men, when he came upon a band of some six hundred Sioux under White Cloud, the great Sioux war chief, who immediately attacked him and drove him into a ravine, the sides of which North lined with two thirds of his men, one third of them being detailed to hold the horses.

The Sioux he said fought well, riding up to the edges of the ravine, and firing as calmly as if shooting game, though they were falling fast, the Pawnees being much better armed; they were, however, gradually driven back, having more than a hundred killed and wounded, and at last they drew off, when North retreated to the Fort as fast as he could go, having lost sixteen men and many more being wounded. He told me that all White Cloud's men were drilled by that chief and always charged like cavalry, using their rifles and revolvers, as they had no sabres.

The fight made it very unlikely that the Sioux would remain in the same neighbourhood, as after a loss of this magnitude they generally return for a time to their villages to mourn for the dead, so that I should only run the risk of meeting small parties, and I was willing to take my chance with them. Bidding my friends adieu, I rode back to Martin's and remained there one day, trying to get a pony; but he had none to spare, and I had not been able to get one at the Post; so as my horse was already much improved by unlimited grain, I determined to take him back again, carrying a bushel of corn behind the saddle.

Mrs. Martin put me up all kinds of good things for my journey, such as cold chickens, bread and butter, and hard-boiled eggs, and I left the ranche on the 3rd of July, with a thick fog all round, which made it a poor sort of day for one to find the way over a wild country; but I had been away so long that I feared my companions would come to look for me, when we might very easily miss one another. I knew the direction which I had to keep, and rode on for some hours, the fog getting thicker every minute, and on reaching a small stream about midday, I camped for dinner, and remained for two hours, when I started again. I intended camping that night on the Little Blue River, but could not find it, so I rode far into the night, when I saw something which at first startled me very much.

I was in a totally uninhabited part of the country, and yet there above me was a house with a bright light shining from several windows, and it was not until I got nearer that I made it out to be a deserted house, which had lost its roof, and the moon was shining through where the windows had been, only showing for a few moments through a rift in a cloud, and then all was dark again.

This place I thought would do to camp in for the night, so I rode up the hill on which it stood, disturbing an old buffalo bull which was lying asleep near it, and which looked enormous in that light and against the sky line. I found that nearly all the roof was gone, and all the doors and windows, but there was enough left to shelter me from the heavy dew, which was almost like rain, and I ripped off some remains of flooring for a fire, and having made the room look quite cheerful with a bright blaze, I off-saddled and brought in everything, picketing

"Jeff" where I had found the buffalo, as it was most probably the best grass. There was, of course, a good chance of my fire being seen, as the house stood in such a conspicuous place, but the fog was thick, and it was too great a temptation to resist, so I ate a good supper and turned in, and nothing happened during the night.

The morning was anything but a promising one, the fog having turned to rain, and I did not start till after dinner, by which time it had cleared up. On consulting my compass, I came to the conclusion that I had kept too much to the east, as I found that the house I was in had been formerly a stage station; so I now turned south-west, and towards evening struck the Little Blue River, and camped in the midst of a thick clump of trees close to the stream, and tied my horse's picket-rope to a large bush where the feed was very good. It came on to rain again in the night, and in the morning there was another dense fog, so being wet and cold, I got up early and went to bring in "Jeff" and water him, but both he and the bush to which I had tied him were gone. I could track him for some distance, as he seemed to have gone back the way we had come on the previous day; and thinking he would not have gone far on such a night, I followed him at once, not stopping to eat breakfast. The trail became very indistinct as I came to a hard ridge, and I soon lost it altogether; but as I thought it most likely that he had gone back to the ranche, I kept on in that direction. It was still pouring, and the mosquitoes were simply awful, rising out of every small hollow in clouds, and it was impossible to keep them off.

I now began to feel the want of my breakfast, but I buckled my belt tighter, and tried not to think of the cold chicken which I had left behind me, walking faster so as to get back to the ranche that evening if possible, having thirty-five miles to do, if I went straight, and this I was not likely to do in such weather. I halted for a few minutes now and then, sitting down on the ground, where there was now more water than grass.

Night came and found me still tramping on, though very tired, the going being very slippery, especially as I was wearing moccasins, and about ten o'clock I lay down and went to sleep, with my hat over my eyes, and slept nearly all night in spite of rain and mosquitoes. I was so stiff in the morning that I could hardly get up, and had to rub my legs for some time before I could start again. About noon I reached the stage road, and the question now, and a very important one, was, had I struck the road above or below Martin's? If the former I was all right, as the Fort was on one side of me and the ranche on the other; but if the latter and I took the wrong direction, there was nothing between me and Lincoln city, a distance of about eighty miles, which probably meant death. I therefore determined to leave it to chance, tossing up a coin, and deciding that it should be "heads up" and "tails down." It came heads, so I turned up, and struggled along till about nine at night, when I saw lights ahead, which proved to be the ranche. Here I was so done that I could not mount the three small steps to the door, and fell against them. The rattle made by my rifle brought them all out, when a few words explained the state of affairs, and I was carried upstairs and put to bed. Mrs. Martin made me some soup and fed me, as I was so stiff that I could not do it myself. I slept sixteen hours, and on waking could not turn myself in bed, everything having to be done for me, and nothing could exceed the kindness of the whole Martin family. They made me all kinds of good things, and came and sat with me nearly all day; it was only on the fourth day that I could walk down stairs, and then with difficulty.

Having now been away from camp so long, I insisted on starting, and Miss Martin kindly lent me her favourite pony, whose name was "Libb," and I promised to bring her back before leaving for St. Joe, so about noon I left the ranche, the little pony carrying me capitally, though she was somewhat lazy. I reached the Little Blue River that night, passing a fresh Indian camp, the marrow-bones which lay about all over the camp being still moist.

As I happened to recognize this part of the stream, and knew that I was not far from where I had left my saddle and pack, I rode down till I reached it, when what should I see standing within a hundred yards of where I had slept, but the horse I had lost, with the rope still round his neck, and a portion of the bush to which I had tied him at the end of it. He had evidently been unable to find his way back to the ranche, so he had returned to where he had been tied, and had remained about there for the last seven days. At first I thought that the Indians must have caught him, and that they were somewhere near; but when I saw that he was loose, I knew that this could not be the case. He was as glad to see me as I was him, and galloped round the pony several times, very nearly throwing us down with his rope. I camped on the old spot, and in the morning started at a good pace, riding Jeff and putting my small pack on the pony, Jeff being so much more comfortable to ride, as my feet almost touched the ground when on Libb.

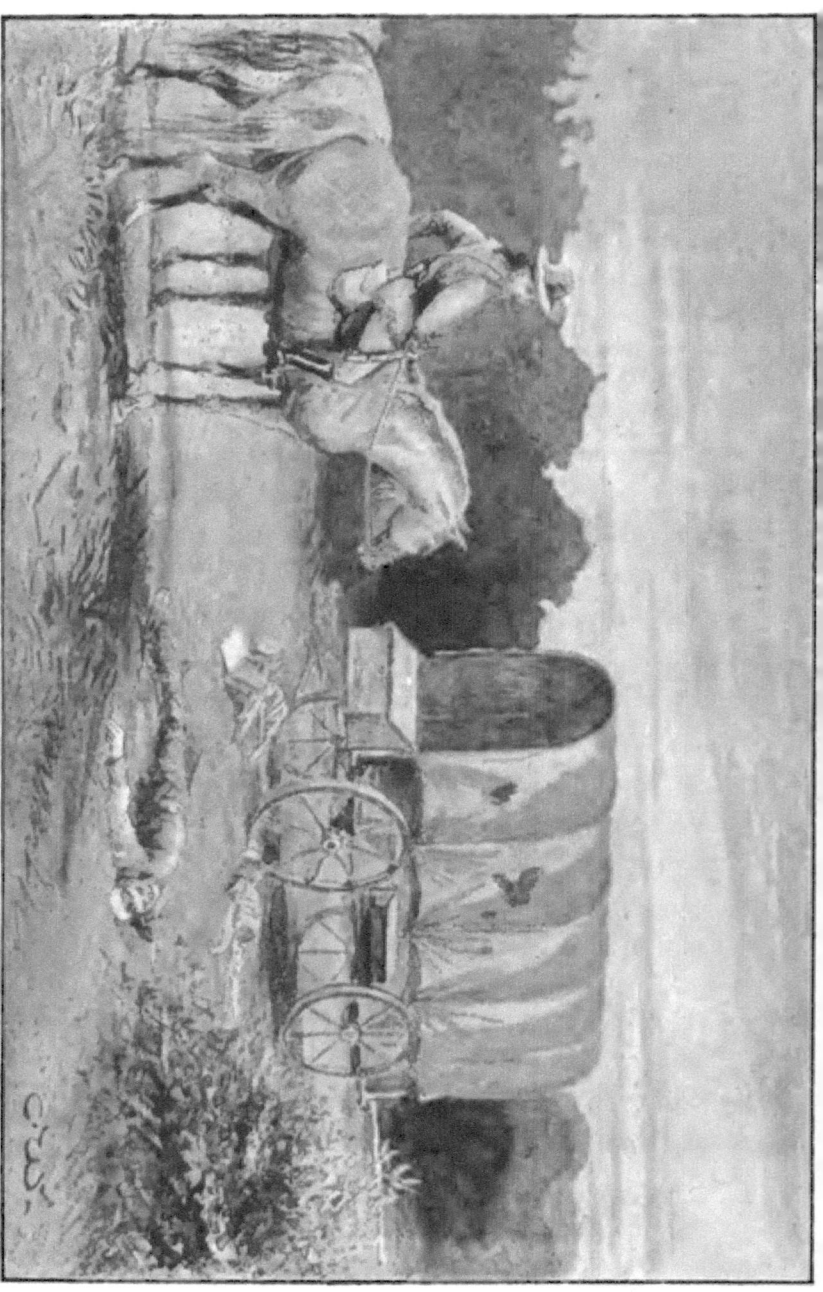

Page 151.—I was surprised to see a waggon on the bank.

A HORRIBLE SIGHT. 151

I had my dinner in the deep bed of a stream, feeding the horses with corn; and it was lucky that I did so, for on going up to look round before starting, I saw a band of Indians, evidently running buffalo, about two miles ahead of me. I lay down and watched them for about two hours, by which time they had all crossed a high divide on my left, when I started again, taking care to reconnoitre before crossing any high ground, tying the pony and Jeff together while I did so, when they would remain patiently till I returned.

I saw nothing more of the Indians, and struck the Republican River about six o'clock in the evening, and was surprised at seeing a waggon on the bank among some bushes. On reaching it I found it had been plundered, while round it lay the bodies of five men and four horses, all of the former being scalped, and one who lay under the hind end of the waggon had had the top of his head chopped off down to the eyes. There were no signs as to who they were, but a small note-book which I found in the pocket of the man under the waggon, in which was written "J. Ralston," and the book contained accounts. It was time to camp, but I could not do so there, so I crossed the river and camped about a mile from the waggon, dreaming during the night of the horrible sight, and jumping up several times, thinking I was attacked by Indians. The men looked as if they had been dead about a fortnight, and as they were partially eaten by wolves, they were not pleasant to look at. I heard afterwards that the party had consisted of an American major and five men, who had been out on a hunt, and who had been attacked and murdered by the Sioux, only one man escaping, as he was on outpost duty at the time of the attack. The major had incurred the hatred of the Indians when they had visited a fort, at which he commanded, during a temporary peace, and they had shown this by treating him more barbarously than the others.

I found all well on reaching camp. F—— had had good sport and had seen no Indians, having been hunting chiefly to the south.

CHAPTER XII.

Awful thunder-storms.—Bad water-supply.—Life in camp.—I leave for St. Joe.—Come across two Indians.—Arrive at Lake Sibley.—Swarm of grasshoppers.—Apprehensions of the settlers.—A man wishes me to engage him. I decline.—I make the acquaintance of a detective.—A plan to rob me. I manage to frustrate it.—Meet F—— at Martin's.—Sioux steal Pawnees' horses. Pawnees and Whites try to recover them. A fight and repulse of Pawnees.—Mrs. Martin's reminiscences of her husband.—Poor sport.—Return to St. Joe.—Intend to winter in Texas.—Billy Breeze. His history.

A FEW days after my return we had some of the most awful thunder-storms I ever saw even in America, where they are always much more severe than in Europe. The rain came down in sheets, and the lightning was incessant, and the thunder seemed to be just over the ridge-pole of the tent. We got a good deal of water inside owing to the ditch, which we always cut round the tent, not being deep enough. In the morning we found one of our ponies dead: it had evidently been struck by lightning and killed at once; the head was folded under the body, and seemed, at first, to have been cut off, so entirely was it hidden. On such a night as this the wolves seem to be very much frightened, their howling being incessant, and the sound seems to be even more melancholy than usual, combining with the storm to keep the traveller awake.

As the water in the stream was very bad and muddy we hunted for a spring, and found that what we had been drinking had all filtered through the ribs of a buffalo which had been dead some months, and which lay right across the channel. Why we were none of us ill I cannot understand, as we had been drinking this water for weeks. Water in the autumn was always the great trouble, as nearly all the streams dry up and leave stagnant pools, out of which we often drove buffalo, and the edges were as much trampled as if a flock of sheep had been there. Along the banks of the larger rivers there are some beautiful springs, especially on the Republican River, where we found a number of them as clear as crystal, and as cold as anyone could wish. Most of them had been carefully cleared out and covered with stones by the Indians.

Our life in camp here was very pleasant, game was plentiful and in great variety, and we sometimes tried to make elaborate dishes, as the one told off to keep camp had plenty of time on his hands; but, as a rule, the "game pies" and "vol-au-vents" were not successes, the pastry being hard to make and very much so to swallow. The bulldog, too, was a good deal of trouble to us, as he would always attack any porcupine he came across, coming into camp very often with his mouth a mass of quills—it took us sometimes fully an hour to pull them out—and in spite of this he would attack the next one he met, so that we thought of shooting him. He was a strange animal; on our way through the settlement he had allowed any dog to bite him, hardly seeming to know what fighting meant, and yet on our return he thrashed every dog he came across, and did it scientifically, knowing exactly where to take hold.

As we wanted a good many things from St. Joe, including money, I made up my mind to ride in on the horse which had kicked me, as he had become very thin and not fit for camp life, intending to sell him before I returned and to buy another; and as F—— was going to move camp to Martin's, it was arranged that I was to go up from St. Joe by steamer to Nebraska city, which would shorten my return journey. I left about the end of July, taking as little baggage as possible; and yet I found that I had nearly seventy pounds, including my saddle—a heavy load for so long a journey with nothing but grass for the horse. It took me two days to reach Lake Sibley, and on the second I was riding along the Republican River looking for a ford, when two Indians came down on the opposite bank and began to prepare to cross. Now they might be friendly, but this was not likely, and as there was no way of ascertaining this, the only thing to be done was to keep them where they were, so I waved them back with my hand, and as they still came on, I pointed my rifle at them. They made friendly signs, but of course this proved nothing, and I continued making gestures to indicate that I should fire if they entered the water. Instead of going away they sat down, holding their horses by the bridle, and now and then making signs to me, of which I took no notice. For several hours I had to sit there behind a log till it was quite dark, when instead of continuing my journey down the river, I struck out into the prairie for some miles, and then turning rode for the river again, much lower down; and this ruse succeeded, as I saw no more of the Indians.

I reached Lake Sibley the following morning, having camped for the night on the river, and found the settlers very much depressed at the arrival of a swarm of grasshoppers, which were destroying their crops and against which they could do nothing. Even while I was there, I saw a perceptible difference in a field of corn, which was simply swarming with them, and some of the neighbouring fields had lost every leaf. All the men I spoke to had made up their minds to leave at once, having no supplies for the winter, meaning to work for wages for some months and make a fresh start in the spring.

The people here had been so often attacked by Indians during the summer, that my saying I had seen two on my way in caused a considerable stir, as the people assured me that it meant another raid on the settlement, the two Indians being probably scouts, sent in front of a larger body.

I was three days doing the distance between Sibley and St. Joe, where I arrived safely, and found letters waiting for me. The supplies I needed were soon procured, and it only remained to sell my horse and buy another. I luckily soon found a customer for mine, a gambler who bought him to race, as I had said so much of his wonderful bottom; but getting a good pony for myself was difficult. A great number were brought for me to look at, but most of them were stable raised and of no use. At last I heard of one some miles from the town, and on going to see him, as I liked his appearance, I bought him.

Having executed all my commissions, I was ready to start on the third day after my arrival, and on the morning of the day on which I intended to take the steamer for Nebraska city, a fine-looking man came to see me and wished me to engage him

INTERVIEW WITH A DETECTIVE. 157

in any capacity I thought proper, telling me that he had got into a scrape, the nature of which he would not explain. I replied that we had all the men we wanted, and after he had tried very hard to induce me to change my mind, telling me that he was an old plainsman and that I ought not to ride so far alone, he left me, and I went down to the boat leading my new pony, on which I had packed my small outfit. It took me till the boat had started to make the pony comfortable, and to put my saddle, &c., in my state-room; but on going on deck I was much surprised to see the man who wished me to engage him, on the boat.

I went up to him and asked him where he was going, and whether he had found something to do, on which he told me that he was going up the river to Omaha, where he had a friend with whom he could stay, that place being about seventy miles above Nebraska city.

I thought no more of him, and soon got to know a number of my fellow passengers, who were very much interested in my proposed ride, thinking that anyone going on the plains when the Indians were so bad must certainly be killed. Amongst others, there was an old American general going up to Fort Benton with his wife and daughter, who did their best to induce me to go on with them, the general promising me an escort to camp from Benton; but this would have involved a very long ride, and I had no time for it.

On the morning of the day after we left, a stranger, whom I had not noticed, called me on one side, and first giving me his card, from which I saw that he was a captain in the New York detective police, said that he had something very important to tell me. He then asked me if I was not an Englishman who had come into St. Joe for letters and money, and was now on my way to rejoin my companions on the Platte River. I replied that I was, wondering what was coming. He then told me that seeing one of the passengers whispering with a deck hand late on the previous evening, he had crept forward and had listened to their conversation, which, it seems, was about me. The passenger was the man of whom I have spoken, and the two men were discussing a plan for following and robbing me. Captain T—— offered to help me in any way I thought best, and it was decided between us that if the man got out at Nebraska city after saying that he was going on to Omaha, we should hunt up the city marshal, and arrange to have him detained till I was well on the road.

Captain T—— had come from New York on the track of a murderer who had fled from that city, and was supposed to have gone up the Missouri, which was a fortunate thing for me, for had he not been there to overhear the conversation, the man might easily have joined me *en route*, and I could not have sent him back, as he had as much right to travel on that road as I had, when nothing would have been easier than for him to have shot me in the back as we rode along.

When we reached Nebraska city that evening, Captain T—— and I went ashore, he having arranged with the captain of the boat to detain it for two hours; and instead of walking into the town, we remained on the wharf for some time, when we saw the man who wished to go with me land and go into a whiskey-saloon near the wharf, so Captain T—— went to find the city marshal, and I remained to keep an eye on the house. On the arrival of the marshal, we went into the saloon and had a drink, and lest the man might suspect something, I asked him to join us, which he did. I then inquired what made him change his mind as to his destination, on which he said he had a friend in Nebraska, whom he wished to see. The marshal asked him the friend's name, and after hearing it we went out, a policeman in plain clothes being left to shadow the man.

When we were well away from the place, the marshal said that he had never seen this man's face before, but he said " I know his friend well and he is a great scamp, and has undergone one sentence, I know, for horse-stealing." We had a long talk about it, and it was finally arranged that I should see the man again and tell him that I was going to start in the morning; but in reality I was to be off that evening, so as to reach Lincoln city, fifty miles away, by daybreak, leaving a letter at the hotel at which I was supposed to be stopping, to say that I knew of his plan and would shoot him "on sight" if he followed me. In the evening I went to a billiard-saloon, where I heard he was, and had a talk with him. He asked me when I was going to start, and I told him that I thought it would be about ten o'clock the next morning, and I also mentioned where I was stopping. It came out, in the course of conversation, that he had been champion prize-fighter of Montana, and therefore a very awkward man to have met even without weapons.

I was off about seven o'clock, and rode all night, the road being luckily a very plain one as it was the old stage road, and before morning I was in Lincoln city, and had to wait some time for the hotel to open. I had a note for the marshal here, telling him to stop the man should he discover my ruse and succeed in evading the police in Nebraska city; but I never saw him again.

My ride from here was an easy one, and I could have followed the road the whole way; but as it turned north to avoid a rough bit of country I took a straight line, hoping to find game, and as it was more interesting than following a road about sixty feet wide, which the stage road then was. I was three days doing the eighty or ninety miles, and killed two antelope on the way, besides seeing many more, and a good many ducks and grouse.

On reaching Martin's I found that F—— had arrived three days before, and was enjoying the fare as much as I had done, while the animals were getting all the corn and oats they could eat.

One evening we were sitting out in front of the ranche, when we saw a body of mounted men cross the end of the valley in which the house stood, about two miles away. It was dusk, and it was too far off to see what they were, so young Martin and F—— rode down the valley to examine the tracks, and came back before dark to tell us that it was a mixed party of Indians and white men, which was easy to see from some of the tracks being made by shod horses, though most of them were unshod, and some days later we heard the explanation of this.

A small party of Sioux, numbering about twenty, had made a dash at the Pawnee horses near the reservation, and had succeeded in driving off a large band of them. About thirty Pawnees had immediately mounted, and accompanied by three white men who happened to be at the camp, had followed the Sioux. They came up with them not far from where we saw them cross our valley, and managed to creep up to the Sioux camp unperceived. The Sioux evidently did not know that they were pursued, and were sitting round their camp fire smoking, when a volley was fired into them at close quarters and several fell. They were picked warriors, and instead of being demoralized they took cover at once, and a fight began in which the Pawnees and their white allies were beaten, and compelled to fly on foot, losing the horses they had been riding.

These Pawnees were, at one time, a very warlike tribe, but, as is the case with the Navajoes, no sooner were they partially civilized than they became cowardly, excepting where they had been disciplined like the six hundred at Fort Kearney.

Mrs. Martin amused us very much with an account of the doings of her husband at the time of the American civil war. He was a southern sympathizer, and had to get all his supplies from a fort garrisoned by northern troops, so that as everyone knew his sentiments he had things said to him which, with his love of fighting, he found it hard to bear. When leaving the post one evening with his wife, as they drove past a whiskey-saloon, some one called out to him and wanted to know when that d——d little Johnny Bull was going to leave the country, as it would soon be made too hot to hold him. On which Martin asked the speaker to step outside, and he at once did so, proving to be a big settler from a ranche on the other side of the fort. Martin told him to take off his coat, and then, although he was himself a small man, he proceeded to give him a sound thrashing, taking only a few minutes in doing it. One of the bystanders saying something he did not like, Martin very soon treated him in the same way, offering then to fight any man in the crowd, on which a cheer was raised for the little Englishman, and he was never again insulted by anyone at

M

the fort. Shortly before our arrival, a soldier was continually coming to the ranche courting one of Martin's daughters; he was told that he was not wanted, but still came whenever he could get away, so at last Martin lost patience, and seized him by the collar and threw him out of the door, when he took the hint and had not been since.

We left the ranche about the beginning of August, and struck up the Republican River, but found nothing but old buffalo bulls, the Indians having driven all the cows and calves south; the water of the river, too, was very bad, as it was almost like liquid mud; there were some beautiful ice-cold springs about, but the Indians having camped near them so often, there was no grass left, and the only game was turkeys, so our sporting experiences are not worth recording.

During my absence, F—— had bought a horse from some professional hunters, which was the only one I ever saw which would eat meat. His former owners had spent the last winter in trapping on the Republican, and had been burned out by the Sioux, and all their horses died but this one, which had taken to eating any scraps of meat he found lying round camp and to gnawing the bones. He would still eat a little if he came across it, though it had by no means agreed with him, as his coat had nearly all come off and never regrown, except in patches.

We remained till the beginning of September, and then returned to St. Joe, having decided on wintering in Texas, then a wonderful country for game. We sold off everything but Polly, as I intended to take her with me, and we bought a number of dogs, chiefly pointers and setters, as we hoped to find a great deal of small game where we were going. We engaged an old Welshman to look after these on the way down the river, whose name was Billy Breeze, and who had quite a history.

He had, first of all, been a policeman in London, but was dismissed for drinking; then he had returned to his native village and turned poacher, and had been sent out to America by means of a subscription raised in the neighbourhood, where he was very popular in spite of his bad habits. On arriving in America, he had gradually drifted West, never working long anywhere, and had settled at St. Joe as a professional hunter, at which he had done well, as game was very abundant and he was a good shot. When the war broke out, Billy had joined the northern army and had fought bravely, being wounded twice; the last time a bullet broke his leg and caused him to limp ever after, so that he was discharged and returned to St. Joe, where he took up his old calling again, adding to it the breaking of dogs, at which he was very good. Here we found him, and taking a fancy to him engaged him to go with us as dog-keeper and general factotum.

CHAPTER XIII.

Voyage down the Missouri.—Wild-fowl shooting.—Objectionable freed slaves.—New Orleans.—My companion dies of cholera. I also am attacked. I recover.—Meet some Confederate generals.—Gambling-saloon.—Galveston.—Several shooting-trips.—An expensive night's lodging.—A young Englishman joins us.—A New Yorker and his supper-party.—The lone tree.—Difficulties with the waggon.—The town of Richmond.—We are fined. But do not pay.—F—— has an accident.—A useful doctor.—General Sheridan's horse.—Buy a wild horse.—A stream in flood.—Racing in Texas.—A racing mule.

The voyage down the Missouri and Mississippi was somewhat monotonous, especially as far as St. Louis, the banks being as a rule low, and the only trees cotton-woods. There were, however, many incidents to enliven the voyage. We often ran on a sandbar, as the river was very low in the autumn months, and we had to be poled over it; this was done as follows: Two poles were stuck in the sand one on each side of the boat's bow, which was then hoisted between them by ropes fastened to the sides of the deck and passing over the tops of the poles, the ropes being hauled upon by the engine. When the bow was sufficiently raised the engines were sent ahead full speed, and the boat was thus thrown forward several feet, this being repeated till the bar was past. When the water still proved too shallow, the vessel had to be forced backwards off the bar.

The chief amusement of the passengers was wild-fowl shooting. An immense number of all kinds of birds go down the river every autumn, on their way to the south for the winter, and these would settle down for the night on the sandbars. We used, therefore, to get up a party among the passengers, when the boat was moored for the night (as the river was so shallow, it did not pay to run after dark), and having borrowed the small boat which was generally towed astern, we rowed to the nearest sandbar. Here we hid ourselves behind snags or logs which had become imbedded in the sand, and for about an hour at sunset the firing was often incessant, the crew retrieving the birds which fell into the river, and becoming so excited that they did not hesitate to plunge into the water to get them. In this way we often got thirty or forty ducks in an evening, besides some geese, not to speak of those which we shot during the daytime, as our captain was good-natured enough to allow us to take the boat to recover any which fell. This shooting from a moving steamer required a good deal of practice, as it was necessary to allow for the speed at which the boat was going, and at first we missed a good many.

We passed Fort Leavenworth, which, when I first came to America, was on the border of the Indian country, but which had now been left far behind by the settlements, and was used only as a depot. At St. Louis we changed steamers and remained one day, putting up at the Lindell House, a very good hotel, which was burned down soon after we left, with the loss of many lives.

From this place we had a splendid steamer, doing twenty miles an hour, as comfortable and with as good fare as an hotel: the banks of the river, too, became more interesting; towns were frequent and, as we got near New Orleans, fine plantations were very numerous. These we heard were much more prosperous-looking from the boat than in reality, as since the war so many of them had been deserted, and none were kept up as they had been in the slave times. Since the emancipation, the negroes, or "gentlemen of colour" as they called themselves, had become most objectionable, as I had many opportunities of seeing, and as was to be expected from suddenly freed slaves. They put on great airs and took every opportunity of taunting and lording it over their late masters. In some cases they remained on the plantations, but worked or not as it pleased them, and could not be punished in any way.

We were much taken with New Orleans; it had a very French look, and it was a relief to get away from towns where the streets were always at right angles to one another. We put up at the St. James' Hotel, and caused quite a commotion in the streets as we walked to it, leading more than a dozen dogs and the mare.

The state fair was going on when we arrived, and I went out to see it a day or two later with a very nice young fellow, whose acquaintance I had made on the steamer. His father had been a rich planter before the war, and my friend had been educated at Heidelberg; but while he was there the war broke out, and his father and he were ruined, losing nearly

ATTACKED BY CHOLERA. 167

six hundred slaves. Soon after his father died, and he sold the plantation for less than half its value to a Northern man, and now lived an idle life in New Orleans. On the way back from the fair, he complained of feeling a great deal of pain, so I called a cab and took him to the hotel, where I sat with him till near midnight, going to bed then as he said he felt better; so my astonishment may be imagined when on ringing in the morning to inquire after him, I was told that he had died of cholera about four o'clock and was already buried, as is the law in such cases. We had not heard of cholera being in the city, and now I found that people were dying at the rate of two hundred a day. Two days afterwards I felt the same symptoms myself, and on sending for a doctor I found I was down with the same complaint. In a few hours I was very bad, but the doctor told me, on his leaving me at night, that if I was there in the morning I should do; and this I determined to be if possible, which I have found to be one half the battle. In the morning I was much better, but I was very ill for three weeks, and just when Billy Breeze would have been a great deal of use to me, I found that he was in prison for fighting, leaving the dogs to look after themselves.

While in the city I was introduced to a number of Confederate generals, including Beauregard, Jeff Thomson, and Morgan, and one night was taken by them to a fashionable gambling-house, where everything was on a sumptuous scale; the servants all wearing elaborate liveries, the rooms beautifully furnished, and a first-class supper being served every night at twelve o'clock, free to all who chose to partake of it, when every kind of wine was to be had for the asking. I would not stay for this, as I was not going to play, but my companions did. The host was much more like an English country squire than a gambling-house keeper, and discussed sport with me as if fond of it.

F—— and I remained in New Orleans for five weeks, chiefly on account of my illness, and then left for Galveston, the capital of Texas, in a miserable little steamer, with poor accommodation. Galveston is a very prettily situated place, being on a long island off the coast of Texas, with, on the land side, the finest beach I ever saw. It is eight miles long and at low tide half a mile wide. We put up at the Palmetto House, kept by an Irish lady, a Mrs. McDonnell—there was a Mr. of that name, but he was a mere cipher in the establishment. Here we had to wait some time for letters from home, so we made numerous excursions into the surrounding country for quail, pintailed grouse, and ducks.

On one of our first trips to the mainland we stopped at the house of a man named Gallagher, an Irishman, and happening one day when shooting to come on the railway, we went into a small store, which was also a railway-station, to buy something which we needed, and got into conversation with the man who kept it, who introduced himself to us as Captain Richardson, late of the Southern army. On our saying where we were staying, and that the fare was bad, he very hospitably pressed us to come back and stay the night at his house, where he said he could give us something better. He so evidently wished us to come, that we consented, Billy Breeze being with us, and walked with him to a very pretty little wooden house, covered with creepers and standing in a garden, where he introduced us to his wife and daughter, who seemed very nice also. Everything was beautifully clean, and our room was all we could wish. They gave us a capital dinner, insisting on opening all kinds of canned things, such as peaches, apricots, and pine-apples, besides a number of bottles of Scotch ale. In the morning we fared equally well, and wished him good-bye with effusion, hoping we might have the pleasure of seeing him again, when, to our horror, he presented a bill nearly as long as one's arm, in which every tin and every bottle was entered at a fancy price, our board and lodging for one night coming to close on twenty-nine dollars, or six pounds, more than double what it would have been at the Lindell House at St. Louis. Of course we had to pay, and I remember had to send Billy back for the money, as we had not brought enough with us. I do not wish my readers to take Captain Richardson as a type of a Texan, as he was not so by any means, he, and one other, of whom more by-and-by, being the only two specimens of his class that we met. Texans are generally very hospitable and generous to a fault.

We found a great many quail almost everywhere, and also grouse, the three of us often getting seventy odd brace of the former in one day, and half that number of the latter. There were in addition always deer to be found, and we often jumped them when after small game. No one seemed to shoot in those days, and deer they seemed to think were not worth eating, and people did not even thank you for a present of venison, living themselves almost entirely on pork.

As soon as our letters came we fitted out for our trip to Denver, intending to go by way of San Antonio, Fort Mason, and Fort Belknap, but meaning to take our time to San Antonio, as we did not wish to get there till the spring grass was up. Our waggon and mules we decided to get at Houston, but we engaged most of the men before we started, the first being a man named Brown, whom we found as a waiter at one of the restaurants, taking him to drive the waggon, our chief trouble being to find a cook.

One day, however, as we were walking along the main street of Galveston, we saw a man coming towards us, who, though dressed chiefly in rags, yet had put them on so that you hardly noticed what they were, and was walking along with a jaunty air, as if in the best of spirits. We spoke to him, and found that he was a Frenchman who had been in the Chasseurs d'Afrique, and, later, had joined the force got together by the filibuster Walker, in Mexico. On the death of his leader he had drifted into Texas, where he had lived by his wits. There was so much "go" in the man, in spite of the emptiness of his pockets, that we engaged him as cook, as he said he was a "Chef," and we sent him out to the camp which we had formed between Galveston and Houston. On following him to camp, we were asked by Billy, what had made us engage a "frog-eating mounseer" who thought of nothing but his appearance and could not speak English? Billy and Louis, as the cook was called, were always falling out and having to be separated, and gave us endless trouble, and later on we were obliged to send Louis away.

Meaning to complete our outfit in Houston we left for that place early in December. A railway running for some way on a high trestle viaduct connects Galveston with the mainland, and a few hours took us to Houston, then a town of some ten thousand inhabitants. Here we bought a waggon and a pair of mules, harness, saddles, and supplies, besides seven horses— I having four and F—— three. Here we added another to our party, a young Englishman whose name was H——, who agreed to remain with us till we reached Denver. We also got two more men, "Bill" and "John," both of them from the old country, and good fellows they were, and our party was now complete.

While getting our outfit together we made the acquaintance of a New Yorker who had been sent to Texas for his sins, his friends refusing to give him any more money unless he went to Texas, and into some business there; so here we found him as a saddler, not that he knew anything about the trade, but he had a manager who conducted the business, and he passed his time in going about in a velvet suit making calls on his acquaintances. He invited us to supper one evening, saying that his friends had just sent him a hamper of good things, and when we went about eight o'clock at night we found that he had forgotten to tell his housekeeper that he was expecting guests, so that she had gone home for the night, and had locked up everything; consequently the supper consisted only of pâté-de-foie gras and champagne, and as I was the only one of the party who could eat the former without bread I finished the tin.

Our new friend H—— was a good shot at small game and a good rider, but had never killed anything bigger than a hare, or done any camping out; but he soon took to it, and before long was as good a man in camp as any of us, beating us all in one particular, which was as a trencherman, where we were simply "not in it," as he would eat as much as any two of us. Louis's cookery was anything but satisfactory, in spite of the grand names which he gave his dishes, his bread being especially uneatable. I remember the first lot he gave us.

which appeared in the form of cannon-balls and of the same colour, and though he called them "Petits pains à la Parisienne" we none of us could eat them; we therefore very soon sent him back, and installed John, who had been first a pastry-cook and then a prize-fighter, as cook, but not before Billy and Louis had had some rounds, in the course of which the latter was knocked into the fire.

From Houston we started north for a place called Richmond, getting into trouble on our second night out. There was a landmark going by the name of the "lone tree" standing out on the prairie, away from all timber, which had served as a directing-post for ages. It consisted of a large dead tree, and it stood in what was in wet weather a swamp. On the second evening we found ourselves not far from this tree, with our animals tired and the wheels half buried in the swamp. We managed to reach the tree, which was on a small dry mound, but could get no further, so we had to camp, picketing our animals out round the tree, and making our fire up against it, and also using some of it to burn. There was not room for all of us to sleep on the mound, so some slept in the waggon; but I was one of the former, and in the night we were awoke by the heat, and found the tree on fire to the top, and it was all consumed when we left it in the morning.

On hitching up we found the waggon was firmly imbedded, and our team could not move it an inch, so hearing the creaking of wheels on the opposite side of a small rise, we rode there, and found a negro driving four span of oxen to Houston, and promised him five dollars if he would get us out of the swamp, but this he refused to do, telling us that he had no time. As another team might not pass all day, we told him that we should take the oxen, on which he brought two span and took us out at once, oxen being very much better in mud than mules. We passed through Richmond, which was then a miserable little place, and camped on a creek some eight or ten miles on the other side, choosing that spot as it was near a cabin where we could buy butter, milk, &c.

When riding through the town we met an Irishman named Gallagher (no relation to our late host), who told us of a wonderful race-mare he had, which was said to be the fastest animal in Texas, so a day or two after pitching our camp F—— and I rode in to have a look at her, going most of the way at a gallop. We saw the mare, with which we were disappointed, and were returning to camp when a man came up and told us that the Justice wanted to see us, so we accompanied him to the court house. Here we were informed by that official that we were fined one sovereign each for riding fast through the town. Now Richmond was a straggling place, and what they called the principal street had no houses for some distance, and then only one now and again at long intervals, the street itself being a sandy track; so we told him that we had seen no regulation about riding fast, and had not even known we were in the town, so we should not pay, on which we walked out and rode off at full speed. As we were leaving the town, we came across a herd of cattle, which separated to let us through, and we were almost past them when a yearling calf, finding, I suppose, that its mother had gone in the opposite direction, crossed right in front of us, and F——, who was ahead, ran into it, going at full speed, turning a complete summersault, horse and all, and landed with a loud thud in a cloud of dust, sending the calf some ten yards in front of him. On pulling up and going back to him, I found that his collar-bone was broken, so I helped him on to his horse and took him to camp, and returned at once to Richmond for a doctor, whom I had great difficulty in finding, coming on him at last in a whiskey-saloon playing cards. He returned with me and bound up the shoulder, but just as he was finishing H—— came in from shooting, and seeing how the bandages were put on, told the doctor he could not know his business, as they did no good at all as they were, the bones not being united, and that the arm was not supported round the neck. The doctor immediately flared up, saying that he knew his own business best, and demanded twenty-five dollars (£5) for what he had done, but as we could feel that it was as H—— said, we refused to pay him anything. On this he got very abusive, called us swindlers and other names, when we told him that if he did not leave the camp in five minutes we would put him in the creek; so he rode off in a furious rage, saying that he would come back with some friends and clear us out, but he must have thought better of it as we never saw him again.

I have said nothing as yet of our horses, so I will do so here. F—— had three capital ponies, much better bred than the common run of them, and just the right height for hunting. H—— had two, but they were too large, being nearly sixteen hands high. I had my mare Polly, a bay horse I had bought in Galveston, and a black horse, which has been immortalized in a poem, being the one ridden by General Sheridan in his twenty-mile ride before the battle of Lexington, when he retrieved the fortunes of the day by doing that distance in the hour. He had been sold as going blind; but this proved to be a mistake, and he was one of the best horses I ever sat on, and was very handsome, being a black about fifteen hands and a half high and three-quarters bred. While in this camp we had an opportunity of seeing how rapidly streams can rise; we had been told of a small rivulet becoming a roaring torrent in a single night, but had not believed it, and we were now to see a proof of this.

Some men came into our camp one evening, and told us that near where they lived a horse had just been re-captured by lassoing from a wild band, which they thought would suit us if we could tame him. He was, they said, thorough-bred and very handsome, but owing to his having run wild for two years, he had not come to his proper growth, being only fourteen and a half hands high. This was the size we preferred, so tempted by the description H—— and I determined to go and see him, and as they stayed the night in our camp we went with them the next morning. A ride of twelve miles brought us to a farm, where we found the horse tied in the middle of a field, and he was so wild that they had put three lariats on him fastened to different posts. On going up to him he trembled all over, and the sweat poured off him, nor would he allow us to touch him, crouching down when we attempted to do so; but he was so handsome and so well made, that I bought him, giving two hundred dollars (£40) for him. He was a bright chestnut with a skin like satin, showing a network of veins all over it; he had splendid shoulders, was well ribbed up and very big under the knee, and when we had had him some time he filled out wonderfully. The great trouble was, how to take him to camp; so I bought him on condition that he was to be delivered safe at our tent.

During the night a storm came on, lasting the greater part of the next day, so that we had to remain two nights at the farm, but it cleared up towards evening, and the following morning we started, two men leading the horse, which I called "Henry," that being the name of his sire; each of the men having a raw-hide lariat round his neck and fastened to the horn of the saddle. There was some desperate plunging at first, but finding he was powerless, he at length submitted and came quietly. On reaching our creek, which we had left about three yards wide, and so shallow that we often went for milk to the cabin in our slippers, we found it was now a torrent fully sixty yards wide, and as there were trees on each side, between which the water was rushing, crossing it would be very awkward, as you would almost certainly be dashed against these. We therefore camped where we were, and picketed "Henry," sending the men back.

We had arrived about dusk, having come very slowly, and had been very much surprised at getting no answer from camp, nor could we see the tent or waggon, though we were just opposite to where we had left them; so in the morning we fired some shots, on which F—— appeared on a small hill some way off, and came down to the other side of the torrent, telling us that all was well, but that they had had to shift camp suddenly. H—— and I made up our minds to swim it on horseback, taking off most of our clothing, and leaving our rifles and saddles behind; so we plunged in, and the horses did not seem to mind it much; but we at once found that we could not make any way at all, as we were carried down the stream and bumped against the trees; so we jumped off and struck out for the opposite shore, leaving the horses to shift for themselves, having merely knotted up the reins, and by swimming from tree to tree, and resting to recover breath, we at last reached the bank five or six hundred yards lower down than where we started from, the horses getting over before we did.

F—— told us that he had been asleep in the tent, and was lying on a feather-bed—lent him by the wife of the owner of the cabin on account of his broken collar-bone—when being woke by the awful rain, he had put out his hand to feel if any water had come in, and had found that there were about two inches in the tent. He at once jumped up and called the men, who were sleeping in the waggon, and they had hitched up and moved to high ground, losing a number of things which were not noticed in the dark, and which were of course washed away by the stream, which was now four feet deep where our tent had stood.

The water subsided as rapidly as it had risen, the creek being in its normal condition on the second day after our return, and even on the morning after the flood it had become low enough for us to ride over and water "Henry;" but we left him on the other side till the stream had quite subsided, as he refused to enter it. We very soon made him much quieter, by feeding him with corn and standing by him while he ate it, and he would now let us groom him, if we did not do anything suddenly. From the first he did not mind a gun being fired, and a fortnight made him like an old horse. It took seven of us to lunge him, and sometimes we were all on the ground together, and would be dragged several yards. I rode him first, putting on breeches and boots for the occasion, but beyond running away for a few miles he did nothing, and was very quiet after that.

We made two more camps on this creek, as feed was good and game of all kinds close at hand; and then we moved north, stopping where we could find game, ducks and geese being in thousands, as they had now all arrived from the north. I used to do most of my grouse-shooting from the saddle, when I rode Polly, who would always stop suddenly when I raised my gun to fire, and who very often saw game before I did.

Hearing that we had brought her with us from the north, everyone thought it must be for racing purposes, and many horses were brought to camp to run against her; but we refused to race, as it nearly always led to some unpleasantness, and frequently to a fight with revolvers. All races in that part of the country were very short, from three to six hundred yards, and the horses started at the report of a pistol.

While in Galveston I saw a heavy-looking, badly bred animal, belonging to some gamblers, which required a whip when being ridden as a hack, but which when on a race-track I did not recognize, being all fire and spirit; it ran a quarter of a mile in eighteen seconds, and beat a fine chestnut thoroughbred, which had a great name as a mile horse. This kind of racing is most unsatisfactory and leads to a great deal of trickery and cheating, so that we never went in for it, after our first trial. Everything depends upon the start when running so short a distance, and the gamblers, who are nearly always the racehorse owners "out west," will take any advantage they can of you, backing one another up if you object. I saw in Texas what I had never heard of before, which was a racing mule; and it was said to be as fast as any horse for six hundred yards, and being such an unlikely animal to run, had taken a number of people in.

CHAPTER XIV.

Move to Clear Lake.—A bankrupt railway.—Abundance of game.—Stalking wild geese.—Invitation to a bear-hunt.—A norther. Story of a norther.—Lynch law.—Bear-hunting poor sport.—Great abundance of snipe.—Good shooting.—Extortionate landlord.—Semi-wild hogs.—Wild bulls. Narrow escapes from them.—Our dog Booze. His fighting capabilities.—Invitation to a plantation. Melancholy appearance of it.—A good afternoon at the ducks.—A Masonic tip.—A Texan ball.—Buying mules.—Fishing in Texas.

Towards the end of November we moved on to Clear Lake, a very pretty camp, and only a mile and a half from a railway station. This railway was a source of much amusement to us. It was only forty miles long, running from Houston to Alleyton, and it was in a bankrupt condition; there was only one engine, which made the journey to Alleyton one day and returned the next, and was very uncertain as to its time of arrival and departure. The engine was an old shunting one from New Orleans, with a leaky boiler, which after running four or five miles, and sometimes less, had to stop to get up steam. On one occasion I had started from camp on horseback, carrying a deer on the front of the saddle, and a quantity of small game being hung round it, intending to be at the station when the train arrived, and to send my game by it to Galveston. As I came in sight of the station, which was then a mile distant, I saw the train just leaving it, and anywhere else should have returned to camp; but I knew the peculiarities of that engine, and that it was bound to stop near a certain tree about four miles from the station, so I cantered across and met the train, asking the engine-driver to pull up so that I might put my game on; this, however, he refused to do, so I continued alongside and chaffed him, telling him that he would have to pull up soon, and might as well do it then, but as he still refused to do so, I cantered on and stopped at the tree and waited, when sure enough the train came to a standstill near me.

We had splendid sport at Clear Lake, as all kinds of game were in great abundance; snipe especially were very plentiful, also ducks and grouse of two kinds—pintailed and pinnated; but what we enjoyed most was shooting geese, which were very numerous, and could be found scattered all over the prairie feeding on the grass. If you stood on any high point you could see hundreds of flocks in every direction, and our way of stalking them was as follows :—We would each take a quiet pony with only a bridle on him, and describe a large circle on the prairie, stooping so as to be concealed behind him from all those inside this circle. Of course we put up a good many, but this did not disturb the others, who merely ran together towards the centre; we gradually contracted this circle, getting nearer and nearer to the middle, till within perhaps a hundred yards, and the geese began to put up their heads and cackle, when we jumped on the ponies and galloped in as hard as we could go, and in this way often got within forty yards before they were well on the wing, firing over our pony's head and getting three or four with the two barrels. Another way was to drive an ox up to them, lying flat on a raw hide, which was attached to the yoke by traces. By driving as if you were going to pass them, you could frequently get very near. Another way was to stalk them with a pea rifle, when you got some very pretty shooting. Beside geese there were a good many sand-hill cranes, standing about four feet high, which could be stalked in the same way, requiring, however, much more caution to be used in order to get near enough to them, as they are such shy birds. When wounded you had to be careful how you approached them, as when their legs were not broken they would jump at your face in a moment, and the beak being about six inches long and very sharp, could inflict a bad wound.

Soon after camping on Clear Lake we received an invitation to a bear-hunt on a large scale, which was to come off in the Brazos bottom (a strip of timber six miles wide lying along the Brazos River) from an old settler named Estes. He was quite a character, living the life of a hunter in a house far removed from any neighbour, and cultivating only enough land to supply himself with flour and vegetables and his horses with corn. He had served in the Southern Army during the war, and when the South had to give in, he had taken an oath not to cut his hair till she had had her revenge, so that it had not been cut for more than three years and was like a rough mane. When we reached his house we found a number of men collected, and a great variety of dogs, most of them curs, which, however, answer better for that kind of hunting than well-bred hounds.

A NORTHER.

In the course of the evening, when we were sitting in the verandah in our shirt sleeves, we had an opportunity of seeing a storm peculiar to Texas, called a " Norther." It was very warm, more like summer than November, and we were enjoying it, when Estes, happening to look towards the north, told us to get our coats as we should need them very soon; and looking in the same direction we saw a long black line, which as we watched it seemed to be coming nearer; then we heard a whispering among the leaves, which increased in loudness till it became a roar, and the norther was on us. In this case it consisted of only a very cold and strong wind, against which it would have been very difficult to ride or walk if on the open prairie; but sometimes it is accompanied by a snow-storm of terrible violence, and then if caught in the open it often means death unless shelter can speedily be found. This storm lasted about three hours, but they sometimes continue to blow for three days.

A half-breed, whom I met in Dacotah, and who seemed to have wonderful powers of standing cold, told me that once when carrying despatches between Fort Wadsworth and Fort Abercrombie, in company with another half-breed, they had been overtaken by a blizzard, which much resembles a Texan norther, excepting that it may come from any quarter, and that as they happened to be near some timber they had ridden hard and had time to off saddle and get under their blankets before the worst of the storm reached them. Under these they remained for three days, the storm being accompanied by snow, which buried them and helped to keep them warm. At the end of that time my informant had come out from under the snow and had found his companion dead and frozen stiff;

and this he said was owing to his being a drunkard, while he himself took no spirits of any kind. They had plenty of food with them, though they had to eat the meat raw, so that it could not have been starvation which killed the man.

But to return to our bear-hunt. Later in the evening, when the norther had blown itself out and we were again sitting on the verandah, a young fellow rode up, whom most of those present seemed to know; and on his joining us some one said to him—"Well, did you get him?" on which he answered "Yes, but we did not bring him in"; and then the subject was changed, as if everyone knew what this meant. Now men are inquisitive sometimes, though of course very seldom, and F—— and I (for H—— was not with us) were curious to know what this meant, so we crossed to where the young fellow was sitting and asked him.

It seemed that some weeks before, he had gone into Galveston to buy his winter supplies, taking with him two negroes, who had been with his family all their lives, and who, when all slaves were freed, had chosen to remain as servants, getting wages; and that while in Galveston two women returning from market had been set upon by negroes and robbed, besides being badly beaten. For some reason one of his servants was suspected, and was arrested and lodged in prison. On hearing this he had gone to him to say that if he was innocent he would provide counsel to defend him, and as the negro assured him that he was so, he saw a lawyer and arranged matters with him. However, before the trial came off, this negro had managed to escape, thereby proving himself guilty. Knowing how stupid negroes are, and how they often when pursued go to the very place where you would be sure to look for them, he felt certain that his man had gone straight home; so he went by rail to within forty miles of the place, and then hired a horse to ride the rest of the way, telling the people of the place where he got the horse what he was going for. The man had done as he expected; so he seized him, put him on a horse, and was bringing him in to the railway, when, as he expressed it, "The boys met me and we put him up." I asked what that meant, on which he leant forward, and pointing to his horse, which was still standing saddled at the fence, he asked us if we could see a raw-hide lariat on the saddle, and on our saying that we could, he said, "Well, that is what we put him up with." They, it seems, had hung him to a tree. When we asked his reason for so doing, he said that since the war it had been almost impossible to get a negro punished, the usual plan being to send any who had committed a crime to a black regiment, and that therefore in this case they had taken the law into their own hands. He added that when we had been longer in the country we should often hear of troublesome negroes having disappeared, and of having gone on a visit to their friends in the north, which meant in reality that they had gone underground.

The following morning we started, about twenty men on horseback, for the bear-hunt, Estes and two or three more going in one direction while we went in another, the idea being to beat up to us. One of the party, who was an old hand at this kind of thing, placed us, telling us to fire at nothing but bears. For some time not a sound was heard, but after waiting more than an hour I heard the dogs coming, and then a shot, followed by another, and all was still. It seemed an age before I heard them again, and when I did they seemed to be coming my way, and something passed by my right, though the bushes were too thick for me to see what it was, and a few seconds later my two nearest neighbours, shouting that it was a bear, left their posts, and followed the dogs, on which I did the same. This kind of riding I soon found required a long apprenticeship, for though the ground is as a rule free from brush, yet long vines hang from the trees, and oblige a man to lie flat, and be very quick about it, as he passes under them, or he will be swept off his horse.

The Texans are fine horsemen, almost all of them being able to pick up a hat off the ground when passing it at a gallop; and I have more than once seen a man, when going at a walk, stoop and pick up his hat which a branch had knocked off without stopping his horse.

I soon found that I could not keep up, and arrived about five minutes after the bear had been shot, and had fallen from the tree in which he had taken refuge. Sometimes they get into a cane brake, in which case you must dismount, tie up your horse, and cut your way through the dense canes to the bear, which is very hard work, and necessitates the carrying of a large knife made for the purpose. Two bears were killed on this occasion, and were of the small black variety, and neither F—— nor I got a shot at either; the only game of any kind which came our way was one deer. We returned to camp the next morning, not caring for any more bear-hunting of that kind. The favourite way of killing deer among the Texans was by driving them with dogs, and taking stands as in bear-hunting, the deer being generally found near the edges of the wood, while the bears are much further in. The Brazos bottom was a grand hunting-ground, consisting as it did of six miles of forest on each side of the river. The number of snipe here was astonishing, and I heard of one man who killed more than a hundred couple to his own gun in one day. We never cared to give up so much time to snipe-shooting, so did not get such large bags, but forty or fifty couple in a morning was common.

One day, just as we were going to dinner, a man rode up and stopped to speak to us, so we asked him to join us. We happened that day to have a specially good bill of fare, and he enjoyed his dinner thoroughly, and remained with us for some hours discussing Texas and the game to be found there. He told us that he lived about twelve miles away, and that there were thousands of snipe all round his house, and that if we cared to shoot such small game, he would be very glad to put us up. We at once accepted his invitation; and taking Billy Breeze with us, to look after the horses, we rode over to his house a few days afterwards. It proved to be a very dilapidated place, many of the doors being gone and most of the glass broken in the windows. This he explained by saying that he had been ruined by the war, and had never had the heart to put things right since. After a meal consisting of very bad salt pork, most of which was melted, and which he and his wife dipped up with corn bread, coffee without milk and sweetened with syrup, we went off to a large field near the house, which was very undulating and contained a number of small marshes; and here we found the snipe as plentiful as he said, every hollow containing twenty or thirty, and they were so tame that they would fly from one hollow to the next and then back again, so that we soon had a large bag, and sent Billy back to get a lot of them ready for supper, not caring for any more of the liquid pork. This meal was a great improvement on our dinner, and I think we must have eaten a dozen snipe apiece, after which we had a long discussion on the war, and on the part our host had played in it, where he seemed to have done wonders for an ungrateful country, and then we turned in—sleeping in our own blankets on the floor.

The next day was a repetition of the preceding one, the snipe being equally plentiful and equally tame, and our bag was a very large one. We had another meal of snipe and then saddled our horses to return to camp, telling Billy to remain behind, and see if he could, in a delicate way, and without hurting his feelings, induce our host to take something for the corn our horses had eaten. We said good-bye and rode off, but had not gone far when we heard Billy calling after us, and saw him coming as fast as he could shuffle (for his wounds, received during the war, prevented his running), and on coming up, we found that when he offered to pay for the corn our host presented a long bill of which I forget the amount, but I know that ten dollars (£2) which we had given Billy was not nearly enough to settle it, so that our delicacy had been wasted.

We were very much annoyed by the semi-wild hogs, which then ranged about the country in immense numbers, as they would come into camp and eat up the corn meant for our horses, driving them away for it. To be even with them we shot a fat one now and then and put him through the sausage-machine. Of course all these hogs belonged to some one, but they were so numerous and worth so little, that all travellers acted as we did; indeed, most men passing through the country seemed to think nothing of killing a "beef" when they wanted meat, and when we went to a settler who owned several thousand head of cattle and asked if we might kill an old bull now and then for our dogs, he said we were the first men who had ever come to ask leave, everyone killing what he thought proper. Some of the bulls are very dangerous to a man on foot at certain seasons of the year, and no Texan will go among them unless he is mounted.

F—— was stalking some fine turkeys one day, when he heard a noise behind him, and found a bull working himself up for a charge, pawing the ground and lashing his sides with his tail, and he had to shoot the bull instead of the turkeys. I was once charged by one—a white one, I remember; he came straight at me when I was snipe-shooting, and I had to kill him with snipe shot, firing both barrels at once, and making a hole in his forehead into which I could have put three fingers; he fell so close to me that he threw the mud all over me, and I had to jump back to avoid being knocked down.

Having so many dogs in camp, we could consume a great deal of meat, and very little was wasted. The cattle were small, and one lasted us only about three days. The Texans kept a great number of large dogs, of no particular breed, using them for holding their hogs by the ear while they were either branded or killed, and these being very fierce caused us a great deal of trouble, fighting with our pointers and setters and laming them. To prevent this we bought a large dog, part bull, as a sort of guardian for the others. He rejoiced in the name of "Booze," so christened by his late master Billy Breeze, of whom we bought him. This dog was the best fighter I ever saw, as he would face any number of other dogs, and behaved in such a dignified way until he was attacked, that they as a rule left him alone and went away. When a number of big dogs rushed out at him from a house we happened to be passing, he would sit down in the middle of the road and look straight before him, allowing them to come up all round him, and never moving, and their pace would usually get perceptibly slower as they got near him, and they were very often satisfied with a look at about three feet distance; but if they touched him there was a sudden transformation scene: the nearest dog was seized and shaken like a rat, no regard being paid to the others, who were probably biting him behind meanwhile; then another was treated in the same way, and then another, when they generally turned tail and fled. However much he was hurt himself he never uttered a sound or seemed to care anything about it. Booze was a splendid dog for hogs, holding the largest with ease, and by keeping always close alongside the hog he avoided his tusks. It was so much trouble to get him off when he once had hold, that we used to beat him when he went after hogs, on which he became so crafty that he would drive one into a stream or pond, where we could not follow him, and there he would hold the hog's head under water until he had drowned him. He would throw the largest bull in a moment, catching him by the nose, and an Irish water-spaniel, which F—— had brought from England, used to assist him by holding on to the tail, and this he would do so firmly, that I have seen him dragged fifty or sixty yards over the prairie before he would let go his hold.

While at Clear Creek we had an invitation from a Captain Duncan, who lived on Caney Creek, which runs into the

Brazos, to pay him a visit; he had been very rich before the war, having owned some four hundred slaves, a racing-establishment, and a fine house in New Orleans. When his negroes were freed and left him, he had no money to work his plantation, and had, like most Southern planters, always lived beyond his income, so that now if a Northern man had not taken part of his ground at a low rent, he would have starved, as there was no sale for his land.

On the way to his house, we came to a cabin with a lake in front of it, and this was full of wildfowl of many kinds, which, as they were swimming about a few yards from the house, we supposed had been raised by the settler; but, on asking him if this was so, he told us that they were wild, but as they were not fit to eat he never fired at them. Not agreeing with him, we dismounted and had a splendid afternoon's sport; the only drawback was our having to retrieve our own ducks, as we had not brought a dog with us. We found the same prejudice everywhere among the uneducated Texans against eating wild ducks, though of course they were as good there as anywhere else. We took those we had shot to Captain Duncan's and found them capital. His plantation was a melancholy sight, the two negro villages were falling into ruins, as also were the racing-stables, and the Captain and his son seemed to have lost all spirit, wandering about disconsolately, and doing nothing but eat and sleep. Miss Duncan was charming, and had all the spirit left in the family, but she could not induce her father and brother to exert themselves, though she tried hard to do so.

On returning to Clear Lake we determined to start for San Antonio as soon as we could find another team of mules, those we had being too small for our load. Hearing of some that were to be sold near us we attended the sale, and I should have bought them, if the neighbour of the man selling them, finding that I was a mason, had not warned us—merely saying "Don't;" so we didn't. He turned out to be a good sort of fellow, and invited us to a grand dance, to be given at his house in honour of his son's wedding, so we went. It was an extraordinary affair in every way, the dancing being quite unlike anything in civilization, and every man had at least one revolver buckled round his waist under his coat or in a pistol-pocket behind. We left early, but we heard that later in the evening there were several little troubles among the guests, whiskey being very plentiful, and partaken of by both the gentlemen and their fair partners.

As good mules were very scarce, it was arranged that I should go to Galveston and buy some, as we had seen a great many good ones in the streets while there. Accordingly I took the railway to Houston, and after I had tried to find some there and failed, I went on to Galveston and put up once more at the Palmetto House. As I found it very difficult to get any here also, I at last, in desperation, stopped every dray in which I saw a good mule, and so secured a fine team of four. These I put into the train and took them to camp, and very soon after my return we made a start for San Antonio, travelling slowly so as to keep our animals in good condition for their long journey.

I have said nothing of the fishing in Texas, there being none worth mentioning; the principal fish is the "cat-fish," a miserable bony monster, only eatable when made into "fish chowder," a sort of stew compounded of fish, with all the bones removed, potatoes, pepper, and salt, which when one was hungry and when eaten hot, on a cold day was not bad. At Galveston you get blue fish, which are very good, and the finest prawns I ever saw. There are besides fairly good and very cheap oysters in enormous shells, costing one dollar a barrel, the barrel meant being the one used for flour, holding two hundred pounds.

CHAPTER XV.

San Antonio and Texas in 1868.—Horse-stealing. Its punishment.—Shoeing and breaking wild ponies. Negroes the best breakers.—Mexicans and their mode of life.—Part with Billy Breeze.—Move to Fredericksburg.—Too hot for the dogs. Death of one.—Trying the men's courage.—Halliday, his history.—A real frontiersman. He declines to go with us.—H—— has an adventure while on guard.—Fort Mason.—Indians catch and torture a man.—Big-foot Wallace. Refuses to go with us.—Leave Fort Mason.—Fight between horses.—A refractory mule. His cure.—An over-confident major.—Start for Fort Belknap.—A plundered waggon.—I meet with Indians. I am pursued. Shoot an Indian's horse and escape.—Difficult country.

SAN ANTONIO in 1868 was a very interesting town, still very Mexican in appearance, having two fine plazas, which on market days were full of Mexicans in their picturesque dress. At the stalls you could get a good dinner of "Chile con carne," frijoles, and tortillas, cooked on a brazier, though you could not always be sure what the meat you were eating was, Mexicans not being very particular.

From the Gulf to this point Texas is very level, but from here the country rises, and the scenery improves, till you pass

Fort Mason, one hundred and twenty miles north of the town, where the prairie begins. This was the great place for buying ponies, many men owning hundreds of them, which ranged over an immense extent of country, and sometimes took weeks to find. As it would be very easy to steal any number of these, it had been made a hanging offence, and any man caught stealing a horse was lynched at once, the usual way being to make one of the animals he had stolen the executioner. The horse-thief was put on one of the ponies, with his hands tied behind him, a rope was fastened round his neck and the other end tied to the bough of a tree over his head, it being then merely a question of time as to when the pony would move off to feed and leave the man hanging. Since this became the unwritten law of the land, horse-stealing has gone out of fashion. We remained several weeks in San Antonio, getting supplies, having our animals shod, and allowing them to recruit before starting on our seven hundred miles journey to Denver.

We had here an opportunity of seeing how they managed to shoe the wild ponies which were always being brought in. This was done by pushing them into a strong frame, just wide enough to hold them, where they had bands passed round them, and were then lifted off their feet, rendering them quite helpless. "Henry" was shod in this way, the country north of the town being too rocky to pass through with unshod horses. We saw here, too, some wild-horse breaking, the best riders being negroes. Sometimes the bucking would go on for half an hour or more, the rider bleeding at the nose and mouth when it was over; and we were told that very few men can break wild horses for more than two years, and they then are wrecks for life, and a good many are killed or maimed by horses falling on them.

Having a good deal of time on our hands, we went about among the Mexicans observing their way of living, and found that, though opposed to the use of water for any purpose, they were as polite as Spaniards, though it did not mean much more than it does in Spain, most of them being ready to knife you for a very small sum.

Before leaving San Antonio we were very reluctantly compelled to send Billy Breeze back to St. Joe. He found that his wounds prevented his riding, and he could not possibly do the seven hundred miles on foot. We were all of us very sorry to see him go, as, when anywhere away from whiskey, a better man we never had. He returned by stage to the end of the railway at Richmond, and from there went back as we had come.

Having driven round and collected our numerous purchases, we left San Antonio about the end of March; three days taking us to Fredericksburg, a German settlement forty-five miles further north. This we found to be like most of their settlements—very clean and well ordered. The houses were large and comfortable and the land well cultivated and fenced. The country we passed through was almost entirely covered with low brush, in which were more quail than we had ever seen before. We put them up continually on the sandy track which did duty for a road, and if it had been the shooting season we could have had splendid sport. The heat was already so great that, combined with the dust, it was too much for our dogs, who were utterly unable to travel, and we had to give several of them away to save their lives. One of our greyhounds came to a very sad end. One day, as he seemed to be suffering from the heat, we tied him under the waggon, as it was a shady place, and soon after doing so we rode ahead for some purpose, supposing that the men would keep an eye on him, as there were three of them behind the waggon leading horses, and when we rejoined the party we found the poor dog dead and stiff, having evidently been dragged for some distance by the neck.

The next settlement we reached was a very small one on the Jan Jaba River, where we were told that there was a first-rate man to take as guide, as we had hitherto failed to find one, everyone objecting to go across the plains through the Comanche Indian country with so small a party. This man was away when we arrived, hunting for strayed horses, so we camped there to wait for him.

While there F—— and I rode to a house some way up the river, to try and buy some milk and butter, and on our way back, hearing some of our men bathing in the river, we thought we would try their courage, so we galloped through the bushes giving the Comanche war-whoop. On emerging on the bank, we could see five or six naked figures going for cover at a great rate, and I cannot say that they exactly blessed us when they saw who we were. Hearing that John, the cook, was the only man in camp, we went into that in the same way and very nearly got shot, finding John under the waggon with a repeating rifle in his hands, aiming in our direction, and only just seeing who we were in time to avoid firing.

I have forgotten to mention that we had picked up another man in San Antonio, whose name was Halliday. He had been a miner in Montana, where he had made about £2000; with this he and a companion had fitted out a slaver for the West Coast of Africa, where he had been seized by a British cruiser, his vessel being condemned and he and his crew turned adrift. He had worked his way back to New Orleans, and from there to San Antonio, where we engaged him to look after the horses. He was one of those men who were always saying what they would do if we met any Indians, having got used to them, as he said, in Montana. How he really behaved will be seen later on.

On the morning after our arrival we came out of the tent to find, leaning on his rifle by the camp fire, which he had made up, the best-looking specimen of a frontiersman I had yet seen. He stood over six feet high in his moccasins, and was dressed in a buckskin suit and a fur cap. His face was handsome and he had a short beard. On seeing us he came forward, and said that he had heard that we wanted a guide, and knowing the country as far as Denver, he had come to offer himself in that capacity. He seemed just the man we wanted, and had lived most of his life on the frontier, and had fought the Comanches and Kiowas. He had lately returned from a hunt after strayed horses, during which he had been driven into cover by a small party of Indians, having to remain there over twenty-four hours, when he managed to crawl through them at night. These Southern Indians will never dismount to pursue a man, having been brought up to consider their horses as part of themselves, and always running away when he is shot. We had nearly concluded our bargain with this man, when he suddenly asked where the rest of the party was, and on hearing that it was composed of the seven whom he saw, he declined at once to go, saying that no smaller party than fifty men could hope to get through. He remained with us all day, but would not be tempted, so we made up our minds to go on alone, though none of us knew one yard of the country. He told us that we might expect to see Indians any day, as they frequently came as far south as this, and that a party had been killed near Fort Mason a few days before. This turned out to be only partially true.

We left the Jan Jaba the next morning, travelling over a horribly rocky country and only making about sixteen miles. That night we arranged the guards, each of us taking two hours, and being seven we got two nights off in the week. The first man went on at eight and the last came off at six, the first and last having an easy time of it, as we often did not turn in till nine and were up by five.

The second night H—— had an adventure during his guard. He was going round to see whether all the horses were right, when he suddenly fell on something which seemed to heave up, H—— being thrown up in the air and coming down with considerable force; he then found that he had walked on to one of his horses when asleep, and it had suddenly jumped up, making him think there had been an earthquake. We found that sometimes the last man would have what seemed an extraordinary long two-hours' watch, it being so long before daylight appeared, and the sun seemed to rise later every morning; and this, we discovered, was owing to one of the men having always put on the hands of the watch, which he was given when going on guard, to shorten his own two hours.

As we got near Fort Mason the character of the country changed, the dense brush giving way to mesquit grass with numbers of small thorny mesquit trees scattered about it. This grass is dry-looking stuff—very short and curly, but it is wonderfully fattening for cattle and horses; and we noticed one very curious thing with regard to it, which was that if any of our animals were picketed so as to be able to reach the sandy road we were travelling on, they would always feed on the dusty grass beside it and on the little ridges between the tracks. Another thing we noticed was that whereas up to this time we had noticed no rattlesnakes, we now found a great many of them, lying as a rule under the mesquit bushes. This was the only wood we could get, unless we came to some small river, where there were other varieties, and fortunately it would burn equally well whether green or dry.

On reaching Fort Mason we camped close to the officers' quarters, and went to call on Captain Thomson, who was in command, and were very hospitably welcomed. We found that the news we had heard of the Comanches being in the neighbourhood was correct, some men having come in a few days before, who had reported that when about a day's journey from the post, bringing two cart-loads of supplies for the sutler, they had been set upon by Indians and one of their number captured, the remainder of them having managed to escape into some bushes which happened to be near, and that while lying there they had heard the agonized shrieks of their companion, whom they afterwards found had been almost entirely flayed alive. This story Captain Thomson confirmed, as he had lately returned from the scene of the fight, where he had found and buried the body of the man referred to.

We heard here of a celebrated guide called "Big-foot Wallace," but on going to see him we found that he also would not risk himself with so small a party. This man had lived on the frontier serving as guide to the troops, and it was said that he could smell an Indian at a distance of several miles, but we had no opportunity of proving this. There was no guide to be had here, so we determined to go on without one, trusting to a very bad map and our compasses; so we left Fort Mason on the third day, the country gradually changing to open prairie, with clumps of trees and brush here and there—capital ground for hunting had the season not been over.

At one of our midday halts we had a good deal of fun— matching H——'s horse called the " Rig " to fight the stallion of a small band of semi-wild horses, which were branded, but were still so wild that they had to be lassoed when required. We discovered them feeding about half a mile from our camp, and the " Rig " noticing them also, galloped to the end of his rope and pulled up the picket-pin, when he joined the band and began making friends. The stallion, resenting the intrusion of a stranger, attacked him at once, and at it they went, rearing up and seizing one another with their teeth, and then whirling round and kicking at one another, and this went on for fully twenty minutes, and they were so earnestly engaged that we walked up close to them without the stallions taking any notice of us. By the end of this time, H——'s horse, finding that he was getting the worst of it, as the other was a much more powerful animal, returned to camp looking very crestfallen, but not otherwise much the worse for the fight, his antagonist having no shoes on.

Not wishing to kill game we lived now almost entirely on stray cattle, which had escaped from the large herds which were driven every spring over our present route to California.

Some of them had been deserted as being too lame to go any further, and having led a solitary life for some months many of them were as wild as buffalo and much more fierce. F—— had a very close shave from one which charged him furiously as he was going through some bushes, though a dose of small shot cooled his ardour very much.

When buying our new team of mules we had retained our small pair in case of a breakdown, or of very bad going, when we could put them in front; and one of these, when he found he was being worked again after a long rest, hit upon a plan for avoiding this. When anyone of us went for him in the morning, and was pulling up the picket-pin and wiping the mud off it, he would walk up and look on, as if waiting to be led to camp; but as you coiled up the rope he would suddenly start off at a gallop, pulling the rope out of your hands, and it was of no use to hold on, as he would then drag you along the ground, tearing your hands and clothes. When this had happened several times, and F—— and I and the men had suffered in consequence, H——, after laughing at us for our clumsiness, said that he would show us how it should be done, so he started for the mule the following morning, all of us going with him to see the fun. He began by petting the mule a good deal and giving him some sugar, it being, he assured us, a great thing to give the animal confidence in you; and he then proceeded to lead him to the pin, which he pulled up, and was winding up the rope, when away went the mule, and in a few seconds away went H—— also, bounding over the ground, his braces breaking and most of his clothes coming or being torn off. We told him that we did not notice much difference in the result of his system and ours, and his required a new suit of clothes each time, whereas ours did not. His only answer was a request for leave to shoot the mule, but he was too useful, so at last we hit upon a plan which cured him at once. Tying his rope to the stem of a strong mesquit bush, which we cut down on purpose, we pretended to drive in the pin as usual, and in the morning, on seeing it pulled up, off went the mule, the rope throwing him over backwards with almost force enough to break his neck; indeed for some minutes we thought it had, but he eventually got up and was cured of that trick for good.

One morning when F——, H——, and I were riding ahead of the waggon, we came on a party of soldiers out on a scout, and the lieutenant in command said that although he did not know any of us, he did know the horse I was riding, it being the Sheridan horse, and that he had been one of Sheridan's four aides-de-camp who had had to follow him those twenty miles, all four having been left far behind. He said that he was out scouting from a post called "Buffalo Spring," which was then in course of erection, and which was commanded by a Major Davis, an Englishman by birth, and was now on his way back, so we joined him and reached the post that afternoon. The major received us most hospitably, letting his smith shoe our horses and repair the waggon, the awful country we had come over having broken a good many bolts.

He told us that as yet they had seen no Indians, and thought that the reports they had heard of them had been very much exaggerated. We told him of the man who had been skinned near Fort Mason; but this did not convince him that there was much danger, as there were always one or more small bands of

Indians in the country horse-stealing. He said that he always had mounted troopers round the horse band, and yet some months afterwards we heard that the Comanches had run off every head from the post without losing a man, and not a single animal was recovered.

From Buffalo Springs our course was almost due north, our next resting-place being Fort Belknap, a distance of about a hundred and forty miles. We got all the directions we could from the guides attached to the post, not one of them thinking we should get through; and they told us to look out for wood roads, which, as Belknap was an old post and wood was scarce near it, extended for thirty miles or more round it. We should, they said, pass the deserted posts—" Phantom Hill" and "Camp Cooper"—which would serve to show us that we were in the right direction.

Nothing of any consequence happened for some days; the country was alternately prairie and wooded, and game was fairly plentiful, and we were obliged to kill a few deer for food, as we did not find any cattle. About the fifth day we came across a plundered waggon and broken boxes lying round it; but there were no signs of a struggle having taken place, so we supposed that the men must have escaped. There had been rain lately, consequently all tracks had been washed out, so there was no way of telling how long ago it had happened. In one of the boxes we found some corn meal and part of a jar of syrup, which the Indians had probably left fearing poison, as it was a common thing in those days to poison any food which had to be abandoned. We tried them, and as they seemed all right we appropriated them.

The same evening we reached an abandoned post, which,

from its position under a high cliff, we concluded was Phantom Hill, as it had a very ghostly appearance, especially at night. It was a beautiful moonlight night, and everywhere else it was almost as light as day, but here the cliff threw a dark shadow over the post, which, with its empty door and window-frames and its fallen-in roof, looked as if it might well be the abode of ghosts. A branch of the Brazos River ran close to it, and here we camped, thinking that we were near enough now to begin the hunt for the wood roads running into Belknap and intending to remain some days and do so.

On the morning after our arrival, F——, H——, and I rode off in different directions, I going north-east, following for some miles the Brazos River. For several hours I saw nothing but some turkeys and antelope, and had eaten my dinner and started again, riding along a low bluff, about two hundred yards from the river, when I heard a shout, and looking into the bottom I saw a party of seven Indians, evidently camped for a meal on the bank, as their horses were tied near them. From the rush which they made to their horses I knew that they would very soon be after me, and that I had no time to lose if I wished to save my hair. I was riding a very slow grey pony, but I put the spurs into him and got him along at a pace which he had never before equalled, I am sure, and was about half a mile from the bluff, when I saw the Indians ride up on to it. There was no cover of any kind to hide me, so they were after me at once, urging their horses along with yells and blows. The ground was very rough, and at any other time I should have hesitated to go over it at a trot, but I clattered over it now at full speed, the stones flying in all directions; but I soon found that it was of no use trying to ride away from them—their horses being bigger and better than mine, so on coming to a large rock I jumped off and dropped behind it, on which they stopped, being now about a hundred and fifty yards from me. One of them was ahead of the others, and stood facing me on a tall bay horse, so I fired at his chest, using a twelve-bore double rifle and a Metford shell. I suppose the horse must have raised his head for, as I ascertained afterwards, I hit him in the neck, making a huge hole in it, on which he reared and fell sideways on his rider, and as he fell I fired again at a second man, but missed him, the whole of them making off at once, not even stopping to help the man whose horse lay on him, and who was some moments in extricating himself. I could very easily have shot him in the back as he limped off, but it seemed to be so like murder that I could not do it, so let him go, merely shouting to hurry him a little. I at once started for camp, as there might be more Indians in the neighbourhood, and found all safe on my arrival. F—— had come in, having found no road but plenty of fresh Indian sign; and H——, about whom we began to be anxious, returned late—having lost his way, but happening to strike the river had followed it to camp.

As this country was too full of Indians we started the next morning, the road consisting of a mass of stones, and came to a second deserted post, not more than two miles from the other; and this we supposed was Camp Cooper, so that we were going right so far. We ought to have found buffalo here, but they seemed to have been all driven away, which was a bad sign; deer, too, were very scarce, so that we were short of meat and had to kill quail for food.

We came one evening to a small muddy stream, which we

Page 206.—I fired at his chest.

hesitated about crossing as it was late and the mules were tired, so we camped on the near side. During the night a storm came up and the heavy rain lasted till morning, by which time the stream was impassable, keeping us there for three days, and giving us a good lesson—always to cross a stream and camp on the further side when arriving on the banks of one at night, as the storms are so violent and sudden in the south, which cause the streams to swell very rapidly. From this point we had a very unpleasant time of it, there seeming to be no end to the streams, almost all having muddy bottoms and requiring bridges to be made over them; and in a distance of forty miles we must have made quite seventy of these, sometimes not advancing a mile in twenty-four hours, and in one case being four days in crossing one stream. This one had banks about thirty feet high and a very bad crossing, and we had to cut down about sixty trees to make the bridge with. When this was ready, and a road, though a very steep one, cut down to it, we unloaded the waggon, took off the leading mules and led them across so as to have them ready to pull it up the opposite side; then we tied ropes to the back of the waggon and passed them round trees, two men holding on to each, chained both hind wheels, and then the driver went forward riding the near mule. For some yards all went well, when suddenly both ropes broke at the same moment, and away went the whole thing. We were afraid to look over and see what had happened, till a shout came from below, when we found that the driver, hearing the ropes snap, had at once put in the spurs, and had landed his mules on the bridge in two desperate leaps, both of them coming down, but luckily there was no damage done to either mules or waggon.

The mosquitoes were a great nuisance while we were constructing these bridges, as they were in millions, making life a burden, and driving our horses and mules nearly mad. We often said we would never return to Texas; and yet we had no sooner left it than we wanted to go back, as there was so much to make up for the few drawbacks. After this the country became more open and the streams fewer, water being sometimes hard to find; but quite by chance we hit on a wood road which took us into Fort Belknap.

CHAPTER XVI.

Fort Belknap.—Buffalo dance by Tonkaways.—A-sa-ha-be. We agree to his coming with us. His suspicious conduct. He leaves us by night.—We turn back.—Appearance of Indians.—A-sa-ha-be comes to propose terms. They are rejected.—The Comanches attack us.—We still move on.—We kill and scalp an Indian.—A reinforcement of Indians.—Downfall of A-sa-ha-be.—Arrival of three Caddo Indian scouts. We send one of them for help. He is pursued, but escapes.—Our casualties.—Halliday's courage.—Arrival of troops.—We reach Fort Arbuckle.

AT Fort Belknap we found four companies of cavalry, under the command of General Sturgess; and here we remained several days, and were allowed to replenish our stores from the commissariat. At the Post were a number of Tonkaway Indians, some of them being employed as scouts; they were the remnant of a tribe which had been very much thinned by small-pox, and the day after our arrival they sent us an invitation to a buffalo dance, which is a ceremony to insure success in hunting. On going to their camp we found about sixty Indians collected, besides twice that number of women and children, and the festivities commenced with a talk, in which they said they had heard that we came from the land of the

"Great White Queen," and that we were very welcome to their country, all in it being at our service, and then hinting that anything coming from us would be very much valued: on which we said a few words through an interpreter of the pleasure it gave us to see a tribe of which we had heard so much; that we thanked them for their welcome, and hoped they would accept some tobacco and beads, which we handed round.

After this the dance began—two old Indians playing on the "tom tom," and chanting a very hideous accompaniment. The men and women danced together—a thing I had never seen before among Indians—forming a circle, and going through some shuffling steps, repeating a prayer to the Great Spirit for success in their next hunt, and for protection against their enemies the Comanches. This was kept up for about an hour, some sitting down and others taking their places, even the elder children joining in. We were asked to take part in the dance, but the partners were not sufficiently tempting, so we contented ourselves with looking on. One old fellow whom I sat near had a necklace made of the finger- and toe-joints of a Comanche he had killed some years before; and he was evidently very proud of it, refusing to sell it to me, though I offered what to him was a long price. Killing a Comanche seemed a very rare event, for they had divided the man amongst them—one having the scalp, another the ears, which he had dried and hung round his neck.

These Indians never trust themselves far from a fort, except when acting as scouts, dreading the Comanches and being despised by them. We tried to get one of them to act as our guide, but no offer would tempt them when they heard that we were only seven in number. One of the soldiers told us that there was a Comanche chief at the Post who might go with us. He had, it seemed, quarrelled with his brother "Queen-a-ha-be," the war chief of the Comanches, and had to leave the tribe in consequence. We sent for him, and found him to be an immense man, standing six feet four and broad in proportion, with a very ill-tempered and treacherous face, the hair growing close down to the eyebrows. He seemed very willing to go, saying that he knew the country well nearly to Denver, and should we meet any of his tribe he thought that he could protect us from them, and that he would fight for us if necessary. It was at last agreed that we should take him, and he was to receive on our getting through safely two horses, a rifle and ammunition for it, a revolver, and twenty-five dollars in money. At first he wished payment in advance; but this we positively refused, giving him a pair of blankets and some ammunition only. We left Belknap on the eighth day, and our next point was old Fort Cobb—a deserted post, about a hundred and forty miles further on.

As we had now one more man it made the guards at night much easier, each of us getting three clear nights in bed. It took some time to make A-sa-ha-be understand how long he was to remain on guard; but he soon got into it, and used to measure his two hours pretty correctly. We had been out about six days when one of the men told us that he had gone out of the tent during A-sa-ha-be's guard, and had found him absent, so we spoke to him about it, when he replied that having seen some suspicious sign that day, he had gone during his guard to see what it meant. Now this was highly improbable; for as the nights were very dark just then, he could not possibly follow a trail, nor would he have had time to go very far during his two-hour watch. So we told him that we allowed no one to leave the camp during the night, and that he must do his scouting in the daytime, when one of us would go with him.

We had mistrusted him from the first, and now were almost sure that he meant to betray us; but it was nearly impossible to get proof, or we would have shot him at once. As he only knew a few words of English, it was difficult to explain anything to him, the only other means being by signs, which he was wonderfully quick at understanding.

Things went smoothly for two days, when one night F——, who was on guard, woke me to say that A-sa-ha-be had just left the waggon, under which he slept, and had gone towards his horse.

Getting my rifle, F—— and I followed him very cautiously, keeping under the shelter of some bushes which grew round camp, and we saw him go to his horse, put on the saddle, and prepare to mount. We then ran forward and called to him to stop, on which he sprang on the horse and rode off at full speed. Being convinced then that he meant treachery, we both fired at him; but the night was dark, and we missed him. The shots roused the men, and we held a consultation as to the best thing to do. To turn back was what we thought wisest; but this neither of us proposed, hoping that some other plan might be devised. If we had been travelling with pack-animals we could have pushed on quickly, having probably a good many hours' start; but with a waggon this was of no use—four miles an hour being as much as we could manage. In any case we had to move at once to a better position, as our present camp was on a flat plain covered with bushes, affording capital cover to Indians creeping up to fire at us; so we hitched up at once and moved on to a ridge, about a mile further on, where we remained till morning, carrying up water in every vessel that would hold it, in case the Indians should come sooner than we expected.

Morning came, and no sign of the Indians; so we had another talk, and all the men being for an immediate return to Fort Arbuckle, we were at last compelled to agree to it; so we put the mules in and started about eight o'clock. We calculated that we were about seventy-five miles from the Post, and that, unless hindered by the Comanches, we could do it in two days and a half, throwing away some of our load if necessary. About ten o'clock F——, who was acting rear-guard, called to us that they were coming; and on looking back we saw about forty Indians on some high ground to our right. We kept on as fast as we could go, pulling up when on a bare hill a short distance further on, as it was a good place for a fight if we were to have one. We had nine Winchester repeating-rifles with us and three thousand rounds of ammunition for them, having bought five hundred rounds per man in case we had any fighting; then we had four double rifles and several hundred rounds of ammunition for them; and, lastly, we had a double eight-bore duck-gun, which loaded with about two ounces of buckshot in each barrel would be grand at close quarters.

The Indians galloped up to within two hundred yards of us, when we waved them back, A-sa-ha-be advancing alone, with a branch in his hand as a flag of truce. On his arrival at the waggon he dismounted and calmly seated himself, made signs that we should do the same quite with the air of a superior addressing his inferiors. We, however, sat down, A-sa-ha-be beginning the talk by saying that he had not betrayed us, but that finding signs of a party of his tribe being near us, he had ridden away in the night to find out their intentions and to do the best he could for us, and this he was still willing to do, in spite of our having fired at him. He said that he had found about forty of his tribe camped a few miles away, and that he had made the best possible terms for us, which were as follows :—That we should give up our waggon and outfit, all horses but one apiece, and that then we should be given a rifle to kill game with, and be allowed to return to Fort Arbuckle, or go in any direction we wished. Now there was not the smallest doubt that if we did as he wished we should all be dead men within the hour, as Indians never spare anyone who is in their power, as they thought we were; so we replied at once that we should give up nothing, but that as the country we were in belonged to his tribe, we were willing to purchase permission to pass through it at a moderate price. A-sa-ha-be answered that the terms he had mentioned were the only ones which would be accepted, and put on a very insolent air as he said it; so we told him we would give him two minutes to leave our camp, and that if he was not gone by that time we would shoot him, and would not miss him a second time, and that if his tribe wanted our outfit, they must come and take it, but that so long as we had a cartridge left they should have nothing. He jumped up in a furious rage, waited till we had finished speaking, and then mounted and rode off, shaking his fist at us; and we could see that on rejoining his companions he was making the most of what we had said, to rouse them, as otherwise forty Indians might hesitate to attack six well-armed white men. I am speaking of twenty years ago, when a rifle was very seldom seen in an Indian's hands, and when the few they had were of a very old pattern, and the supply of ammunition for those was scanty.

In the meantime we started again, throwing out of the waggon several sacks of flour to lighten the load, the Indians remaining where they were for nearly an hour, two messengers being sent away at full speed, we feared for reinforcements. About one o'clock, when we were thinking of halting to rest the animals, the Indians appeared again, coming at a gallop and, passing us at a distance of about four hundred yards, fired as they passed, and several balls came unpleasantly near, one of them going through the side of the waggon. On this we gave them three or four volleys from the Winchesters, the result being the wounding of a horse, which bolted, and was only stopped after going about a mile, when the rider dismounted and got up behind one of his companions. This seemed to show them the range of our rifles and the rapidity with which they could be fired (a Winchester rifle firing its fourteen cartridges in less than as many seconds if in good hands), and for some hours they contented themselves with keeping us in sight. We drove on till nearly dark, filling buckets and kettles at a pond we passed and watering all the animals, so that we might camp in the middle of a prairie, where there was no cover of any kind to hide a crawling man. Here we had supper, and arranged that one half should keep guard while the other half slept.

The Indians let us know that they were near by firing now and then, the bullets going far overhead, but they did not try to attack us, and at daylight, after a very hasty breakfast, we were off again. We had a number of creeks to cross that day, and always rode ahead to find out whether they were lying in wait for us, but saw nothing of the Comanches, except in the distance, till we came to a stream having very heavy timber and bushes on both banks, when F——, H——, and I rode along, about a hundred yards from the timber, going at full speed, and lying, Indian fashion, on the side of our horses, having one elbow in a noose round the horse's neck and one foot on the saddle, and we had not gone more than a few hundred yards when five or six shots were fired at us, all of them going wide. We immediately turned and rode in for the creek, hearing the Indians making their way through the bushes but seeing none of them; till one, thinking he was concealed, came out on the opposite side and ran along in the open, loading as he went. We all jumped off and waited till he passed an open space, when we fired together, and over he went, seeming to die at once.

We now beckoned to the waggon and got it across, not far from where the Indian lay, and on going to see how he had been killed, we found that a bullet had passed through the shoulder and a no. 12 Metford shell had burst low down in his back, making a hole almost as large as the crown of a hat, and nearly cutting him in two. We had all said that if we shot an Indian and could get at the body we would scalp him and think nothing of it; but when the time came to do it, each one tried to get out of it, till the driver of our waggon came up and, asking why we made such a fuss about such a trifle, took it off at once, removing merely the scalp-lock and the skin under it, about the size of, and in the same position as, the tonsure of a priest.

When Indians have plenty of time, they like to take the whole skin of the head, beginning behind, skinning the head and the whole face, including the ears; and the scalp when thus taken presents a ghastly appearance when stretched. Soon after we left the stream we could hear the Indians howling over the body of the man we had scalped, and they came by a few minutes later, yelling their war-whoop, and placing their closed fists against their foreheads and then opening and shutting them, which means " war to the knife." As they passed we fired a good many shots, and three horses went down, their riders getting bad falls, though it was impossible to tell whether any of them were hit, as when a man has fallen and seems hurt, two of them will at once gallop by him, one on either side, reaching down and catching a limb, when they swing him on to the saddle in front of one of them and ride off.

The scalping of their companion had evidently made them frantic, as it is their belief that a scalped warrior has to act as servant to the others in the happy hunting-grounds; and they, in consequence, came much nearer, several times gathering as if for a rush, and then giving up the idea on our firing a volley at them. Towards evening a large party of Indians suddenly appeared and joined the others, making their number up to about two hundred. They all met and had a short consultation, we in the meantime camping, as we were in a capital place to receive them—a clump of timber standing on a rise about two hundred yards from a stream, and there was no other cover near but a few small bushes, which we at once cut down. We drove the waggon in among the trees, and all set to work to cut down some of the smallest of these to make a breastwork.

Our stopping seemed to disconcert them, as they did not care to attack a fortified position; so they began to taunt us, and made insulting gestures, and fired a number of shots, one of which killed one of the mules, the poor brute being hit through the stomach, so we had to shoot him. We had a very quiet night, and were off by daybreak, keeping as much as possible in open ground, even when we had to make a detour to do so. We calculated that we must have done nearly half the distance, and as yet no one was hurt, our loss being one mule; and as we put a horse in his place, this did not much matter.

That day the Indians were bolder than ever, coming within two hundred yards, and losing five horses during the day, besides one man, whom we were sure of, as we shot him as he ran away when his horse was killed. We had offered a reward of fifty dollars to our men if they could shoot A-sa-ha-be; but he would not come within range, galloping by on a fine black stallion at a distance of five or six hundred yards. That day, however, he suddenly turned his horse, and lying over so that we could see only one elbow and a foot, he passed within two hundred yards, firing as he did so. We all ran forward as he came near, and, kneeling down, gave him a volley, the black horse being killed almost instantly, and turning a summersault, giving his rider so rough a tumble that he lay where he fell, and we made a rush for the body. The Indians, however, seeing their chief in such danger, closed in from all sides; and as we dared not risk a hand-to-hand fight we had to retreat, but we did so firing as we went, and four more horses fell, causing great confusion, some of the men whose horses were shot crawling away, as they did not dare to rise and run. The Indians drew off, and we were left in peace for some hours, when about three in the afternoon we saw them all galloping to one point, apparently in chase of something; and in a few minutes later we made out, with the glasses, three men making straight for us at full speed, closely followed by the Comanches. On their reaching us, we found them to be three Caddo Indians, speaking English very fairly, and they told us that, being on a hunt from Fort Arbuckle and hearing the firing, they had come to see what it meant, and finding that it was their enemies the Comanches, and knowing from our waggon that we must be whites, they had ridden through to see if they could help us in any way. We camped at once and held a consultation, and it was at length decided that one of them should take " Polly," and try to get through the Comanches and bring us help from Arbuckle.

The distance was, they thought, eleven miles, and the only question was, could the mare do it? The Caddos were all of them small men and very light, but some of the Comanches seemed well mounted, though A-sa-ha-be's stallion—the animal we most feared—was now dead. We promised a very large reward should help arrive in time, and all three of the Caddos were willing to go, so we chose the one who seemed the lightest.

He prepared himself by taking off everything but a shirt, a breech-clout, and moccasins; and, provided with a raw-hide whip and holding a green branch in his right hand, he started, riding slowly, so as to give the Comanches time to collect at one point. This we saw them doing, thinking, no doubt, that he was commissioned to treat for peace. On getting to what seemed to us to be about a hundred yards, he threw away the bough and struck off to the left, and we could see that he had passed them; but so near, that every moment we expected to see the mare fall, struck by one of the bullets which were being fired at her. A few seconds after this, the Comanches shut him out from us, and an anxious time began. Would he succeed in distancing them, and could the mare hold out, thin as she was, and having had nothing but grass for so long?

We hitched up and went on again, all the Indians being out of sight, and must have made three miles, when we saw some of them coming back, the slow pace at which they came making us feel sure that our messenger had got through, and very soon they were all collected together, apparently consulting, about half a mile from us. We knew that they would now do their best to get us, as they could pretty well calculate how long it would be before the arrival of the troops; so we made all preparations for a rush, loading every weapon we had and laying ammunition handy.

The country here was alternately wood and small prairies, the former being open and not affording much cover, and we were passing round one of these small woods when the Comanches made a rush at us, coming on in a double line and yelling their war-whoop. Our men were excited and fired wildly, not a man dropping, till they were within about a hundred yards of us, when the horses fell fast and the Indians wavered. Our magazines were empty, but just at this moment the cook gave them six ounces of buckshot, which, as they were pretty close together, told well on the horses, many becoming quite unmanageable, and the whole party turned and galloped off into the timber, leaving seven horses and two men on the ground. As they opened fire upon us from cover,

Page 222.—The Comanches made a rush at us.

we turned and drove for some thick bushes on our left, losing another mule and two horses before reaching them, one of the latter being my bay horse. He was wounded in the side, and breaking the rope with which he was fastened to the waggon, he galloped off, falling after going a few hundred yards.

Our casualties were as follows:—One of the Caddos had a groove cut in his left arm by a bullet, and the other was hit in the left arm below the elbow, but the arm was not broken. One of the men was very slightly wounded in the calf of the leg; another (Brown) got a bullet through the side, six inches above the hip, and although we did all we could for him, and laid him in the waggon, he died just as we got into Arbuckle, and everything in the waggon was saturated with blood. F—— got an arrow in the back, but not making a serious wound; and I got a bullet in the right shoulder, which F—— that evening cut out with a razor, and an arrow under the knee.

But to return: we soon got out of shot of where the Indians had posted themselves, and they seemed to have had a lesson and left us alone. We now put one of F——'s ponies and the Sheridan horse in harness, and got on slowly, the going being very bad. The country, too, began to be more heavily wooded, so that it was difficult to keep a straight course. Our two Caddos had behaved bravely in the fight, standing well out in front, and using their Spencer carbines with great effect, and they were now very useful in showing us the road to the fort. When within about four miles of it they left, riding to meet the soldiers, to show them where we were; and shortly afterwards we decided to camp, so we drove in among some scattered trees and began to make a barricade, when it suddenly occurred to us that we were a man short, Halliday having disappeared. It seemed impossible that he could have been left behind without our knowing it, and we were on the point of trying to ride back to the spot where the rush had been made, when the cook, who was standing at the back of the waggon, beckoned to me, and on going up and looking into the waggon I saw a pair of boots, with the soles towards me, standing upon their toes—an impossible position for boots which had not feet in them; and the same thought occurring to each of us, we suddenly caught hold of a foot each, and pulled Halliday—all covered with flour—from under some sacks, bedding, &c., jerking him over the tail-board of the waggon and letting him fall on the ground. He at once shammed ill, calling us inhuman wretches for treating a sick man in that way; but a look at him was enough to let us know what his illness was—the man was simply shaking with fear. It came out now that he must have been there some time, no one having seen him when the rush took place, and the other men said that he had been of no use all through, giving out that he felt very unwell. We made him work at the barricade, and it was wonderful how soon his illness passed off.

About six o'clock P.M. two companies of cavalry rode up, the Indians still remaining within sight, as they knew that the cavalry horses could not catch them; for these large eastern horses when sent west and living on grass and half rations of corn, beside being constantly on scout duty, where they hardly get any, soon fall away to nothing and can hardly carry themselves. About two hours' travelling took us into the Post, where we arrived nearly worn out, having been fighting for three days, with very little food and less sleep.

The young Caddo returned with the troops, but left the mare at the Post, as she well deserved a rest. She had behaved splendidly, having run away from the Comanches in the first two or three miles; so that most of them had turned back, and only three or four had followed nearly to the fort.

CHAPTER XVII.

The Caddo Indians.—Story of their chief and the Comanches.—An insolent blacksmith. His punishment.—Our camp fired into.—Discovery of the culprits. Their punishment.—Leave Fort Arbuckle.—Chase of a wolf by a pointer.—Difficulty of crossing the Red River.—I return for provisions.—Difficulty of carrying eggs on horseback.—An Indian reservation.—Incivility of an Indian. We become better friends.—Thirsty oxen.—Our party breaks up.

On arriving at the fort we called on the commanding officer, and found that he was away on leave, but the officer acting for him kindly gave us an order to have our horses shod by the cavalry smith. The garrison consisted of one company of white infantry, and two of white and one of negro cavalry.

We next rewarded the Caddo who had ridden to fetch us help, and had a talk with him about his ride. He said he had never ridden so good an animal as my mare, and that after the first two miles she had run away from the Comanches without any need of a whip. He then tried to buy her of me, but of course I would not sell her. We found that there were forty Caddos in the service of the Government here as scouts, who were paid, armed, and mounted as soldiers; and most excellent scouts they were, and belonged to a tribe which boasted that they had never killed a white man. Their chief had gone into the Southern army at the beginning of the war, and had risen to the rank of captain and gained a name for bravery.

I heard here a story of him which will show the kind of man he was. It seems that some time in the summer of the previous year, he and seventy of his men were out on a hunt, in the course of which they came across the Comanche chief Queen-a-ha-be and about three hundred warriors of his tribe. Now though the Comanches were at war with the whites, they were not so with the Caddos, so they fraternized and camped together.

One day as the Caddo chief was walking about the Comanche camp, he came upon a horse with the U.S. brand, showing he belonged to the Government, and on asking how he came to be there, he was told that shortly before meeting the Caddos, and after the latter had left Fort Arbuckle, the Comanches had made a raid on it, and had carried off some ten or twelve soldiers' horses. On hearing this the Caddo chief went to Queen-a-ha-be and asked if what he had heard was true, when Queen-a-ha-be said that it was an affair between the United States Government and himself, and with which he had nothing to do. The Caddo chief replied, that as head of the scouts he was answerable for the safety of the fort and all its horses, and that those which had been stolen must be given up to him that he might take them back. Queen-a-ha-be flatly refused to do this, on which the Caddo chief said that if they were not given up to him by the next morning he should come and take them. Queen-a-ha-be laughed at the idea, saying that he had three hundred warriors to the Caddo's seventy, and that it would be folly in him to attempt it. The Caddos immediately left the Comanche camp, and formed a separate one on a small hill in the neighbourhood, and in the morning sent a runner to ask what the Comanches had decided to do, and on hearing that they meant to keep the horses the seventy Caddos attacked their camp, and after a desperate fight, lasting some hours, utterly routed them, killing seventeen and capturing most of their horses as well as those stolen from the fort. They then went back to Arbuckle and returned the stolen horses, giving a pony to everyone who had temporarily been deprived of his horse. This attack on the Comanches meant a great deal to the Caddos, for from this time they could no longer go hunting to get buffalo-robes and deer-skins, which are to Indians what money is to white men—being exchanged for everything they require.

Having got leave to have our horses shod, we sent them in charge of one of our men to the forge, from which they returned in the evening, nothing having been done to them. This happened again next the day, so on the third day I rode up to the forge and saw the smith, a brawny negro, who said in a very insolent manner that he had enough to do without shoeing the horses of everyone who came along. The smithy was a high one and the door large, so I rode in to remonstrate with him, telling him that whereas the order entitled us to have our horses shod for nothing, we meant to pay him what we should have paid an ordinary smith. This had no effect on him, and he ended by ordering me out of the smithy, enforcing his words with an iron bar with which he advanced on me, but the muzzle of a revolver made him think better of it, and he contented himself with bad language. I at once rode off to the officer who had given us the order and reported what had occurred, on which the matter was inquired into and the negro was condemned to work for a month with a ball chained to his leg.

I left that day for the Caddo village to visit H——, who had ridden there two days before and had been taken ill and had been unable to return. When I got back on the following day, I found that F—— and the men had been very much startled during the night by a volley which had been fired at the tent, but fortunately had gone high. They had turned out and remained on the watch for some time, hearing bugles blowing at the Post and the troops mustering in haste. Shortly afterwards the Caddo scout arrived at our camp, having been all round the fort and found no signs of Comanches, and asked our party whether they could explain the firing. The thing remained a mystery until the morning, when one of the negro troopers went to the commanding officer and confessed that he and seven or eight of his comrades had crept out in the night, their men being on guard, and had fired at the tent in revenge for the punishment of the smith, of which we had been the cause. There were not enough officers at the fort for a court-martial, so the men concerned were imprisoned till the commandant returned, when they were tried and most of them were sent to the Dry Tortugas, islands off the coast of Florida, and answering to our Botany Bay as it used to be.

We had now recovered from our fatigue, and our remaining animals were in good condition, having been fed on corn since our arrival at the Post, so we determined to start for Fort Smith in Arkansas, sell off our horses and mules there, and then go down to Memphis, on the Mississippi, where our party would break up. We had still four mules, though we had lost two of our best, and four horses—fortunately neither my mare nor the Sheridan horse had been hurt—so that we still had enough for our present journey. We left the fort about the middle of July, and travelled slowly through a very pretty country, killing a deer now and then for food, as there were then no cattle in those parts. Our dogs had dwindled to two, our camp dog and a pointer, and the latter caused us a good laugh soon after leaving the Post. We jumped a wolf from some bushes, on which the pointer gave chase, the wolf doing his best till he was on the other side of a small valley and out of shot, when he turned round and waited for his pursuer, who on coming up and finding the wolf waiting for him, seeing, too, that he had some very formidable teeth and was altogether a different animal from what he appeared to be when running away, he now stopped, and then the two sat down face to face, putting out their noses to smell one another, one of them making a step forward when the other would take one back; and this continued for some minutes, when they got up and separated, the dog returning to us with a very sheepish air. All this time we had been trying to set Booze on the wolf's track, but without success, and we found soon afterwards that the great heat during our journey had made a coward, at all events temporarily, of one of the pluckiest dogs I ever met with.

In a few days we passed the first ranche, and from this point we came across a good many, getting milk and butter now and then—great treats when you have been without them for months. We reached the Red River without any incident worth relating and found the water low, so, notwithstanding it abounds with quicksands, we began to cross at once. It was here about a hundred yards wide with a sandy bottom and very muddy water, and soon after entering it the mules sank in a quicksand, and after struggling for a few moments quietly lay down and refused to pull any more. We unharnessed them with a great deal of trouble, made them rise and got them out of the river, and then tried to draw the waggon out backwards, but it had sunk till the bottom of it rested on the sand, and it would not move; the mules, too, were demoralized and would not do their best. So F—— rode to a rauche, which we had passed some three hours previously, and returned bringing the owner and three span of good oxen. Fortunately it was still only midday, so that we had plenty of time before us. While F—— was away we all stripped, and with nothing but our hats on unloaded the waggon, carrying everything over on our heads; and if one of my readers will take a sack of flour weighing a hundred pounds, or a portmanteau of about the same weight, on his head, and will wade a river a hundred yards wide under a broiling sun, and keep this up for two hours, he will know whether we had a pleasant task or not; but by the time F—— returned, all our things, including a heavy stove, were piled on the opposite bank. We first had our dinner and then, following the advice of the owner of the oxen, we dug away the sand as much as possible from round the wheels of the waggon—and the digging under water was very hard work; then we fastened a rope to the hind axle and brought the end of it on to the bank, the waggon being about twenty yards from the edge of the water. The oxen were fastened to this rope and the whip applied, and out the waggon came. We then put the mules in again, took off all our clothing once more, and by keeping sticks going and running alongside, shouting like madmen, not allowing the mules to rest for a moment, we got the waggon across.

It was arranged that the rest should go on and camp at the first grass, while I should return with the settler and bring back some milk and eggs, taking a gallon keg for the former and a handkerchief for the latter. The only mistake I made was in choosing the horse I did for this ride, taking the wild horse we had broken ourselves. He had turned out a fine horse for hunting, letting you fire off his back; but he had one peculiarity, for though used to a gun, if you pulled out your handerchief suddenly, he would jump violently and try to bolt; even if you took off your hat quickly he would do the same. We reached the settler's house about four o'clock in the afternoon, filled my keg with milk and put four dozen eggs into the handkerchief; then I mounted and was handed the keg, which I hung round my neck with a strap, taking the handkerchief in my hand, the settler showing both to the horse before handing them to me. For some miles all went well, as I kept the eggs in a straight line behind his head, holding them high so as to avoid hitting the pommel of the saddle. This was very tiring to do for any length of time, and I presently felt the eggs go bump and knew that at least one was broken. Then the same thing happened again, so I tried holding them on one side, and had no sooner done so than the horse sprang five or six feet sideways, bringing the eggs with a tremendous bang against my knee, and I had hard work to save any of them and quiet the horse. Each time, too, that he jumped the keg would swing outwards and come back against me with a thump; this happened so often that I was thankful when I reached the river. Now, however, came the worst part of it, as I had to ride across as fast as possible to avoid the quicksands, so that by the time I had reached the other side my eggs were a soft mass and the contents of the handkerchief streaming down the horse's shoulder and on to my boots. The waggon had been taken some distance, and as it was by this time dark, I do not know how I should have found it had they not hung a lantern in a tree to guide me, the trail being indistinct even by day. On reaching camp the eggs were examined and only four sound ones were found among them; we, however, cooked the yolks which remained in the handkerchief, making them into an omelet, of which a large portion was broken egg-shell.

We were now in the Indian reservation, and met a good many of the semi-civilized ones, and very bad they looked in white men's dress. An Indian will not cut his hair short before he puts on a wideawake, and his long black hair hanging down, in many cases far over his coat collar, quite spoils him. And, again, their copper-coloured faces are not suited to our dress, and an Indian who is grand-looking in his own costume is a scarecrow in ours, and though in some of the larger towns, where they have become doctors, lawyers, &c., they have almost transformed themselves into white men, their hair is "shingled," as American barbers call it, and some of them have become great dandies. Those we came across were as a rule rough specimens, and at many of the houses they refused to sell us anything; in some cases not even answering our questions.

It had been pouring all one day and the country was little

better than a swamp, when towards evening we reached a good-sized ranche, and we determined to stay there instead of putting up our tent in the water. On riding up to it we found an Indian sitting in the verandah, so we asked him whether we could remain the night if we paid for all we had. He answered very roughly that we could not do so, and nothing more could we get out of him. It was such awful weather that we made up our minds we would stop, and told him so, on which he got up and went away. We drove the waggon up close to the verandah and got out our food and cooking-things, no one coming near us. We then went into the house, where we found two women who would not speak to us, so we made up a fire in the stove and boiled some coffee and cooked some meat, retiring then to the verandah and sat down and ate it. Later in the evening our host returned bringing some other Indians with him; but he seemed to have calmed down and talked to us about where we had come from and our object in travelling till bed-time, being especially interested in our fight with the Comanches, and he became quite friendly when he heard that we had killed and scalped one of them. In the morning the women of the house did our cooking for us, and our bill on leaving, including corn and fodder for our horses, was reasonable.

The road was now very heavy, and as we intended to sell our animals at Fort Smith, and did not, therefore, wish them to arrive looking thin, we hired a span of oxen to take our waggon there, coming down from three or four miles an hour to barely two. I know of nothing more tedious than having to keep with a waggon and being obliged to check your horse continually, for his slowest walk is much too fast for them.

In dry weather, when they have gone for some hours without water, they are the most obstinate animals in the world, mules being nowhere when compared with them. On one occasion as we neared Fort Smith, we had gone from morning until late in the afternoon, finding no water and passing no house where we could have got it from a well, so that the oxen were very thirsty and their tongues were hanging out, when suddenly we came on a large pond having a bank on our side of it, and in one minute, in spite of all we could do, they were over the bank and into the water, which came almost over their backs, the bed of the waggon being submerged and most of our things wet through. It was impossible to go back, so they had to be forced through the pond, which fortunately became no deeper.

When about seven or eight miles from Fort Smith we camped in a very pretty spot to allow our horses to recover from their fatigue, and after a stay of some days we had them taken into the place where sales were always held, which was a large open space in the middle of the town. A large crowd collected seemingly to decry our animals, and everything sold very badly; but we were obliged to let things go, as we wanted to get away and had a long journey before us, and wished to reach the mountains before the winter set in. I retained the stallion and mare, meaning to take them with me.

From Fort Smith we went by rail to White River, and down that to Memphis, where our party broke up. H—— remained there. F—— and I went north, and the men were paid off and left behind. I was very much surprised to hear years afterwards that one of them had gone into a lawyer's office and that he is now a lawyer in St. Louis and doing very well, and another had set up as a butcher in Chicago.

CHAPTER XVIII.

Account of Julesberg. A specimen of the manners of Julesberg. Our lodgings. Seeing the town. Its inhabitants.—Gambling-saloons.—We start for Sheyenne.—Description of hotel accommodation.—A citizen shot by an officer.—Start for Elk Mountain.—Reach Willow Springs.—All Houston.—Camp at Willow Springs.—Woodchoppers, bad characters.—Story about Houston.—Obliged to hunt singly.—We go together to hunt.—A deserted hut and grave of occupant.—A visitor.—Polly's behaviour.—F—— starts for Sheyenne.—Snowed in.—Villainous-looking visitors. They are induced to go.—Precautions.—F——'s return.—I return to Sheyenne.—F—— goes to Virginia Dale.

From Memphis F—— and I took the steamer for Omaha, by way of St. Louis—a long journey of nearly sixteen hundred miles—and thence we went by the Central Pacific Railway to Julesberg, which was then the temporary terminus of the railway. Julesberg was a most extraordinary place. In a few months it had grown out of nothing, and on a bare prairie, to be a town of three thousand inhabitants, most of whom were the offscourings of the western cities. Two houses out of every three were either saloons and gambling-dens or dance-houses, while the remainder were shops. There was no hotel at the time I am speaking of, and when we got out of the train and made inquiries for a place to stop at, we were told that there was an eating-house, where they had a lean-to on each side, divided into pens, some seven feet square, and that we might with luck get one of these.

While walking along the street we had soon an opportunity of seeing what kind of a place we were in. A man more than half drunk rushed out of a saloon on the opposite side of the street, followed by another in the same state, with a pistol in his hand, which, on his catching the first man, he put to his head and tried to shoot him, but was too drunk to do it; and when we were going to run across and interfere, a bystander told us not to be fools, but to remain where we were, as the more of such men there were shot the better.

The streets were composed of small one-storey wooden houses of all shapes, and placed anyhow, some projecting many feet further into the street than others—no two being alike—and the intervals between them were filled with empty tins, broken crockery, old boots, broken kettles, bottles, and all kinds of rubbish. Some men had put a short piece of board sidewalk in front of their houses, and some had not, which made the walking at night very awkward, especially as there were no street lamps, and the only light came from the lanterns hung in front of saloons to light up some transparency. On arriving at the eating-house we found that we could have one of the pens between us, every bed here being meant for two, and we were to get our meals in the centre room, our bedroom being just big enough for a bed, chair, and a very small wash-stand, with barely room to stand when dressing, making it necessary for one of us to dress while sitting on the bed. The people who came for meals were a very miscellaneous collection—gamblers in black frock-coats, diamond breast-pins, and rings, sitting next to ox-drivers and railway labourers, clerks in the different stores, and ex-prize-fighters, who were now keeping saloons; and these last were quite the "upper crust," no men being more thought of in the West, and there were also a few women. The food put before us was such as you might expect in such a place—half cold, and all tasting alike, and served up in tiny oval dishes, which were placed in a semicircle round your plate, and everything was brought at once. The charge was one dollar, and paid on the spot, as no one was trusted.

The first night we were there it began to rain, and almost immediately F—— and I felt water pouring on us; so we lit the candle, and then found that the roof was only composed of boards laid side by side, the chinks not being stopped in any way, and that consequently there was nothing to keep the rain from coming through. Having a mackintosh sheet with us, we put it over the bed, but it was not quite large enough, and, besides, the water collected on it so rapidly that there was soon a small lake in the middle, and in shooting it off from time to time we at last shot one lot into the middle of the bed. This settled it; so we hastily put on a few clothes, and gathering up our belongings and such bedding as had escaped the deluge, we went into the eating-room, where we found a number of people, of all ages and both sexes, in similar dress, or rather undress, looking very miserable, and as there was nowhere else for us to go, we turned in under and on the tables.

The next day we went round to see the town, as it was very unsafe to do so at night, and by dinner-time we quite agreed with a man who at supper the night before had said that "this place was only removed by the thickness of a sheet of writing-paper from a certain hot place," which shall be nameless. The swells were the gamblers, who seemed always to have plenty of money, with which they were continually treating their friends, and they generally drove a fine pair of trotting-horses and had some good dogs. We had met many of them in St. Joe when fitting out for our various trips, and had always found them very civil, giving us many invitations to "drop in and see them some evening," for which we thanked them, but did not take advantage of. As there were some four thousand men working on the railway and getting good wages, never less than eight shillings a day, and as, being the terminus of the railway, all miners from the mountains when on their way home for the winter were obliged to come there to take the train, there was a great deal of money to be made by these gentry, many miners bringing in several thousands of dollars, and losing them all in one night, working at anything they could get till spring, and then beginning again. Nearly all the saloons had some attraction to tempt people to go in—long-distance walking-matches against time being the craze when we were there, most of the saloons having some such notice as the following, in a transparency:—"Walk in, gentlemen, and see John Smith, the champion long-distance walker of the world, who is doing one thousand miles in one thousand hours, and is now fresher than when he began last week.—N.B. Don't be taken in by the shams at the other houses." The said John Smith when you went in to see him, paying one shilling for doing so, looked wonderfully fresh, which was not surprising, as he went comfortably to bed on the house being closed, and resumed operations when it opened at eight the next morning. Almost every night there were fights in these saloons; a good many men were shot, and no notice was taken of it, as there were only three policemen in the place, who took particularly good care to get out of the way as soon as a row began.

Two days in such a place satisfied us, so we went to a livery stable and bought a waggon and two ponies and a small outfit, and started for Sheyenne—a place to which Julesberg was beginning to move on to, as the railway was finished to within a few miles of that town. It was about ninety miles further west, and we were three days in reaching it, and on arrival found it to be just such another place as Julesberg, but rather more substantially built, and possessing two wooden hotels, to one of which we went, putting our ponies in a livery stable together with "Polly" and "Henry," the daily bill for the four being eight dollars (32 shillings). The excuse for such an outrageous charge was, that nothing was grown in the country, and everything had to be brought from such a distance. I forget the name of our hotel, but it was kept by a Mr. Gildersleeve, and it contained only one room for men, in which there were twenty-seven beds, each meant for two. You never knew who you were going to have as companion—very frequently a half-drunken waggon-driver, who before he got into bed deposited a loaded revolver under the pillow, which you found yourself lying on in the course of the night. As we were two we were spared this, though having a number of such men in the room with you was quite bad enough. I have said there was only one room for men; but divided from this by rough unplaned boards, merely put up side by side, were two small rooms for ladies or married men, though the number of the former coming to Sheyenne was extremely limited. We found this to be quite as rough a place as Julesberg, and of the same size, and the description of one will do for the other.

There was a good deal of excitement when we went there about a young officer having shot a civilian under the following circumstances:—He happened to be officer of the day at Fort William Russell, three miles from Sheyenne, when in going his rounds, accompanied by an armed soldier, he heard a quarrel going on in a small house, in which lived an old couple, the husband being a mule-driver to the post, though not a soldier. The man who was with the officer told him that the old man and his wife were always quarrelling, but that it never amounted to anything more than words, so no one took any notice of it. The officer, however, opened the door and called to the old fellow to be quiet, but got a rough answer, on which he went in and abused the couple, the old man giving him as good in return; whereupon the officer got in a rage and told the soldier to shoot him, and as he refused he took the rifle from him and shot the old man dead. He was arrested and tried by court-martial, but was acquitted, because he pleaded that the man put his hand behind him to pull out a revolver, and that he had shot him in self-defence. This verdict did not satisfy the people of Sheyenne, and they sent to demand another trial, the chief reason for their animosity being that the same officer had shot another man under somewhat similar circumstances about a year before, when he had also been acquitted. On receiving the demand the commandant of the post sent the officer east to be tried, and I saw him come into Sheyenne under a strong escort, without which I am sure he would have been lynched. The soldiers had very hard work to save him as it was—a huge crowd surrounding them from the entrance to the town to the station, who were only kept off by the fixed bayonets which the soldiers used freely.

We only remained a day or two to complete our outfit, and then set off along the proposed line of railway towards "Elk Mountain." F—— drove the waggon, while I rode one horse and led the other, as we had not cared to engage any man we had seen in Sheyenne. We had a small tent; but as there was no wood from the town to the mountains, and as we had no poles, we did not put it up, but slept in the waggon, which was very risky, as the Sheyennes and Sioux were often in the neighbourhood, and had run a man into a town a few days before.

We had bought a log of cedar as firewood, about six feet long and six inches square, for which we gave three shillings, and which we made last us for four or five days; as our meat was cooked, and we had only to boil coffee, using crackers for bread. At the end of that time we reached a small settlement called Willow Springs, which had sprung up to supply the woodchoppers—who had gone into the mountains to cut cord-wood for the railway—with whiskey and provisions. As engines in the west always used wood in those days, an immense supply was needed, and these men made it pay well, cutting three cords a day, and getting ten shillings a cord. The only drawback was the high price of provisions, everything being seven or eight times its price on the Missouri River

Here we met a man named "All Houston," one of the best hunters and best shots at game with a rifle that I ever came across. He was only twenty-seven or eight, but had been all his life in the mountains, and had never done anything but hunt. He had, too, a pony with almost as great a reputation as himself. She was about the size of Polly, and so fast that he had run down elk over rough ground with her. We tried to engage him to go with us, and pass the winter somewhere in the mountains; but this he refused to do, as he made all the money he wanted by killing antelope and elk and selling the meat at the stage stations. This was a stage that ran between California and Sheyenne. He gave us a good report of game, especially antelope, which then swarmed all along the stage line. There were always some in sight; and Houston would at any time back himself to kill an average of five a day, and would often get more. He agreed to go on a hunt for a few days with us, riding his pony, and being armed with an "over and under" rifle weighing eighteen pounds, which carried a ball sixty to the pound; and we got off the following morning, taking it in turns to drive the waggon. Houston knew every foot of the country and acted as guide, and as he was a very quiet young fellow and free from brag, he made a very pleasant companion.

Willow Springs lay at the foot of the first range of the Rockies—a long line of glaciers being visible from it, and the wooded hills which intervened formed a lovely country to hunt in, as they were full of little prairies, surrounded by timber, and with small streams running through them, where at that time you could find game. You very seldom came across a hunter, as most of them were too much afraid of the Indians to venture far into the mountains, though there was really very little danger, as these always went south when the cold weather set in. We camped in a narrow valley by a small stream, with a glacier filling up the end of it, and an enormous rock formed a capital shelter for the camp. The first day we all went out together, and left the tent and horses to look after themselves, the only danger being from the many outlaws among the woodchoppers, as a great number of men who had escaped from justice took refuge here, as it was a perfectly safe asylum.

For some time we saw no game, till suddenly we heard a rattling among the stones, and on looking up saw seven or eight deer (whitetails) galloping along the side of the mountain through some fir-trees, and about a hundred yards above us. Houston was off in a moment, and the eighteen-pounder raised and fired, the buck he aimed at being evidently hit, when waiting till he passed an open spot about fifteen feet wide Houston fired again, and down he rolled into the track we were on. Later in the day F—— killed a second buck, seeing several more, as game was very plentiful, and we saw elk-tracks in all directions. The next day F—— and Houston went out, and I remained to take care of camp, and when they returned, bringing one whitetail, F—— told me that the only chance Houston had during the day was at this deer, which stood behind a large tree so that only the head and a small portion of the shoulder was visible, and though the distance was more than two hundred yards, he killed it at the first shot. Before Houston left camp we tried to get him to run his mare against mine; but he refused to do so, as he said he should feel so badly if she were beaten.

He left us on the third day, and we were very sorry to see him go. Some months afterwards an officer, who had been moved from Fort William Russell to Fort Laramie, happened to say one day that the best hunter in the west lived at Willow Springs in Colorado. Now as there was a celebrated Indian hunter, who supplied Laramie with game, the officers there offered to back him against Houston, if he would consent to hunt on the Indian's ground. He was sent for, and on hearing the terms of the wager agreed to do his best, if given a fortnight to learn the ground. The terms were arranged, and they then set out on a hunt, the agreement being that whichever brought in most game at the end of a fortnight was to be considered the winner, and was to get half the bet; and at the expiration of the time Houston had beaten the Indian badly. This was probably done by good shooting, as I have never yet seen an Indian who could shoot well.

As the valley in which our camp was pitched seemed very central for hunting and the keep was good, we determined to put up a cabin; so we began cutting logs, and had got together a good many, when a passing hunter told us of a much better place, so we abandoned the idea, meaning to remain some weeks longer where we were, and to move to the place he recommended later in the autumn. As it was unwise to leave camp without anyone to look after it now that the woodchoppers knew of our being in the mountains, we had to hunt singly, and found a good many deer, a light fall of snow making it easy to track them. F—— had a very long chase after an elk which he had wounded, following it for eight hours far into the mountains, and he told me on his return that, to judge by the sign he had come across, elk must be much more plentiful there than where we were, and advised our going there later. It seemed to have been the great Indian hunting-ground during the summer; for he had seen several small camps, where, from the number of bones lying about, they must have had great sport. He had seen no bear-tracks, so they had evidently holed up, and we only came across one during our stay, when the bear had probably come out for a time, as they often do in the winter when there is a spell of open weather.

One day we determined to let the tent take care of itself and have a hunt together; so we hid most of our valuables on the top of the rock against which the tent was pitched, and rode far into the mountains. When crossing some of the stony ridges we had some desperate scrambling, and frequently we had to lead our horses over places which were only fit for goats. For this kind of work we always found horses better than mules. They no doubt fall more at first; but when used to mountain work they are much quicker and pleasanter to ride than the latter; for though a mule very seldom falls, he is continually catching his toe as if about to do so. We had ridden some miles when we came into a beautiful little valley about a mile long—wooded hills and picturesque rocks surrounding it, while the grass was first-rate, making it and the small valleys which ran out of it an ideal hunting-ground.

On our way up the valley we passed an enormous rock, which had at some distant period fallen from above, and which was now covered with a dense growth of small fir-trees. It lay close to the side of a wooded mountain; but something made me ride round to see whether there was room to pass behind it, when I found that there was a circular hollow between it and the mountain, in which stood a cabin, having a grave in front of it, with a piece of wood, on which was cut a cross placed upright at one end. The grave told its own tale very plainly. Some hunter had put up this cabin to pass the winter in, but had been murdered by the Indians, and someone finding the body had buried it and erected this rough tombstone.

We had dinner here, and soon after leaving it saw two elk going over a ridge on our left; so F—— set off to stalk them, and I remained holding the horses. At the end of half an hour I heard a shot; so I mounted and rode after him, and found him in the next valley standing over a fine young bull. Having now plenty of meat, the fancy took us to remain the night in the hunter's cabin; so we cut up the elk, and loading both horses led them back to it, picketing them out, and setting to work to repair the roof, most of which had fallen in, as it was only constructed of fir-boughs. This we soon made water-tight; then we cleaned out the inside, putting down a carpet of pine-branches; made a saddle-blanket into a door, and had everything snug by sunset. We had only venison and water as food and drink, and one saddle-blanket as covering; but as the end of the hut was solid rock, and as we had made the fire against this, the inside was almost too warm: so we passed a very pleasant night, sitting up late to discuss Indian fights and hunting. There was something very romantic in the situation of the place, and we very nearly made up our minds to winter here, the scarcity of water causing us to give up the idea. Now that that country is settled, and the Indians have been driven out of it and placed on a reservation, I can fancy that valley making a beautiful farm, and I hope that some day I may revisit it and stay with the owner.

On the second day after our return to camp we had a visitor. It was about dinner-time, and both of us were at home, when a big, rough-looking woodchopper walked into camp, and after saying "How d'ye?" sat down by the fire. It seemed that he had heard from Houston of our being here, and of our having some medicines with us; so he had come to know whether we had anything which would do good to a very bad toothache which he had now had for some days, and which had made his face as big as two. It was a hollow tooth, and F—— was able to relieve the man before he left, ending by giving him a glass of Santa Cruz rum and water—a most insinuating beverage, and one which he seemed to appreciate thoroughly. He was most grateful, and as he was not allowed to pay for the medicine, he wanted to know what he could do for us, but we could think of nothing; so, after having dinner, he left, warning us that there were some very bad characters in the mountains, and that we ought to keep an eye on our horses. We were certainly living in a very careless way, keeping no guard; and our only reliance was on "Polly," who, if anything strange came near the camp at night, galloped to the tent and neighed. We had made a great pet of her, never tying her up, as she would always stand to be caught, and if we were late in the morning she would put her head in and pull our blankets gently, as a hint that she wanted her sugar. When we sat by the camp fire, too, at night, she would come and stand by, taking the greatest care not to tread on anyone, and every now and then rubbing her head against us.

Soon after this it got very cold, and as we had brought no great-coats it was arranged that F—— should ride to Sheyenne and buy some soldiers' overcoats, returning as fast as he could. We killed game enough to last a week, so that I should not have to leave camp, and he then started, meaning to try to do it in six days—the distance being about a hundred and twenty miles. The morning after he left I got up, thinking it seemed very much colder than the day before, and on trying to open the door of the tent I found it was held down by a mass of snow, as it was banked up against the canvas to the height of four feet. This was a pleasant prospect for a man left quite alone in the mountains, forty miles from anywhere. However, I had to have breakfast; so I waded out, and after feeling about with my feet for some time I found the shovel, with which I cleared away the snow for a fire, and found the cooking-things and axe, which of course had been buried. Fortunately there was any amount of pitch-pine—a grand wood in a cold country, as it is full of resin—and I soon had a large fire and some steaks on it, when I began to feel comfortable once more. Having finished my breakfast and warmed myself with about three pints of hot coffee, I hunted up the horses, which I found looking very miserable; but Polly had omitted to come for her sugar, and had got into the middle of a thicket. The picketed horses had turned their tails to the storm, and had stood so still that they had a sharp ridge of snow several inches high all along their backs. I brought them to the fire, and threw on a great quantity of wood, making a grand blaze, which they appreciated as much as I did; and I then turned them loose, as they could find some feed among the trees, and would be sheltered at the same time.

I was sitting near the fire doing some mending, having a goodly collection of stockings lying by me, when I heard the horses neighing down the valley, and a few minutes later Polly appeared and galloped up to me; so I took a double twelve-bore rifle, which I kept loaded, and walked down towards the stream where the horses were, when I met two villainous-looking half-breeds, mounted on small ponies, and carrying rifles and revolvers. They had evidently from the tracks been examining our stock, and were now on their way to see how many we were. They asked me where the camp was and what we were doing there; also of how many the party consisted; and as I did not like their looks I said that there were several, but that my companions were away hunting, though I expected them back at any minute. They accompanied me to the tent, and telling me that they had eaten very little breakfast, they cut some steaks off one of the deer which I had hanging up, and I gave them some coffee. They then lit their pipes and made themselves comfortable round the fire, asking me all kinds of questions—as to where I came from; what our object was in hunting; evidently not believing me when I said we were out for pleasure, but thinking we must be looking up land claims, as it was incomprehensible to men of their kind that anyone should find pleasure out of a town. When they had sat a short time they said that they would go into the tent and take a sleep; so, as there were many things in it which would have tempted them very much, and which if they did not take at once they might come back for that night, I told them that it was so small that our beds entirely filled it, and that we did not allow anyone in it. On this they said that I did not seem to be very hospitable, and that they would come again when my companions were at home. I replied that they were welcome at any time to all they could eat, and I warned them not to come at night, as with so many bad characters about we always fired first and asked who it was afterwards. Fortunately they did not see "Polly," and the other two horses were looking so miserable and were so thin—every hair standing on end from the cold—that they did not seem to think them worth the risk of being shot for. After they were gone I brought up the horses and picketed them where I could see them from the tent, and before dark fastened them to the waggon, and kept this up till F—— returned. I could cut no grass, as the snow was nearly two feet deep; but when animals have been feeding all day, they do not eat much at night. I also kept a gun loaded with buckshot handy, as it was a much better weapon at night than a rifle; but I saw no more of the half-breeds.

F—— returned on the evening of the sixth day with the coats, and very poor things we found them. Soldiers line theirs with blanket, when they are fairly warm. Our "toothache friend" paid us another visit before we left this camp, evidently coming in hopes of getting some more Santa Cruz rum, for he led the conversation round to it at once. I told him of my late visitors, whom he said he did not know, though he told us that some of the worst men in the mountains were half-breeds. He also said that if I had owned to being alone I should have had trouble most probably. In spite of the cold weather I had been very much troubled with ague; so I made up my mind to go into Sheyenne for a few weeks and try to shake it off, and as F—— did not care to camp out alone, he decided to go into a small place called "Virginia Dale," and make excursions into the mountains from there with a pack-horse, and to wait at Virginia Dale till I rejoined him.

CHAPTER XIX.

Move to Virginia Dale.—Meet my old driver.—Stage drivers.—Abundance of antelope.—Reach Sheyenne.—Vigilance committee.—Election for mayor.—An unpleasant neighbour. Play a practical joke on him.—Life in Sheyenne.—Action of the Vigilance committee.—Stories of various desperadoes.—Joe Riley the prize-fighter.—Racing at Sheyenne.—A railway quickly made.—Leave for England and sell " Polly."

F—— DETERMINED to move to Virginia Dale before I left, as the road was so bad that it required two to be with the waggon; so we started at once, doing it in one day. We found it to be a small place, consisting of three houses, where the overland stage changed horses and the passengers had a meal; and while I was there the stage arrived, when I was very much astonished by the driver's jumping down and shaking me by both hands. He was so wrapped up in furs that for some seconds I did not recognize him, but on his removing his cap I saw that it was Ben my old driver, who went with me on my first trip to the Republican River. He was very glad to see me, and offered to leave the stage company and go with me, but I was on my way to Sheyenne and had no use for him, so we had a drink together and parted.

These stage drivers had a very hard life, though they were well paid, getting from twelve to fifteen pounds a month. They had to drive in all weathers, and were given in many cases unbroken horses, which they had to keep straight over roads which would frighten a European coachman—full of holes and stumps, and in wet weather halfway to the axle in mud; while the bridges were merely trees laid across the streams with poles placed side by side across them, only one in ten or twelve being pegged at the end, and with no rail of any kind, the poles jumping about as the coach passed over them, and looking as if the whole thing was going to pieces. It was very trying to the nerves to sit on the box-seat of one of these stages and turn a corner at a gallop to find a chasm before you bridged as I have described, everything depending on the coachman's keeping his wild team in the middle. Also many of the stage routes were through a part of the country where there was always a chance of attack by Indians, the driver and conductor having rifles beside them and revolvers in their belts, as it was by no means uncommon for every soul on the stage to be murdered and scalped. Many of these drivers were very good fellows, who if they took a fancy would keep you amused the whole journey by stories of the different oddities they had carried and the adventures they had gone through, while if they got hold of a "tenderfoot" the amount of information they would give him must have very much astonished his friends on his return home. There were very few accidents considering there was a coach every day, as the men were splendid whips, though their way of holding their reins would astonish a member of the "Four-in-Hand Club."

From Virginia Dale F—— started off into the mountains,

riding my mare and packing a waggon-horse, and I left for Sheyenne the same day, riding "Henry" and putting my bundle on the second horse of our team. I was three days going in, having stopped occasionally to stalk some antelopes. I never saw so many as on that ride, several bands being continually in sight; they seemed very tame, letting you ride up to within a hundred and fifty yards of them. I got two in one stalk, having crawled to within seventy yards of them, and later the same day I tried "Henry's" speed after them as the plain was level for miles. I tied up the pack-horse to a bush, and by riding down a hollow I managed to get near a single buck, running him for fully three miles, and being as far behind then as when I started. Henry was very game, as he was thorough-bred, but his action was far too high to be fast, and "Polly" could have run away from him easily.

On my way I overtook some miners from the mountains, about eighty miles north of where F—— and I had been. They had done well, but had had a good deal of trouble from Indians during the summer, having had all their horses run off, so that they were obliged to send in to Sheyenne to buy ponies before they could leave. None of this present party had ever seen that place, so I was able to give them a few hints, for it was necessary to be careful as they had several thousand pounds with them in dust. They were on their way to Iowa, where they had left their families, and said they would take the train at once and only remain one night to sell their animals. Many a train has been stopped by "road agents" for a less sum than they had with them; and I know of a case where three of them had emptied the pockets of everyone in a long train and not a shot was fired at them, so much terror

can three desperate men inspire; I have, too, seen a noted
desperado overawe a whole room full of men who looked as bad
as himself, daring anyone among them to say a word, when no
one opened his lips.

On reaching Sheyenne I put "Henry" in a livery stable,
selling the other horse at once, as he would have eaten more
than his value at eight shillings a day, and I went myself to
Mr. Gildersleeve's once more, managing to get a bed to myself
by saying that I had a fever, which though not very dangerous
might be troublesome to anyone who caught it. If I had not
made some such excuse I should have been accused of putting
on airs, and there would have been trouble.

The town had grown very much during the last three months,
and now contained about five thousand inhabitants; but its
moral character had not improved, and a vigilance committee
had just been formed. This was a necessity in such places,
and at first did a great deal of good, the regular police being a
farce; but gradually abuses crept in, many joining the committee
in order that they might denounce some man against whom they
had a grudge, and there is no doubt that a number of innocent
men were hung in this way, as very little proof of guilt was
necessary, the trial sometimes not lasting more than ten minutes,
the supposition being that a man was guilty unless he could
prove himself to be innocent.

I found the elections for mayor and town council going
on, and was urged by some men at the hotel to vote, as
I possessed the only necessary qualification—that is, having
been three months in the territory. Our landlord was
the respectable candidate, the popular one being a Colonel
Johnson, an ex-prize-fighter and owner of one of the largest

saloons. The poll was to be open only one day, and I found that every decent man who went there to vote for our candidate returned without having been able to do so and more or less battered. The gamblers were managing everything, being to a man Johnsonians, so I got a ticket for both, one of them being blue and the other yellow, the blue being for our man; so putting this in my pocket and flourishing the yellow one in my right hand I went down to where the poll was being held. Here among the gamblers I found several of my "old friends" from St. Joe, who immediately shook hands cordially and asked if they could do anything for me, on which I said I wanted to vote, allowing them to see my yellow ticket, but that I was afraid one was liable to meet with rough treatment in doing so. They assured me, however, that with them there was nothing to fear, and they passed me with the greatest ease through a very rough mob to the entrance to a narrow passage between two rails, at the end of which was a small window where the tickets had to be handed in, and on reaching this I passed in my blue ticket and at once left for the hotel, not waiting to see "my friends" again. I was congratulated on being one of the very few supporters of our host who had returned in a sound state. As it turned out, all my strategy was wasted, as Colonel Johnson was returned by a large majority, and I had the pleasure of seeing him driving round the town that evening in a carriage drawn by six horses, with a barrel of whiskey on the front seat, from which he dispensed freely to all comers.

My ague was no better in Sheyenne than it had been in camp, returning every morning about ten o'clock and making me so weak that I was fit for nothing, and this induced an

Irishman, whose name was Fox and who occupied the next bed to mine, to abuse Englishmen in every possible way. This man had been a miner in Montana, but had done something there which had caused him to be hunted out of the country. What it was I never heard, but it must have been something very bad, for it was always said that "a man who was not fit for Montana could only go to one other place," which I need not mention.

Now I had heard Fox say that there was nothing of which he had so great a horror as of finding any animal in his bed, declaring that if he found a skunk there, as a comrade of his had once done, he thought he should go mad. Owing him a grudge as I did, I determined that he should have the chance. I had made myself a wolf-skin cap when in the mountains, with the tail hanging down behind, which had always been too hot to wear and was of no use to me, so going to bed early one night I put the cap in Fox's bed, knowing that as the house was not full at the time he would have one to himself. I also fastened a string to the lower corner of his bed-clothes, bringing it down through a small staple which I had driven into the floor in such a way as to make it appear that the bed-clothes had been drawn off from the opposite end of the room. He came up very late that night, more than twenty men being in bed and asleep before he arrived. It only took him about three minutes to undress, when he put out his candle and jumped into bed. An awful yell followed by another immediately resounded through the room, and though he had a game leg and was lame in consequence, he was out of bed with one leap, pulling out two revolvers which were under his pillow (for in that room everyone had at least one with him) and declared that there was some wild animal in his bed and that he meant to fire at it. On this the men in the other part of the room, who had been awakened by the yells, said that if he did they would fire at him, as it would probably bring up the vigilance committee. One of them then jumped out and drew down the bed-clothes exposing the cap. Fox's rage was awful, and he swore that if he could find out the man who had put it there he would shoot him "on sight." I naturally did not inform him who it was, and no one else knew, so he got into bed again using awful language. I let him lie about half an hour, when I pulled the string and off came his bed-clothes, the string coming away in my hands as I intended it should. He sat up and gasped for breath, speechless with rage, but when he found his voice my pen cannot do justice to his language. I of course pretended to sleep through it all, and was not suspected even when I asked him if he had not had rather a disturbed night, as I fancied I heard some sounds coming from the direction of his bed during the night. He glared at me for a moment, but as I kept my countenance he walked off with an oath.

While I was in the town two Englishmen arrived, on their way to California, and as they were quiet well-behaved men we got to be very friendly, the occupants of the other beds being such a rough lot, so we used to lie awake talking till far into the night. One of these two men had been a prize-fighter who had made money and now meant to go into business in San Francisco. They proposed one evening that we should go round and see the sights, promising to stand by me should there be any need for it. So we first of all visited one of the gambling-dens, which we found so full of smoke that we could hardly see anything. There were about seventy or eighty men in it, about half of whom were playing, chiefly at faro, rouge et noir, and roulette, the stakes being principally silver with a sprinkling of gold pieces. It was early in the evening, so that there was no one drunk and not much noise, but a man to whom we spoke told us to return about eleven o'clock if we wished to see the fun. In the back room was a young girl doing five hundred miles in five hundred hours and looking wonderfully fresh, though she was supposed to have done more than half that distance—the truth being that it was the public who were being done and not the distance, as in the instance I have before mentioned. We then visited a dance-house, where there were three females, two of whom were smoking cigars, and you had to pay half a dollar to dance round the room with one of them, standing drinks afterwards. The room, which was a very long one, was full, a small space being reserved at one end for the dancing, the music for which was a street organ.

I was told a story of one of these places soon after Sheyenne was started, which my informant declared he had witnessed, but for the truth of which I will not vouch. He said that he was standing near the bar in a dance-house talking to a chance acquaintance, when a drunken man got on the bar and began shouting and brandishing a revolver, swearing that he would shoot the first man who refused to drink with him, on which the man to whom my informant was speaking stopped in the middle of a sentence, drew a revolver and shot the man dead, merely saying "that he might have hurt some one," and then finished his sentence.

Certainly human life was thought very little of in such

places as Julesburg and Sheyenne, and often when I have heard shots in the street as we sat round the stove in the evening, and I have got up to go and see what was going on, some one would say "It's only some poor devil gone under; sit still unless you wish to follow him." On several occasions the vigilance committee turned out and went by the hotel in a double line, filling the street and arresting all they met, each man wearing a black half-mask and carrying a revolver in his right hand, and it was wonderful how soon the streets cleared in front of them, even drunken men seeming to become sober at once. One morning I was awakened by hearing a good deal of talking downstairs, and on going to see what it was I found that everyone was looking at the bodies of four men which were hanging from telegraph-poles within sight of the house, having been tried, condemned, and executed by the vigilance committee during the night. While I was there they put a man against a telegraph-pole telling him they were going to shoot him, firing really only blank cartridge, but he was found to be dead from fright.

Among the men hung in Sheyenne was a noted desperado named Hughes, who was supposed to have murdered five or six men, and whose wife was as bad as himself; so after hanging him they gave her twenty-four hours' notice to leave the town, telling her that she would be hung if found there after that time. I heard of this, and also that she was going by the next train, so I went down to see her off. A great crowd had assembled for the same purpose, and when she appeared she was mobbed, most of the men seeming to admire her pluck. She was driven to the station in a carriage (as the line was now open to Sheyenne and was most elaborately got up and wore a great deal of jewelry. The men crowded round to shake hands, and she joked and laughed with them as if she was going to a ball. After getting into the train she alternately cursed the vigilance committee and sang snatches of comic songs, and was kissing her hand as the train disappeared round a curve; and yet this woman had acted as a decoy for her husband and had been the cause of, if she had not actually witnessed, several murders.

One of the quietest men in the hotel was a prize-fighter named "Joe Riley," who was training to fight for the championship of Montana. He was an Irishman but not a Fenian, and had seen better days, his people having been well off. After trying many things and failing he had become what he was, and had won several fights. He and I used often to sit up and talk by the stove when everyone had gone to bed; and we were there one night when some one knocked violently at the door, which stood at the top of three wooden small steps. Riley asked who it was, on which a voice answered that it was some fellows who wanted whiskey, though it was evident that they had had too much already. Riley told them that the bar was closed and that no more could be had that night, but as the knocking still continued he opened the door, when three men, all more or less drunk, attempted to come in; Riley, however, prevented their doing so, saying that they must go away, and on their asking who would make them do so, he replied that he would. One of them then made a rush at him, but was met by a right-hander in the face, knocking him into the road, the second going down on the top of him, on which they made off, not daring to use their pistols, as it was only a day or two after the four men had been hung, which quieted the town wonderfully for a time.

While I was at Sheyenne a ten-mile race was got up between a prairie-bred mare and a thoroughbred, as he was called, belonging to some gamblers, and I went to see it. The gambler's horse was certainly not thoroughbred, though a good-looking animal, and the mare was a nice pony somewhat bigger than " Polly."

There was a great deal of betting, a crowd of gamblers backing their companion's horse, and a good deal of quarrelling as to weights, the gamblers having got a boy from the east, while the owner of the mare, who was a big man, rode her himself. In spite of this the mare led nearly all the way, being only beaten in the last mile. There were many attempts made to induce me to run my stallion; but even if he had been fast enough, which he was not, I should not have had fair play, as they would have thought nothing of giving him a dose before the race.

I had an opportunity of seeing how quickly railways are made in Western America before I left. A branch line was wanted from Sheyenne to Fort William Russell, so they offered the men who were working on the main line extra pay if they would work on a Sunday. The distance was three miles, and they began it on Sunday morning and had some freight cars at the fort by nightfall; the ties in most cases were laid on the grass, a few shovelfuls of earth being put under them when necessary. It was in this way that the Central Pacific Railway was made at first, to get the subsidy from the government, and of course when the storms came most of them gave way and had to be remade.

Just after Christmas I received letters which made it necessary for me to go east, so I had to give up my intention of joining F—— in the mountains, where he remained till early in the spring, killing as many deer as he wanted and a fair number of elk, and then he returned south and I went back to England. I sold "Polly" to him; but it grieved me very much to part with her, as I felt I was parting with an old friend.

CHAPTER XX.

I intend to go up the Wichita and Red Rivers.—Grouse-shooting.—Creasing a horse.—Poor settlers.—A money-lending parson.—Danger of Mexican cooks.—Henrietta in 1874.—A norther.—Rough cowboys.—Lose my horse.—Return towards Henrietta.—Indians about.—A suspicious horseman.—Reach Henrietta. The settlement raided by Black Kettle. The settlers cowed.—A preacher. The preacher and I put up in the same room. The first night he scores; the second I do.—Life of a cowboy. A new class of cowboy. A gentleman cowboy.—A good shooting-ground. —I shoot a puma.—A lucky sportsman.

HEARING from my friend F——, who was then living in Texas, that the game had very much increased since I was there last, I started for Denison in 1874 for a trip on the Wichita and Red Rivers, intending to remain out until Christmas. On the way there, going by St. Louis, Sedalia, and Sherman, I stopped at Parsons and had two days' capital grouse-shooting, they at all events being much more numerous than I had ever seen them in those parts. It is very curious with reference to these birds, that you can very seldom find them in uncultivated portions of the West, but as soon as settlers come and plant crops the grouse appear at once and get more and more plentiful. I have found a few, when after big game, in wild parts of Montana and Idaho, but not enough to make it worth while to take a shot gun; and as in those parts they live during the shooting-season on rosebuds, they taste very strongly of them and are not worth killing. I got more than sixty brace to my own gun at Parsons in a day and a half, besides a few snipe and ducks. Half a day's travelling from there landed me at Denison, which I found to be a very dull little wooden town, with a wretched inn, where the arrival of a stranger was an event. F—— was waiting for me, and we at once set about buying our outfit. We got a two-horse waggon, a tent, two work-horses, and the necessary provisions, beside engaging a Mexican as cook, leaving the buying of riding-horses till we got further into the country, as they were much cheaper there than near the railway. F—— was already provided with a good hunting-pony, and soon after leaving Denison I bought a horse with a history. He had been ridden by a scout in a fight with the Comanches, where his master had been killed, and he had been "creased," as it is called, the ball striking the upper edge of the shoulder—a wound which temporarily paralyses a horse. It was in this way that a great many wild horses were captured before the country was settled, and the shot required a first-rate marksman, as if half an inch too low the animal was killed or ruined for life. About forty miles from Denison we came to a small place called Whitesboro', where I bought a mare out of a waggon, which proved to be an excellent animal in every way.

The settlers in this part of the country struck me as being the poorest and most miserable of any we had come across; no one seemed to have any money, and nearly all of them were very much in debt, having borrowed in many cases at sixty per cent. I met a parson riding along the road one day, and getting into conversation with him, I happened to say how sorry I was for the poor men who had to do this, and what horrible usurers I thought those men were who had asked such exorbitant interest, when he turned to me quite fiercely and said that he could not see it, that a man had a right to make all he could of his money; it was optional with the borrower whether he took it or not, adding that he had lent some money himself at that rate.

From Whitesboro' we drove through a pretty country to Gainsville, a very nice little town built on the Mexican plan round a plaza, as it was a quiet place. There was quite a stir about the time we arrived over a shooting affray which had just taken place. A man who went by the name of "California Joe" had shot a man in broad daylight in the plaza and had ridden off, no one trying to stop him, as he had the character of being a reckless desperado.

We were obliged to send our Mexican cook back from here, replacing him by an American. He was very dirty, like most of his countrymen, and objected to washing our dishes more than once a day, considering a scrape good enough for the other two meals. There was a stage from Gainsville to Denison, and by this he returned, telling the people there on his arrival that he had left us because we put on too many airs. We had heard on our way of another hunting-party, consisting of five Texans, who had also engaged a Mexican as cook, and as they were very much dissatisfied with him, they had at first found fault with and afterwards struck him. The man did nothing at the time, but one day two of the party went shooting by themselves, and found on their return that their three companions had been murdered with an axe by the Mexican, who left a written statement of his reasons for doing it. We had been wise in getting rid of our cook when we did, for the Mexicans are a revengeful and treacherous race, and if any of us had struck him we might have met with the same fate.

From Gainsville we set out for Henrietta, a very small settlement not far from where Fort Buffalo springs used to be, on the Little Wichita River. On the way my rifle fell out of the waggon and remained nearly a day on the road; however, fortunately no one came along the road, and we found it when we went back to look for it. Henrietta was then a place of a dozen small cabins, placed in two lines facing one another, on the bare prairie, and about two hundred yards from the river. The principal man, who was always spoken of as Judge Johnson (I am sure I do not know why, for he was the postmaster and had never been a lawyer), had a long talk to us about our trip, and tried to persuade us to give it up by telling us that the Indians, chiefly Sheyennes and Arrapahoes, were very bad just then, and that they fully expected that the settlement would be attacked before long. A party who had been out "skin hunting" had lately come in with several of the men wounded and their waggon riddled with bullets. We had heard this kind of thing so often before that we did not take much notice of it, generally finding any Indian news to be very much exaggerated, if not entirely untrue.

Our first day out from Henrietta we camped on the bank of a small stream away from any bushes, partly as being a better position, in case Indians should take it into their heads to attack us, and partly as low ground means ague in Texas, and we had both of us had enough of that. During the night a norther began, and if we had not gone out at once and held the two corners of the tent on the side from which it came, it would have been blown to pieces. We were in bed when it began, and had only time to jump into our trowsers, so that in these and a flannel shirt we had to sit for hours holding on with all our strength, and we were quite worn out and nearly frozen by morning.

The following day we passed a cattle-ranche, one of the first which had been started in Texas, the cattle having been allowed up to this time to range anywhere, with no cowboys to keep them within certain bounds. These first cowboys were very rough fellows, being in many cases men who had to disappear for a time, yet they were kind-hearted and hospitable, and would give a passing stranger anything he wanted, or shoot him, should a quarrel arise, with equal pleasure. There were four men at this ranche, which consisted of a square house of logs and a corral for cattle, with no attempt at a garden or field. They told us that they had seen some Indians in the distance a few days before, and that they were not going to venture far from the ranche for some time,—Black Kettle[*], a noted Sheyenne chief, being in that part of the country with a hundred warriors.

At our next camp we found a good deal of game—deer and turkeys,—so we remained some days, when my "creased horse" being missing, I borrowed a pony from a cow-ranche, a short distance from our camp, and rode towards Henrietta, supposing

[*] This was not the celebrated "Black Kettle," chief of the Sheyennes, and who was killed by General Custer's troops at the battle on the Little Wichita River in 1868, but was another chief, who probably took the deceased chief's name after his death.

that in all probability my horse had gone back there. The pony I had borrowed was foundered from too hard work and could only raise a slow canter, going as if his legs were wooden and had no joints. As I passed the first ranche we had come to, I found all the cowboys in it and their horses in the corral. They told me that the evening before they had been out rounding up some cattle, when they were run in by about forty Indians, and had got in only just in time. Fortunately these southern Indians never dismount to fight, so that they were safe when once inside. It was not probable that the Indians would hang about in the neighbourhood, as they would know that the cowboys would not leave the ranche, so I determined to go on, and saw nothing but some antelope, till about five o'clock, when it was getting dark, and then I discovered a man riding along the top of a parallel ridge to the one I was on. It was too dark to see whether he was an Indian or a white man, so I hailed him several times but got no answer, and as I expected to have to camp out, Henrietta being still some miles away, I fired two shots at him, aiming very high, my double rifle being only sighted for two hundred yards, and the distance appeared to be far more than that. He at once disappeared, riding, I presume, down the other side of the ridge. This made me feel rather uncomfortable about camping out, so I determined to reach Henrietta that night if possible, and I blundered on, my pony nearly coming down over every inequality in the ground, till long after dark, when finding that I was lost I camped in some brush, without any water, made a miserable supper of some crackers, and turned in, having nothing but an old saddle-blanket for covering and not daring to light a fire. Before daylight I was off again and luckily struck the Wichita a few miles below Henrietta, and reached that place about ten in the morning. Here I found everything in confusion: Black Kettle and his warriors had passed through the place, hooting and yelling, two nights before, and had carried off every head of stock of all kinds, and even all the poultry, no one daring to fire at them. When we were there before, we had met a much-got-up individual, who was loud about what he would do if the Indians came there, giving us a great deal of advice about how we should act if attacked, and yet this man was one of the first to advise no shots being fired at these Indians when they did come for fear of provoking them. One of the settlers borrowed my pony to follow the trail a little way, to see if he could pick up any strayed animals, but he could not have gone far as he was back in an hour.

A preacher had arrived on the day of the Indian raid, and a meeting was held that afternoon. I attended, of course, and listened to his sermon for more than an hour, when, not being able to stand it any longer, I went out, as the man made me laugh by using long words the meaning of which he was quite ignorant of, and putting them in the wrong places. When the service was over he gave me a long lecture for having gone away, and it was a little difficult explaining why I had done so, without hurting his feelings. He told me his pony had been carried off with the rest, and that he was getting up a subscription to buy another, and he hoped I would give liberally. I replied that I meant to give a sum to Judge Johnson for the poorest of the settlers, many of whom were utterly ruined by the loss of their stock, and that I thought that as he had a salary of twelve hundred dollars (£240) he could afford to buy himself another pony, on which he left me in a rage.

Finding that my horse had not come into the settlement, and thinking that the Indians had probably got him, I determined to wait for the mail, which was expected the next day, and then go back to camp. When night came, Judge Johnson told me that he had been obliged to put me with the parson in a lean-to (which he, by the way, called a room). This was at the back of his cabin, and had apertures for doors and windows; the bed was made of four forked sticks, over which were laid a number of small ones and some grass, and two single blankets were spread on the top of this. I had inspected it, and not being very favourably impressed with its comfort, I sat talking to the Judge till long after his family had gone to bed; and when I did go to my quarters I found the preacher already asleep and with about two thirds of both blankets round him, leaving me so little that, though I lay as close to him as I could, my back was all uncovered. Finding it very cold, I asked him if he had not more than his share, on which he replied that he had barely enough and wished me "good-night," an impossibility under the circumstances. I managed to get through it somehow by continually turning and warming one side and then the other against him, and was thankful when the morning came.

The mail did not arrive the next day, so I passed my time in going round among the cabins listening to the very curious experiences of their owners. Some of the occupants had known a great many ups and downs, the latter predominating. Most of them, coming from the east, had had no experience of Indians, and were thinking of moving back towards the

Mississippi once more, as they were much frightened by Black Kettle's raid. They told me that he had some two hundred men with him, and that they came close to the cabins, in some cases breaking the glass in the windows with their guns and firing into the houses; and that one man, having put up a small fowl-house, in which all his chickens were shut up at night, had had it robbed by one of the Indians, who had taken the fowls and had tied them to his saddle. I think the number of Indians must have been exaggerated, as Black Kettle, I heard later, had only one hundred warriors with him. In the confusion of a night attack it was easy to see double.

I went to bed early that night, the preacher not having yet come home; but about an hour afterwards he arrived, and was much put out at finding me already in bed. He made up the fire, though this did very little good in a place with three big holes in it, and not yet chinked, and then he turned in, merely taking off his coat and boots. He soon found, as I had done the night before, that the blankets were too narrow, as I had taken a liberal allowance and put it well under me; so he pulled, but could get no more; he then asked if I thought he could sleep under so little, when I reminded him that I had said much the same thing the night before. He was quiet for a time and then began again, asking me if I thought it right to make a preacher pass the night in such a manner, on which I said that I had always thought that a pastor should help his flock, but had discovered my mistake the night before. He then got up and sat by the fire on a three-legged stool, and there he remained until the morning, when he would not speak to me.

The mail came in early the next day, bringing some letters

for us, and I left for camp about mid-day and reached the first ranche by evening. I found that they had seen no more Indians, but they had remained in most of the time. They were inclined to think that the man I had seen was an Indian out hunting by himself, and that I might have hit him, but the distance was so great that I do not think I did.

The cowboys led a very hard life in those days, their food being only meat, bread, and coffee, whereas now they have tinned vegetables, fruits, jams, and all kinds of luxuries. The class of man, too, has changed, as there are now many gentlemen among them of good families, learning the business before setting up for themselves. I remember once in Dacotah, when out after deer, meeting a rough-looking cowboy, to whom I spoke a few words, and then, as we were both going in the same direction, we rode side by side for some time without speaking. It was a very hot day, and he suddenly said, " Would not some iced champagne-cup be nice now?" and on my looking hard at him, he said, " You seem to think that I have never tasted it, but, indeed, I have very often. I lived in South Kensington once, and went about in a stove-pipe hat and a frock coat." Yet here he was looking as rough as any of his companions.

I left the ranche early and was in camp by nightfall, where I found my horse; he had strayed off and wound up his rope in a thicket, where the men had discovered him. The next day we moved to Buffalo Creek, and had a great deal of trouble in getting there on account of streams with high banks having to be crossed. We found this place the best we were ever in for deer and turkeys. F—— and I in less than two hours shot nineteen turkeys, and the cook actually shot one while sitting by the camp-fire. Of course we should not have killed so many, but each of us thought he was having all the sport to himself.

I was out one day, some miles up the stream, when I came on a fine buck feeding; I managed to dismount and tie up without his seeing me, and keeping in the timber as far as I could, I then began to crawl, getting to within about three hundred yards of him, when something startled him and he cantered round a point of timber. As he did not seem much frightened I followed as fast as I was able, and crawling round the point I could not see the deer, but noticed a small head with pointed ears above some long grass, watching me. I thought it must be a wolf, so, determined to have something for my trouble, I fired, aiming under it, and the head sank and a long tail lashed backwards and forwards as I walked up, and on getting close I saw that I had killed a medium-sized puma, the first that I had ever seen. It is curious, considering that there are a good many of them about, how seldom you see them, though you often find their tracks, and where they have been at the carcass of a deer you may have killed.

I heard of a shopkeeper from Antonio, in Texas, who came out to a large hay camp, about forty miles north of that place, and who borrowed a soldier's rifle thinking that he might get a shot at a deer, having never killed anything larger than a goose in his life. He was away some hours and returned in a great state of excitement, saying that he had killed two big animals as large as calves, and when some of the men went with him to see what these were, they found that he had shot two pumas—such a chance as might not occur to a professional hunter once in his whole life.

As I might never kill another, I was very anxious to get this one to camp and skin him there; so I tried to hoist him on to the mare, but the thing was like a big cat—so limp that when I got it up on one side it fell off the other. The skin was so loose that it was very difficult to get a good hold of it, so I had to think of some other way. I could have hauled it to camp tied to my horse's tail, as I had often done with deer, but that would utterly ruin the skin, so I first of all hoisted it up with my lariat to a bough about ten feet above me, and then riding under the bough I gradually lowered the body on to the back of the mare, sitting with my face to the tail, and after binding it firmly to the saddle I tied the fore and hind feet to the stirrups, and by keeping my legs very stiff and my feet much further out than is usual, I managed to get it to camp. I supposed it weighed about two hundred pounds, and the skin measured ten feet from the nose to the tip of the tail when stretched nearly square. I saw a much finer one than this when in British Columbia, which had been killed by an Indian, but it had been very badly skinned and stretched. Mine was a light fawn-colour, whereas his was nearly black, shading off to fawn. Pumas have a most unpleasant cry, which very much resembles that of some one in agony; and there are stories of these animals springing on passers by from a tree, but I could not get one of them well authenticated, and do not believe them.

CHAPTER XXI.

Camp on Buffalo Creek.—Awful thunder-storms.—Two cowboys visit our camp. We return the visit.—Description of a "shack."—Stories of attacks by Indians.—A buck-jumper.—A curious shot.—A refractory mare.—Loss of a horse.—A herd of wild horses. Old Bridger's opinion of them.—Camp nearly destroyed by fire.—Poisoning wild animals.—A ghost story.

I do not think that we ever lived better in any camp than that on Buffalo Creek. Turkeys were so plentiful that we only ate the choice parts, feeding our dogs with the remainder. We had as much venison as we wanted, besides ducks and grouse—our only trouble being to dispose of all the game we got, as we never let any spoil if we could help it.

One night we had a succession of the most awful thunder-storms I ever saw. Our horses were used to living in the open air, and yet on this occasion they were so frightened that if we had not gone out and held them, they would have broken loose and have been lost. It would have been an amusing sight for a spectator if he could have seen us, in the light costume of a hat and a pair of boots, holding on to the horses in a pelting rain, and being dragged in all directions by them, and frequently taken off our feet, while, from not being able to see, we were very much knocked about by their knees. The storms came up one after another, barely giving us time to get into bed and warm ourselves before another began, and out we had to go again.

When we had been in this camp about three weeks two cowboys arrived from a small ranche twelve miles down the creek; and very rough specimens they were, as water with them was looked upon as a superfluous luxury, and their clothes were polished with grease and blood. They told us that about a month before one of their companions had been out after strayed cattle, when some Indians chased him. He seemed to lose his head, forgetting that he had a rifle and revolver, and only tried to get away. They went out from the ranche when they saw him coming, but were too late to help him, as almost immediately the Indians overtook him and speared him in the back, throwing him from his horse, when they scalped and mutilated him. One of these men had seen F—— from a distance one day, and not knowing of our being in the country had gone back to report having seen an Indian, after which they kept to the ranche for several days. They had, however, come across our waggon-trail, and had then known that we must be white men, so they had come out to visit us. They remained for a meal, and were astonished at the cooking, everything they ate being boiled in a camp-kettle, and all tasting alike. A day or two later we returned the visit, taking our blankets, as we meant to remain out a day or two and try the other end of the creek for game. A ride of two hours brought us to the "shack," as that kind of house is called, the plan being as follows :—

You first find a sloping bank, out of which you cut an oblong space as large as you wish the inside of the house to be: it is open in front, has sloping sides, and the back is some ten feet high. You then build the front of logs, making it two feet lower than the back, and fill in the ends either with logs or earth. The door and windows are then cut out, and a roof of poles, grass, and mud is put on, and your shack is complete, only requiring the floor to be stamped down to be ready for use. Sometimes a chimney is made; but in many in which I have stayed the fire was lighted in one corner, and the smoke found its way out by a hole in the roof. The spaces between the logs are daubed with clay to keep out the cold; and with a good fire these shacks are very comfortable, when your eyes get used to the smoke.

This shack was a small and very dirty one, and contained a "boss," or manager, and four boys. The food was chiefly boiled beef cut up in lumps, as they had not much time for hunting, and had driven most of the game away by firing at everything they saw. They were a very rough set, and their conversation was dreadfully monotonous, being almost entirely about beef, its price in the market, and the best way to get it there—the whole being seasoned with very strong language. There were some stories, too, of Indian atrocities, several cowboys having been killed lately, though no ranche had been attacked. The Sioux will sometimes dismount to crawl up to a house at night and fire into it; but none of them have been known to do so in the daytime; and I heard here of a rancheman's wife having kept off nearly twenty Indians by using her husband's repeater through the windows of the cabin, though they knew her to be alone.

Every cowboy rode with a Winchester carbine in a sheath on the off side of the saddle, where it could be grasped in a moment, and all of them had one or more revolvers. The man who had been speared was armed in this way; but they said that he was a new hand, and only lately from the east, and consequently lost his head. We remained the night, and in the morning the "boss" told us that we should witness some fun with one of the worst buck-jumpers he had ever come across; so we went out to see him mounted. The horse was a small chestnut, about fourteen hands high, with a very wicked eye; but he came up quietly to have the saddle put on, and we were afraid that there would be no fun that morning; but we were mistaken; for, almost before his rider was in the saddle, he began putting his head between his fore legs, arching his back, and jumping stiff-legged, going up with his head one way and coming down with it the other, turning half round in the air. The cowboy used his spurs well and forced him up the bank out of which the shack was cut; but he came down again, bucking all the way, turning round even when coming down the steep slope. His rider sat splendidly, not seeming to mind it at all, sending him up twice only to return immediately; but the third time, with all the boys shouting and using their whips, he went up with a rush and galloped off.

We tried the country round the ranche, but saw very little game, what there was being very wild; so we returned to camp that night, and found that our cook had shot a fine buck while sitting by the camp-fire.

One day, when F—— and I were out together, F—— made a curious shot. He had stalked a young buck and had fired at him at about two hundred yards, not being able to get nearer. The buck was standing almost directly facing him, a little on one side, and seemed, when F—— fired, to go off as if hit. We had a dog with us that day—a young retriever which F—— had brought, thinking he might be useful after wounded deer; so we put him on the buck's trail, which he took up at once, going off at a great pace and soon leaving us far behind, as we had gone out on foot. We followed as fast as we could run, and after going half a mile heard the deer bleating, and found it lying on the ground with the dog on the top of it, he seeming to think that he must not use his teeth. Now the curious part of it was that the ball had broken the near front leg off above the knee and the off hind leg above the hock, and yet this deer had gone all that distance almost as fast as if perfectly sound. This retriever would have made a good deer-dog with a little more training, and was the second I had seen used for that purpose. The owner of the other one refused twenty pounds for him, which is a large price for a dog in the west.

As we had found a good many ducks at some lakes near camp, we thought we would have a day's duck-shooting for a change; so I went to fetch the mare to ride to them, and was bringing her in when something startled her, and she bolted, dragging the rope out of my hands. As she had sixty feet of rope on her I thought I should have no trouble in catching her, and told F—— to ride on and that I would overtake him; but she always knew when I was close to the end of the rope, trotting a few yards just as I was going to jump on the end of it; so that when F—— returned, three hours later, there was I still chasing the mare, and I only got her at last by driving her into some low brush, where she could not judge distance so accurately, and here I managed to tie her up and give her a lesson. One of my horses met with a sad fate at this camp. We found one morning that he had pulled up his picket-pin and had gone off, and the place being a mass of horse-tracks we could not trail him up. There was a great deal of heavy timber and thick undergrowth round camp, and we hunted this carefully, but could find no trace of him; and it was not until some months later that we heard from a cattle-man that one of his cowboys, hunting for strayed cattle, had found him tied up in some bushes below our camp and nearly dead from starvation. He had given him food and water; but it was too late, and he died.

From Buffalo Creek we moved about twenty miles to Beaver Creek, arriving there late at night, and for some time could not find any grass or water, as the country had been burnt, and the only water in the Creek was in muddy pools. F—— and I were riding ahead and had just entered a small grove of trees, when out dashed a herd of horses. We at once thought we had come across an Indian camp and had stampeded their horses; so we galloped out into the open, getting our rifles ready as we went; but hearing nothing, and seeing that the horses were led by a large roan stallion, we knew that they must be a wild band. These were the only wild horses I had ever seen during eleven years' wanderings in the west. There were a few in Western Texas in 1868, but they were not worth catching, and were killed for their skins. I had a talk with old Bridger some years before on the subject of wild horses, he having lived in the west nearly sixty years; and he told me that it generally ruined a good horse to catch a wild one, and that when broken most of them lost their spirit and were worth nothing. A few were captured by creasing; but nearly all of these were of no use afterwards, the wound in the spine seeming to have taken all life out of them.

We found Beaver Creek by no means so good a place for game as the one we had left. The feed, too, was very bad and the water half mud; so we drove on to the Red River, and were surprised to find this large stream utterly undrinkable, the water being full of gypsum and causing violent colic, though, curiously enough, the horses seemed very fond of it and could hardly get enough, standing in it till you were tired of waiting for them, and looking afterwards as if they would burst.

While on the Red River we were very nearly losing our tent and all in it by fire. When making a camp-fire we usually burned a space all round it, the sparks flying in all directions and setting fire to the grass; but as we had camped late, and it was very cold, we neglected to take this precaution : as the bottom was covered with long grass this caught, and the flames spread so rapidly that by the time we got branches to beat them out with they were beyond our control; so we rushed to the horses and let them loose, and then, by throwing blankets on the fire, which was by this time close to the tent, and stamping on them, we managed to save it, the flames passing us and burning out the whole bottom below us, where we meant to have hunted. It was a grand sight— the night being dark—watching the flames, which were fifteen and twenty feet high, rushing down the valley, the long grass being very dry and burning like tinder; but it might very easily have brought the Indians on us, and it put an end to our hunt in that direction, and obliged us to retrace our steps.

The next morning we moved back to Beaver Creek and there met with a very heavy snow-storm, and the wind was so cold that we could not travel; so we remained there two days, killing one white-tailed deer. Soon after leaving Beaver Creek we saw a huge wolf walking very slowly ahead of us, having apparently no strength to get away, and on shooting him we found that he had been poisoned and was going away to die. When I first went to America I took strychnine for poisoning wolves; but after seeing one dying from its effects I never used it again. The agony must be awful, the animal being in the form of a half circle when dead, his back arched, while his coat stands on end, and the lips are drawn back, showing the teeth. The fur of a trapped animal is worth much more than that of a poisoned one, and the Hudson's Bay Company refuse any which have been killed in that way, as the hair is said to come out after the skin is dressed.

On reaching Buffalo Creek we stopped a few miles above our old camp, and once more had capital sport, especially with the turkeys. We remained a few days here and then went on to Denison, which we reached in nine days, and sold all our outfit. When going round to say good-bye to the friends we had made we heard a very strange story, which I will give here.

When we were fitting out at this place in September, we had bought some things at a store kept by two men (a German and an Irishman); but finding them very rough, every third word being an oath, and both of them generally the worse for liquor, we had got the remainder of our outfit elsewhere. About two months after we left the German died, and when on his death-bed he and his partner had a conversation as to whether there was a future state or not, when the German said—"If there is one, Bill, I will come back and tell you." The man was buried, and the Irishman kept the shop by himself, no change being noticed in him, till what I am going to relate happened. The store was a long narrow wooden building, the front portion of which was the shop, behind which was a railing, and the back portion was used as a bedroom, there being a bed in each corner, and a large stove stood just behind the middle of the railing, which had talc slides, so as to give light as well as heat. The Irishman slept in one of the beds, the other being empty, when one night, having been asleep for some time, he woke, and looking towards the stove saw what looked like a man sitting between himself and it. Knowing that he had locked the front door, and wondering how anyone could have got in, he sat up in bed, when, as he did so, the figure turned round, and he saw that it was his friend the German, who looking steadily at him said, "There is a future state, Bill!" and then seemed to fade away. The Irishman got out of bed and went to the stove, but found nothing, and the doors were both locked and the windows fastened. Our informant added that since that night the Irishman had been a different man, that he had given up drinking and swearing, and conducted himself in every way as a good citizen. So ended one of the pleasantest short trips I ever made. The country we hunted over is now, I hear, thickly settled and all the game killed off; and there are very few places in America now where a man can get such sport as we then had.

CHAPTER XXII.

Resolve to go to the Judith Basin.—Colonel P—— agrees to accompany me.—Start for Carroll.—Delay at Bismarck.—Have some shooting.—Journey by steamer up the Missouri.—Land to hunt every day.—Come upon an old hunter. His history and end.—The remaining Indians concerned in the Minnesota massacre.—Arrival at Buford.—Freak of a lieutenant.—Symonds joins me.—Start with Major Reed for Judith Basin.—The ways of Indian agents described.—Join Colonel P—— in camp.—Good news of game.—Adventure with a bear.—Description of the Judith Basin.—Hunting mountain-sheep.—Reed and Bowles at home.—Visit the Crows' camp. Go with them to meet the Bannocks. —Buy a horse from the Bannocks.

WHEN returning from a duck-shooting trip in Dacotah in the winter of 1877, I travelled with a Colonel Clendenin, who had spent the summer and autumn at Fort Benton, on the Upper Missouri, and was now on his way to Washington for the winter. The conversation turned on sport, and he spoke enthusiastically of the beautiful scenery and the great quantity of game in a portion of Montana called the Judith Basin, lying near the Mussel-shell River, which runs into the Yellowstone. I had hunted years before to the north of this place, and I retained very pleasant recollections of my trip, so

I determined to return the following year and spend the autumn in and about that country.

Colonel Clendenin told me that he had the management of the steamers on the Upper Missouri, and that if I wished he would get my outfit for me—horses, waggon, and men—and send it down from Benton by river, to meet me at a place called Carroll, which he said was about the best starting-point, thus saving me a great deal of time, trouble, and money, besides giving me the benefit of his experience in choosing the men, and of course I accepted his kind offer.

The following spring I was trying to find a companion, when I saw a very good article in the 'Forest and Stream,' from a gentleman who said he had spent the last season in the country to which I wished to go, and that he meant to return again that summer. I wrote to the address given, and got a letter from a Colonel P——, saying that he thought of starting soon and should like a companion; and it was finally arranged that he should share my outfit, and that we should meet at Carroll late in August. When the time came I was delayed by having to go to New York to meet some guns, &c., coming from England, so I wrote to the Colonel asking him to go on to our starting-point, take out the outfit and leave a horse for me, on which I could join him. This he did, and I started for Carroll about a week late, going by rail to Bismarck, then the terminus of the Central Pacific railway, and by steamer to Carroll, this place being about a hundred and fifty miles above Fort Buford, at the mouth of the Yellowstone River. At Bismarck I had to wait a full week for a steamer from below; so hearing that there were a good many black- and white-tailed deer on Big-heart River, I hired a horse and made an excursion up it, though there was a report that some Sioux Indians had been seen there lately. Before starting I went across the Missouri and saw the principal Indian scout at Fort Abraham Lincoln, as to the probability of this report being true. He told me that one of his men had seen two strange Indians in the distance when some miles up the river several months before, and this was all the foundation there was for the rumours I had heard. I had bought a tent, not unlike the French soldier's tent d'abri, weighing only three pounds, and a very small outfit, and this I rolled in my blankets and fastened behind the saddle and then started, going up the valley of the Big-heart River.

The first day I only saw one buck in the distance, and as I did not mean to hunt so near the Fort, where the country was always being disturbed, I did not follow him, camping that night under a large rock, with the beautifully clear river running within six feet of my tent door. One solitary wolf came and serenaded me for hours during the night, asking me probably to kill him something to eat, hunters having been very scarce lately; and in the morning I was off early and rode all day, making I should think thirty miles, and got into a very pretty hunting-country—small wooded hills, separated by narrow winding valleys, where I found plenty of deer sign. On my way I had jumped three deer, and going out on the evening of my arrival I shot a fine buck, getting a grand chance at him as he crossed a small prairie not a hundred yards from me. He ran about fifty yards before he fell, and on going after him into some bushes I put up what I think was a puma, but I only got a glimpse, and the light was too bad to make certain.

U

The next day I hunted on foot, following the bluffs above the river, and jumped a good many deer, shooting one fine black-tail only, as I had then as much as I could carry back to camp. That night I was awoke by what sounded like an Indian's yell, which brought me out on my hands and knees, as I made certain I was in for a fight; but I heard nothing further, and it might have been a puma, though, as a measure of precaution, I took my blankets and slept in the bushes, where I could see the tent. We have often left a light in our tent when in a dangerous country, and then gone and slept in the bushes round it, as it gave us a capital chance of shooting any Indians who came between us and it. I was not disturbed again, and the next morning, after trying for pumas near where I had jumped one the day before, and seeing nothing but two deer, I packed my two bucks on my pony, and finding that he objected to carry me as well, I started on the back trail leading him. Now I found the folly of coming on even so short a hunt as this without a pack animal, as I was about fifty miles from Bismarck, and had three days to do it in, leading a pony who needed to be dragged along. I tramped down the river, making about three miles an hour, and did about twenty miles that day, reaching my first camp-out about lunch-time on the second day, and Bismarck about midday on the third. I saw only a small bear and some deer on the way. The bear got in among some huge rocks where I could not follow him, and having so little time I had to leave him there. On getting in I found that I need not have hurried, as the steamer would not be up the river till late the next day.

Going up the Missouri from Bismarck was even in 1878 a

pleasant experience, though the game had become much scarcer since I came down it in a canoe eleven years before. You could, however, still find some all along the river bottoms, and there was just sufficient chance of meeting Indians to make the hunting exciting.

There was a man on board who was taking up two capital ponies to Benton, and I used to hire one of them and go ashore with it before the boat started in the morning (as we never ran at night), taking with me some bread and meat for my midday meal, in case I should get no game. I would then follow the course of the river, cutting across the bends, and frequently got a deer and some grouse by evening when I rejoined the boat, being always able to find it by its smoke from any high point. I had in this way very good sport, and avoided the monotony of the journey, and saw some very pretty country which was not visible from the boat.

One day when making my way through a dense thicket on the river's bank, into which I had driven some grouse, I came upon a hunter's cabin, made of brush, and so placed that if I had not gone in as I did I should never had suspected its existence. The occupant was a curiosity, and was dressed in an old leather shirt and trowsers, almost black with age and dirt, his hair hanging down fully six inches below his collar, and his face one mass of wrinkles and very like old brown parchment. This old fellow had led a solitary life on the river for years, only going into a town twice a year to buy ammunition and sell his pelts. He told me that he had originally come from the Missouri near St. Louis, which, he said, was then a small town and the rendezvous for trappers, and that when only sixteen he had there joined a party under

Bridger, and had spent many winters in the mountains. He had been wounded twice, and more than once had escaped with the loss of everything. When he was twenty he married a Bannock squaw, and he assured me that an Indian wife was worth several white ones, as they would do more work, and you could always beat them when they did not obey you, and send them back to their people when you were tired of them. He seemed, however, to have been very fond of his squaw, for when she was killed in a fight with the Sioux he left his companions and had lived as a solitary trapper ever since. He was, he said, known to so many Indians that none of them would injure him, and he offered to take me to the hostile Sioux camp, which was then he said about forty miles south of where he was then living, and he assured me that they would not touch a friend of his; this kind offer I, however, declined, neither having time to do so nor caring to risk it. He gave me a dinner of beaver tail, of which he had a great store, but I fear I did not appreciate it, though it is considered a great delicacy, as it was almost solid fat; and I bade him good-bye, hoping I might see him on my way home in the winter; but, poor old fellow! he was dead before then, being found by a passing steamer lying dead near his hut about a month after I saw him. It was thought that he had been killed by a man who had been trapping near him on the river, as they were known to have quarrelled, but there was no way of proving it. Appearances, however, were so against this man, that if he had not left that part of the country he would have been lynched.

Seven days after leaving Bismarck we reached Buford, the steamer having been very much delayed by the low state of the river, as she was continually running on to sandbars. Here I saw some old women belonging to the same tribe which had given me so much trouble in Minnesota in 1863. It seems that after the thirty-three Indians had been hung at Mankato for having shared in the Minnesota massacre, a number of the Sioux gave themselves up; and the Government not knowing what to do with them, they were sent up to Fort Berthold, on the Missouri south of Buford, where within two years they were all killed off by the Sheyennes and Blackfeet, the one tribe hunting to the north and the other to the south of that Fort, and now only these few women remained of a party numbering from seven to eight hundred.

Two days from Buford took us to Carroll, a very small place on the south bank of the river, consisting of three whiskey-saloons, about five small dwelling-houses, and a big store-house belonging to the Steamboat Company. Here I found Colonel Clendenin waiting for me, and a pony had been left in his charge on which I could follow Colonel P——, who had started two days before.

I arrived at night, and made up my bed on the floor of the storehouse, where Colonel Clendenin also slept. In the course of the night we were woke by some loud yells followed by a shot, and in the morning heard that a lieutenant of cavalry and six men were here, who had been sent to a large Bannock Indian camp, where they were to remain and see that none of the hostile portion of that tribe came into the camp, but finding that slow work, the lieutenant had brought his men to Carroll, where they were having what they called "a good time"—playing cards and drinking whiskey; and during the previous night, the lieutenant being drunk had fired at one of the men, who he said had cheated him, but fortunately he missed and only made a hole in the tent.

I found that I could not carry all I had brought with me to camp on my pony, so I waited at Carroll a day, as I heard that a Major Reed, an ex-Indian agent, was going out to a trading-store which he had in the Judith Basin, and as he would pass near our camp he kindly offered to carry my things. I went out grouse-shooting to pass the time, and met two prospectors from the Black Hills in Wyoming, who were on their way to the Judith Basin, where they had a mining claim, but who had lost their way. As I had on a leather suit, they took me for an Indian, and ran away as fast as they could go, leaving their pack-donkey, and I had some trouble in catching them to show them their error.

In the evening a young fellow came up and shook hands with me, saying that he had met me in Bismarck the year previous, when he said that he was a clerk in a bank there. I did not remember him, but as he was a Canadian and seemed in great trouble, I took him to my "bedroom" and we had a long talk. He had got into money difficulties in Bismarck, and had come up here in the spring, living by chopping wood and any odd jobs he could get, having previously been a great dandy, never having done any manual labour in his life. When I met him he had on the remains of a very smart suit —frock coat, light vest, and grey trowsers, with patent leather boots—but it was somewhat difficult to discover what the material was. His shoes had once buttoned, but they were now tied together with tape, and the kid uppers were sewn on to the patent leather with buckskin thongs. He was a good-looking young fellow, and had evidently been well educated, and what he now wanted was, that I should allow him to go with me till a chance occurred of sending him to Butte City, where he said he had friends. One more or less in camp could make no difference, so I bought him a pony and saddle and bridle, and we started together on the second day, Major Reed going with us, driving his waggon and taking my things. My companion had nothing to carry but a mackintosh sheet and what he stood up in. I should have mentioned that his name was Symonds.

We had about forty miles to do, expecting to find Colonel P—— camped at the entrance to the Judith Basin. The first day out we saw no game larger than grouse, the country being rolling prairie with wooded hills every few miles, and we had to camp early as there was no water for some distance ahead; and after supper Major Reed gave us his experiences, which were very varied, as he had begun life as a shop-boy, then enlisted and fought through the war, and at the end of it, when he was a lieutenant, he had been made an Indian agent, and hence the brevet rank of major, this being what agents are always called. He certainly opened my eyes to the way in which Indians were treated, telling us that though an agent's pay was only three hundred a year, yet he must be a fool (or an honest man, which terms he considered synonymous) if he did not make twenty thousand pounds during the five years for which he held his appointment. He told us that he had often landed one half of a steamboat load of flour on the bank of the river, bringing on the other half and giving it to the Indians as all that had been sent, and then had returned and fetched the second half, and sold it as his own, always selling as well half of the coats, blankets, socks, &c., which were forwarded for them.

I had been warned before starting that Reed was an awful drunkard and a dangerous man when he had had too much, who would stick at nothing, and there were many stories of the men he had shot; and yet I found him an unusually nice man, of fair education and very fond of Sir Walter Scott's novels, especially the poetry, which he always had with him, and of which he knew a great deal by heart. For the time he had "sworn off," and was drinking essence of ginger in water, as he said that he must have something hot. He warned me to beware of his partner Bowles, who, according to his account, was equal to any rascality, but who had in some way got a hold over Reed.

On the morning of the second day we had some rain, and thinking that we should see no game I put my rifle in the waggon, which jogged on, the road being good, while Symonds and I rode slowly chatting, and we had in this way dropped about half a mile behind, when we saw a large grizzly bear and a cub leave a ravine on our left and make across the open country for some hills about a mile away. As we had no weapon of any kind, I arranged with Symonds that he should follow the bears, not going near enough to hurry them, while I galloped after the waggon, and got my rifle and returned as quickly as I could. I went at full speed and was not away more than ten minutes, but when I got back I found Symonds at the first small stream which he had come across, and over which he said he could not get his pony to go, and the bears were out of sight. I galloped in the direction in which they had been going, but could see nothing of them, as I came across a good many small ravines full of branches, into any one of which they might have gone, the prairie being too hard for tracking, so I had very reluctantly to give them up and go back. This seemed to have been a very large bear and would have made a good commencement for the trip. On rejoining Symonds and discussing the matter, I was convinced that he had not been anxious to keep the bear in sight, as it was the first he had ever seen, and he had a very exaggerated idea of the danger of hunting them.

We did not overtake Reed till he had reached our camp, and it was a very curious thing that the Colonel P——, whom I only knew through the letter in the 'Forest and Stream,' turned out to be a gentleman with whom I had shot grouse four years before in Minnesota, though I had not learned his name. I brought the tents with me, finding all the party living under a waggon-cover, and we had to pitch them at once as the rain had changed to snow.

The report of game was very promising, as there seemed to be a great many deer, some elk, and any amount of bear-sign, which were what we had come for. The Colonel had two old buffalo killed for baits, at two different points, and with the fresh-fallen snow the tracking would be very easy. Reed left us in the morning, inviting us to visit him at his ranche, near which he said we should find plenty of bears, as no one hunted them.

The three men seemed good fellows, especially the guide, who was a very quiet man and spoke very little, but seemed to know the country well, and was willing to do anything you asked him, which is not the case with all guides, some of those I have had standing on their dignity and refusing to cut wood or to help with the horses.

I had hoped to have found some more blankets in camp,

but they had been forgotten, so I had to share mine with Symonds, which was hard, with snow on the ground, as I had only one pair and a greatcoat, while Symonds had my second pair and his small mackintosh sheet. I have forgotten to say that Symonds had a greyhound when I met him at Carroll, and as it seemed a good way of giving him a little money without hurting his feelings, I bought it of him for twenty dollars (£4), although it could be of no use to us, but he assured me that it was very plucky, and would go in at anything in a moment.

After Reed's departure, the Colonel, Fishel (the guide), and I started off to visit the baits, Symonds preferring a book by the fire—bears in print being more in his line than hunting them. Soon after leaving camp we came across two fresh bear-tracks, going in different directions, so the Colonel followed one of them while we took up the trail of the other, and had gone about a mile when we came to a large swamp, through which the trail went. We were obliged to go round, which we did, one on each side of the cover. On the opposite bank was a thick clump of willows, about fifty yards square, and it did not look large enough to hold so big an animal; and we had just entered this at opposite corners, when the bear rose just in front of me, looking as large as an elephant. He remained a moment on his hind legs and then charged me, uttering a loud grunt. I shouted to Fishel that he was coming, and my pony spun round so quickly that I had no time to fire, so I rushed across a small bottom about a hundred yards wide, crashing through a lot of fallen wood, with which it was covered. Luckily it was almost all rotten, or it would have thrown us down. On hearing my shout, Fishel had started,

Page 298.—My pony spun round so quickly.

and was now doing his best across the bottom, presenting such a comic spectacle that I almost tumbled off the pony from laughing. His hat had come off and his long hair was blowing out behind, while his thin legs were flying about round the pony's sides, and his equally long arms were flourishing his rifle, with which he was beating the pony; at the same time he was yelling at the animal, and seemed to be trying to climb on to its neck. On the opposite side of the bottom was a steep rise of ten or twelve feet, up which we went, and the bear stopped at the bottom and then trotted back to the willows. I jumped off and managed to hit it behind as it entered them, my pony backing quickly and preventing my taking any aim. Fishel in the meantime had galloped on till he had reached the top of a ridge about four hundred yards away, and here he remained and opened fire upon the thicket, being much more likely to hit me than the bear.

Just as I remounted, the Colonel appeared on the opposite side of the swamp. He had lost his bear in a thicket, and hearing our shots had come to see what we were doing. On being told the state of affairs, he at once rode into the bushes, when the bear charged him, and was so close to his pony's tail when he came out that I thought for a moment he had caught him. On reaching the open the bear gave up the chase and returned to the bushes. I, however, got another ball into him, which hit him in the chest, but too much on one side, as it only lamed him. I then drew him out by throwing in stones, when the Colonel hit him again behind, after which he refused to come out again any more. Meanwhile it had begun snowing again, and as the bushes were becoming weighed down by the snow—neither of us liked to go in on foot, as it would have been very difficult to see on account of the showers of snow—so we agreed to return to camp and come back in the morning, bringing the greyhound, which would let us know whether the bear was dead or not.

In the morning, the Colonel, Symonds, and I started for the willows, taking the dog, and on reaching them sent him in. He went in bravely enough, but did not remain one minute, coming out again with his tail between his legs, and making for camp at his best speed, and taking no notice whatever of his master's shouts. On this the Colonel and I tossed up to see which of us should go in, and I lost the toss; so he took both horses and kept his rifle ready, while I cautiously entered, shaking off the snow in front of me as I went. It was difficult to see anything when once inside, but I had not gone far, when I came on a big mound of snow, which I made out to be the dead bear, lying with his head on his paws as if asleep. He was a fine fellow and had a good skin, but the body was already very much swollen and offensive though covered with snow, and we found it necessary after this to open any animal at once, even when coming back to skin him within an hour or two.

This snow only lasted a few days, and then began that most beautiful of all seasons—the Indian summer, which generally lasts six weeks, and is simply perfection, being neither too hot nor too cold, when a beautiful haze covers all the mountains, such as one sees in Italy. The Judith Basin was one of the most perfect hunting-grounds that I was ever in. It is a valley about fifty miles long by twenty wide, and has seven small ranges of mountains round it, all of them wooded, and at that time full of game of all kinds, including buffalo, antelope, white- and black-tailed deer, elk, mountain-sheep, bears of three kinds, wolves and foxes, not to mention grouse and ducks. The ranges average about 8000 feet, and have no snow on them in summer. The valley had grass as high as one's knees, and was intersected by a number of small clear trout-streams which, although only a few yards wide, held trout up to three and four pounds in weight, while in the willows along the banks you could always jump deer.

Bowles and Reed's rauche was the only building in the valley, and neither of these men ever did any hunting, so that the game was very tame, the only hunters being Indians, who did not trouble deer much when buffalo were so plentiful.

We moved camp into the Judith mountains, but found deer scarce, barely getting enough to supply us with food, though we were only about ten miles from where they had been so numerous. It is very curious how the game in this basin moves from range to range, being in one of them one year and in the next one the year after, though there is no apparent reason for the change. We went from this camp into the middle of the range, going up high and leaving our waggon at the bottom, and we put up our tent by a fine spring, which seemed a favourite drinking-place for bears, as their tracks were very numerous. This was a lovely spot, surrounded by peaks which were now covered with snow, and there was just room to picket out the two horses we had with us, the rest of them having been sent on to Reed's ranche in charge of one of the men. Here game was more plentiful than below, and we soon found a band of mountain-sheep and killed two of them. The meat was delicious, tasting like mutton with a wild flavour.

While after these sheep we came across a prospectors' camp, in which were three French Canadians. Two of them were those I met at Carroll, who had mistaken me for an Indian. They were doing badly here and wished themselves back in the Black Hills, and very soon after set off to return there.

Major Reed having told us that he was expecting the Bannock Indians on a visit to the Basin in about a fortnight's time, the Colonel and I determined to pay the ranche a visit and see them arrive. On our way we camped for dinner by a stream, which disappeared underground every few hundred yards, and yet was full of fine trout wherever it was visible. I had never seen a similar case, though our guide said they were common throughout the country, the soil being very sandy. In summer this stream was several feet deep, and is above ground its whole length, only sinking in the manner mentioned when the water gets low in the autumn. We reached the ranche in the evening and found Reed and Bowles at home, the latter being a big rough man, who had married a Blackfoot squaw, who kept house for them. The ranche consisted of a square stockade with large entrance gates, inside which were four or five small log cabins, one of which was the trading-store, another was for Bowles and his wife and Reed to live in, while the others were for strangers and for eating-rooms. The whole place was very untidy and dirty, a squaw having no idea of cleanliness. We were shown into the one meant for passing travellers, where there was a bed and two home-made chairs with raw-hide seats. The floor was earth and the fire was made on it, the smoke going out through a hole in the roof, most of it, however, remaining in the room, so that you had to sit on the floor to breathe.

The Bannocks were camped about three miles away and would be in to-morrow, so that we had come just in time, the chief having been already to the ranche to make arrangements. Near the stockade were the tents of about twenty Crow Indians, who were very busy getting themselves up to meet the Bannocks, putting on all their finery, and giving their faces another coat of paint. We went in the evening into some of their lodges and had a talk with them, Bowles doing interpreter. They seemed very nervous about the approaching meeting with the Bannocks, the two tribes having very recently been at war with each other, and peace had only been made that summer. They feared lest the Bannocks should take this opportunity of getting a few scalps, Indian ideas on the subject of the sacredness of a treaty being very vague, particularly when, as in this case, there were nine hundred Bannocks to the Crows' twenty.

I remained in one of the lodges after the others had left and lit one of those little pellets called Pharoah's serpents, out of which came something resembling a long white worm, causing a regular stampede—men, women, and children tumbling over one another in their hurry to get out of the lodge. In a few minutes a number of heads appeared, looking cautiously in at the door, and seeing that I was unhurt they gradually returned, and made me do it again and again, till I refused to light any more, wishing to keep a few for the Bannocks. On this the women surrounded me, and tried to get them from me by force, and I had quite a struggle to get

x

away, being pursued to the gate of the stockade, while all the men stood round and laughed.

In the morning we rode out with the Crows, forming a line when we came in sight of the Bannocks, who also did the same. Then the Crow chief and ourselves rode forward to meet the Bannock chief, whose name was Tendoi, and we all shook hands in a very friendly manner. This chief, of whom I saw a good deal later on, was a fine-looking Indian, with a good face, though his appearance was much spoiled by his wearing a battered high silk hat, of which he was very proud, and in the front of which he had put a red cockade. The Bannocks were, as a rule, finer men than the Crows, the latter were small and wiry, however, and as active as cats. After we had all shaken hands, Tendoi joined us, and we rode to a place about half a mile from the ranche, where he planted a small flag, and this meant that his wives, of whom he had three, should put up his lodge on that spot, the rest of the tribe erecting theirs so as to form a large circle, the spaces between the lodges being filled with brushwood. Into this the horses are brought at night, three or four of the younger Indians taking it in turn to act as horse-guard. Having seen the lodges put up we returned to the ranche, leaving word in camp that I wished to buy a good horse. I heard from Reed that more than half the tribe had gone on the warpath, taking most of the horses, so that there were not many for sale; but a big grey was brought for me to look at later in the day, which was much larger than the average Indian pony and very good-looking, which I bought for a Winchester rifle and fifty dollars (£10). I thought it odd that so many Indians came with the horse, and crowded round as I mounted, and I fancied, too, that as I rode off they looked disappointed; but the horse went so quietly that I thought no more of it, and rode him to camp that evening.

CHAPTER XXIII.

A nice-tempered horse.—A large band of elk.—Putting out baits for bears. The first a failure. The second a success.—Buy a new pony.—A good bargain.—Fishel goes for letters. Antelope-stalking.—A useless dog.—Fishel has his ponies stolen. He and I pay a visit to the Crow Indians.—A buffalo-run with the Crows.—The Indian game of " Hand."—A visit to the ranche.—Tendoi, the chief of the Bannocks. Stories of him.—Unpleasant quarters.—How Bowles got his wife.

On our return we moved camp to the end of the Judith range, hearing from Bowles that he had seen a good many bear-tracks there when cutting wood for the ranche about three weeks before.

We had brought our horses and man back with us and were soon comfortably established, and we made a capital dining-tent of an old waggon-cover which we had bought at the ranche.

The next morning the Colonel and I went hunting together, meaning to separate when we got into the mountains. It had been raining and I had put my rifle in its case, when seeing some very fresh deer-sign I pulled it out, and was holding it at arm's length, with the cover in the other hand, when the grey gave a tremendous buck, and being overbalanced by the rifle I came off, on which he turned deliberately round and lashed out twice at me, missing my head by a few inches only, and ending by going off to camp as fast as he could. The Colonel followed and brought him back, when I proceeded to give him a lesson with a young sapling, in the course of which there was some grand bucking done. I began to see now why the Indians had been willing to part with so good-looking a horse, and why they had been disappointed when he went off quietly.

Soon after this we separated, and I tied up my horse and began to climb the hill. I had brought a glass with me, as I wanted to see if I could find any sheep. It was a very rough climb as there was so much fallen timber in all these ranges, but about three hours' walking took me to the top, where the view was splendid. The Basin lay at my feet, looking much smaller than it really was, and I could see all the other six ranges quite plainly; but although I remained there about two hours and looked about carefully I saw no game, so I began to descend, coming down a different way, and was about halfway down, when on mounting a small rocky ridge I found myself among a large band of elk, which seemed to jump up all round me. I fired at one with a good head, and was then sorry I had been so hasty, as a grand bull galloped up out of a small hollow where he had been lying and passed me within thirty yards. It was horribly tempting, but I had already more meat than we could eat, so I let him go. The one I had killed had a very pretty head, the horns being perfect, but only about 47 inches long. I took as much meat as I could carry, fetching my horse from where I had left him, and I found that he had his good points, as he would carry anything that was put on him, even allowing me to take home the head across the saddle, and I do not know anything more awkward to carry.

The Colonel came in late bringing one deer, and he told me that he had killed three more for bear-baits, a useless waste of meat, as a bear always carries away a deer, and you see no more of him. The remains of the elk would make a capital bait, being too large to carry far, and would last for several days. I returned to it on the second day, and found that a bear had been there, and after eating what it wanted, had covered the body up most carefully, the skin, which I had taken partly off, was put back again, and the edges were fastened to the ground with mud, plastered smoothly down, the legs being entirely covered with mud also. It looked almost as if someone had done it with a trowel, and one could not fancy the clumsy paw of a bear doing it so neatly.

The next night the Colonel and I watched by the bait, going about an hour before the moon rose, as we always found that their favourite time for coming was within half an hour of its rising; and we had not been there much more than fifteen minutes when we heard some animal coming through the bushes behind us, but unfortunately down wind, so that almost immediately there was a sound something like a sneeze, and the animal made off again faster than it had come. It was of no use waiting any longer, so we returned to camp. When we went to the place in the morning, we found that a large bear had come within twenty yards of us and had then winded us and made off. I examined the place and found a high rock which overlooked the bait, so I went early the following night and lay down on the top of the rock, taking a blanket with me as the nights were very cold. This time the bear was late, and did not arrive till the moon was so high that I feared he would see me, but he came from the opposite side, and the bushes were very thick right up to the bait. He seemed to stand on the edge of these for some time, during which I flattened myself on the top of the rock as much as I possibly could, and then out came his head, his body following very slowly. I waited until he stood well in the light, about thirty yards from me, when I fired at his head under the ear, and he sank at the shot and hardly moved again. This was a very fine bear with a splendid coat, the hair on the crest was fully six inches long and very thick, and the colour black, tipped with grey. I only opened him that night, returning in the morning with Fishel to skin him, when we found that he measured seven feet eleven inches before he was skinned, and we estimated his weight at nine hundred pounds, as he was not very fat.

One day while we were at breakfast in camp we heard a loud hail, and saw a man, whose face seemed all hair, holding a pony by the bridle and calling to us from the top of a ridge, apparently not caring to come down till he knew that he would be welcome. He proved to be a French Canadian, who had arrived at the prospectors' camp at the Black hills after they had left it, so he had come to us for information as to their whereabouts. We told him that they had done nothing and had returned, so that he must have passed them as he came to us. He decided to go on to some mines near Fort Benton, and left us after having a meal. Before he left I exchanged one of my ponies for his, giving him some money as well, and it turned out one of the best and toughest little animals I ever sat on, though it had almost as much hair on it as its late master. I have on several occasions returned to camp with one deer in front of the saddle and another behind, sitting myself in the middle, and he jogged along for miles with this load, apparently making nothing of it.

We had received no letters since leaving Carroll, so we sent Fishel to a place called Martinsdale about eighty miles off, where there was a post-office kept by a brother of Colonel Clendenin's, to which we had directed our letters to be sent. Fishel thought that he could do it in two days, returning in three, and he took two good ponies of his own as we needed a few stores at the same time.

During his absence we went in a good deal for fishing, and caught some trout over three pounds in weight, and we threw in all under a pound. Game was so plentiful that we could only hunt twice a week, and used to explore the mountains or fish on the other days. One day we thought we would vary our sport by having a day's antelope-stalking, Symonds following us in the distance with his dog, in case we wounded any. We had some miles to ride as they very seldom came near the timber, and at last saw a small band feeding on a very bare portion of the valley; the only way to get near them was to wade up a stream which ran within about two hundred yards of them. We left our ponies in charge of Symonds and entered the stream, the banks of which were only about three feet high and the water very cold. Walking against a strong stream in nearly two feet of iced water was not very pleasant, especially when you had to double yourself up to keep below the bank; and my companion soon gave it up, so I kept on by myself, getting at last within about three hundred yards, too far for a hollow bullet from an express rifle, so I waited, hoping that they might feed a little nearer. Finding my feet becoming numbed with the cold, I determined to risk a shot, so making a rest of my soft hat and putting up the two hundred yards sight, I aimed high and fired at a fine buck, standing nearly broadside on. He was evidently hit with the first barrel, and the second bullet passed just over his back, but he went off well, going so as to pass near where we had left the horses and dog; I ran as fast as I could, shouting to Symonds to let the dog go, but on our leaving him he had lain down and gone to sleep, leaving the horses, which were fortunately tied together, to look after themselves, and it was only when I was close by that he woke, and seemed to take in the state of affairs when it was too late. I mounted, and calling the dog galloped in the direction which the antelope had taken, sighting him at last half a mile away, and managed to get the dog to see him also, when away he went, I keeping as near as I could on my hairy pony. The start given to the antelope was too long a one, but the dog went up fast, as the buck was evidently crippled, and very soon he was alongside, barking but not daring to catch hold. I gained slowly, and when within two hundred yards I jumped off and fired twice, but missed, and had a very long gallop before I got near again, hitting him, however, this time with a bullet in the hind quarters, which tore one ham nearly to pieces. It had been a gallop of about four miles, and my new purchase had gone well, being by no means fast but lasting splendidly.

Fishel returned on the sixth day, but astonished us very much by arriving on a miserable rat of an Indian pony leading another, both of his having been stolen by Indians on the night of his arrival. This was very bad luck as they were both of them good shooting-ponies, well trained to stand fire and to remain where they were left. When getting off to stalk any animal, the usual way to ensure your pony's being there when you return, supposing him to be used to hunting, is to throw your reins on the ground, when he will go on feeding till he treads on them, and he will then remain on that spot for hours.

Fishel said that the thieves were supposed to be Crows on their way to the large Crow camp, about fifty miles from us, so he and I determined to ride there and try and recover them, as the Crows were friendly. We started the following morning, the Colonel saying that he would move camp in our absence to the foot of the Little Snowies, a range lying next to the Judiths. We were a day and a half doing the fifty miles, as the ground was rough and a good many streams had to be crossed. I rode my grey and Fishel the hairy pony, which I christened "Brownie," and we took my third pony to pack. Early on the second day we overtook about twenty Indians going our way, and thought that perhaps they might be the thieves, but on coming up with them, we found that they were a party of Bannocks going to the Crow camp to buy horses, and having seen me with their chief they were very friendly. On reaching the Crow camp, where there were about twelve hundred warriors, we were given a lodge, and a quantity of buffalo-meat was sent to it for our use. We went to see the chief, whose name was "Spotted Bear," in the evening and told him why we had come, and he promised to ride with us to the horse-band in the morning, as the grass being all eaten near the camp, they were several miles away under the charge of a guard.

He said that the buffaloes were very plentiful near the camp, and offered us horses if we cared to have a run, which offer I accepted, Fishel preferring to go to the horse-camp, which he could do just as well alone. In the morning I found a wild-looking animal waiting for me outside the lodge in charge of an urchin about five years old, and almost as wild as the horse. These little fellows, though their legs stick out straight and they can get no grip, will ride any horse in camp, and are frequently sent out to bring in a band of them, turning their own rapidly in any direction to head a horse off which tries to escape. I found that about a hundred Indians were going with me, and that we were under the orders of a sub-chief, with whom I rode. We were some hours finding cows and calves, passing a good many old bulls, but at last came upon a large band, and when they began to run, the word was given, and with a wild yell away went all the Indians, I doing my best to keep a good place. I had a pair of sharp spurs or I should have been nowhere, as an Indian pony will not go for a white man without them, and even then I found that I must content myself with a "back seat" as they had given me a slow one, so I waited till the band was separated, and then took after two cows and a calf which had gone off at right angles to the others, all the Indians having left me. I followed the buffaloes into a narrow side valley and gradually crept up to them till I was almost alongside, when round they both came and charged, defending the calf. I fired and hit one of them in the neck as she came on but did not stop her, and had to gallop some way to get rid of her, giving her another shot behind the fore leg, about a foot above the brisket, when she fell. I then turned my attention to the others, which were by this time a quarter of a mile ahead, and a gallop of a mile put me once more alongside, when I shot the calf, letting the second cow go as my pony was nearly done.

After taking the two tongues, I rode back the way I had come, meeting some of the Crows coming to look for me, thinking I was a "tenderfoot" and should lose myself. I told them where my two buffaloes were, and they said that the women would come out the next day and take the meat to camp. On our return I found Fishel in the lodge, having just come back from the horse-camp, where he had not found his ponies, though he said that he was sure that they had been there when we arrived, from some words spoken by the Indians on their way to the horse-camp that morning, which he had understood. An Indian's morality on the subject of stealing generally, and especially stealing horses, is very lax, one of the best Indians I ever knew telling me "that him no wrong to steal, him only wrong to be found out." When you catch them in the act they will only laugh, as if it were a good joke, and are not in the least ashamed of themselves. There was nothing to be done but to make the best of it, though we felt inclined to try and run off a few of their ponies when we left.

That evening we went to an Indian's lodge to see them play their favourite game of "Hand." The game consists in holding a shell in one hand, then placing both hands under a buffalo-robe, which is lying in front of all the players, who kneel in a circle, moving the hands about rapidly, changing the shell from one to the other and then holding them both up closed, your adversary having to say in which of them the shell is, losing a peg if he is wrong. A row of pegs stands in front of each man, who either takes one from or gives one to his opponent according to his loss or gain. These pegs represent so much, and everything an Indian possesses is valued at so many pegs—a wife so many, a horse so many, and so on. An Indian will frequently lose all he has in one evening —wife, children, horses, and lodge—and will leave with nothing but what he stands up in, when his friends will lend him a gun and some ammunition, with which he will in time get skins enough to fit himself out again. Many of those present lost heavily on this occasion, but they all took it very quietly, and you could not tell from their faces whether they were winning or losing. I was told that when a man lost his wife and children they generally went to the lodge of the winner without showing any feeling at all.

In the morning the chief got up some horse-racing, of which all Indians are passionately fond, and many white men make a small fortune by going among them with a fast horse, winning any number of ponies, buffalo-robes, deer-skins, &c. The Indians, however, are very good judges of a race pony, and will refuse to run any which they think too fast for theirs.

We only remained two days in the camp, and then set out to return, getting as far as the foot of the Judiths by nightfall, and as we travelled fast we reached our last camp by the middle of the next day, and by following the waggon-trail we found the fresh camp—pitched at the head of Great Spring Creek, the largest stream in the Basin, which rises in the Snowies. We found the Colonel just on the point of moving again, as he had discovered a place high up in the mountains where game of all kind seemed very plentiful, bear-sign especially being very thick. There were, he said, large thickets of wild raspberries and blueberries, of which the bears are very fond, and round some of these the ground was trampled by them like a sheep-pen.

As Fishel had directed any letters coming to Martinsdale to be forwarded to Reed's ranche, I determined to leave the others to move camp while I rode to the ranche and got our letters. On getting in I found two very rough men staying on their way from Carroll to Bozeman. They were Indian traders, and had brought a quantity of the vile stuff which is sold by them as whiskey, and this they had all been drinking for some days, and were more than half drunk when I arrived. My letters had not come, so that I had to wait for them, and I passed most of my time with Tendoi in the Bannock camp, a good Indian being a preferable companion to such men as there were at the ranche. The chief and I got to be such friends that he lent me his war-horse, a fine roan of about fifteen hands, to ride, which was a great favour.

I heard a story of Tendoi which shows what kind of man he was. When the tribe some months before had held a council as to whether they should go on the war-path or not, and more than half had decided to do so, Tendoi and his son had gone in the night and had warned all the neighbouring settlers, who in their turn had warned others, so that when the hostiles had visited their ranches the owners had fled, and the intended massacre did not take place. They risked a great deal in doing this, for had it become known they would probably have been killed, fully three quarters of the tribe having joined Peggee, the war-chief, against Tendoi's orders.

I slept in his lodge one night and he lent me some buffalo-robes, and I am sorry to say that it took me several days to get rid of what he supplied me with. I tried to induce him to give up wearing the high hat, but could not succeed in doing so; it had been smashed several times, and I took it off his head and sat on it, telling him that he was a fine Indian without it, and a scarecrow with it on. This last word, however, he did not understand, but replied: "Me like um, me; a good white man give um, and me wear um;" and he did not mind my having sat on it in the least.

Bowles told me another story of him, showing how unlike most Indians he was. On a former visit to the Judith Basin, one of his men had hidden himself in the stockade one night before the gates were closed, and waiting until everyone was asleep he cut out the parchment, which formed the window of the trading-store, and began to get in. Bowles happened to be sleeping there that night, and the noise waking him he fired, killing the Indian so instantly that he remained half in and half out of the window. Knowing that the man's relations would make a blood-feud of it, and that unless something could be done at once to prevent it he was as good as dead, he went to Tendoi and related what had happened. The chief told him to bury the man and that he would put the matter straight; so early in the morning he summoned all the Indians in camp to a council, and when they were all assembled he stood up and told them that a member of the tribe had disgraced it by trying to rob a friend of their chief's, that he was dead, and that from that time his name must be forgotten and no revenge taken for his death. He then mentioned the man's name, and said that if anyone disobeyed him he would kill that man; and nothing more was heard of the matter.

As I did not care to remain a second night in camp I returned to the ranche, and found everyone there drunk as usual and very noisy. The cabin in which we had to sit was not more than sixteen feet by twelve, and four drunken men nearly filled it, so when bed-time came I asked Bowles where I could sleep, and was told to lay my blankets in a corner or take the bed, whichever I preferred. Now there was no sign that the drinking was at an end, and it was more than likely to finish up with a fight, so I declined to occupy either of the places offered me, and said that I should sleep in the trading-store, the door of which opened out of the room we were in; on which Bowles replied that he allowed no one to sleep there. I saw that unless I was firm I must pass the night where I was, so I told him that of course I was not going to remain with them in their present state, and that I must have the key of the store at once, on which he gave it to me and I went in and locked the door after me, telling them that I hoped they would not try to come in during the night as I always fired through the door in a case of that kind. I knew the whiskey was in there and thought they might come in for a fresh supply, but though there was a great noise in the next room till far into the night, and some quarrelling, I was not disturbed.

In the store I found a large pile of buffalo-robes which made me a capital bed, though the flavour was a little too pronounced perhaps, as a good many of them were not dressed. In the morning I had a look round the store to see what it was that Bowles guarded so jealously, but found nothing but trumpery common beads and knives, brass wire, sham jewelry, packets of vermilion and blue paint in powder, and pots and pans, everything being of the commonest kind.

The men in the outer room were all asleep when I went in there, so I adjourned to the well, and was getting a fair substitute for a bath in a stable-bucket, when I found that Bowles's squaw was watching me, and I had to bolt, much to her amusement. This woman had come to the ranche with her husband, a Blackfoot warrior, who had three fine horses with him which he had stolen in the settlements. Bowles tried to buy them of him, and failing in this got up a quarrel and shot him over the counter of the trading-store, taking his horses and his squaw, the latter being very well pleased with her change of masters. Reed told me this story, and took me outside to show me the Indian's grave, seeming to think nothing of it, no one in that country looking on an Indian as a human being, but as something little better than a wolf.

The food at the ranche was very badly cooked and very dirty, so I broiled myself some buffalo-steaks for dinner and supper, which helped to pass the time. I had to pass two more days there, as the Government courier was delayed and the mail nearly a week later than usual; and we found when he arrived that this was because his horses had been stolen when one day's journey from Martinsdale, so that he had to walk into that place, carrying the mails on his back, to get more horses to continue his journey.

Y

CHAPTER XXIV.

Reed shoots a grizzly bear!—A splendid hunting-ground.—Wholesale massacre of deer.—The Colonel shoots a grizzly. I get one the next night.—Another bear.—Tendoi pays us a visit. His appreciation of curry.—Suspicious tracks.—Horse-thieves. Expedition to destroy them.—Horses stampeded. The cause.—Fishel and I go to see the Crow war-dance.—Crow sham fight.—Foolish freak of an Englishman.—The war-dance. Unpleasant reflections thereat.

As soon as I got our letters I started for camp, very thankful to get away from such a place. Reed had been ill most of the time, so that I had seen very little of him. He had taken to drinking again, the ginger not satisfying him for long. He told me, during a sober interval, that he had been into Martinsdale since I saw him last, and that, on his way back, he had had to camp out one night without a tent, and that during the night, happening to awake, he had looked up and seen what he took to be an immense bear standing on the opposite side of the fire; so he snatched up his rifle and fired at it, and it fell, and when he went to see what it was, he found he had shot his favourite horse. He was always on the verge of D. T., so that his mistaking a horse for a bear was not to be wondered at.

I slept at our old camp on Spring Creek that night, and reached the new one by the afternoon of the next day, and found the Colonel had just come in from a hunt, and very enthusiastic about the amount of game in this place which he had discovered. He had seen two bands of elk that morning and no end of deer; bear-sign, too, was everywhere. The men said that they had heard elk close to the tent in the night, so that things looked very promising. The camp had been pitched on a beautiful spot, a small plateau at the foot of the Snowy Range about six thousand feet above, and with a view over the greater portion of the Judith Basin. The mountains behind us were a long line of jagged peaks, rising out of dense pine-forests. The Colonel took me to a point close by and showed me a band of elk feeding, before I had been ten minutes in camp; and on my way to where they were we jumped three small bands of blacktails. I got one of the elk after a very easy stalk, and three deer on my way back, taking all the meat into camp, as I had asked Tendoi to come and see us, and knew that he would be glad of it. I never saw so many deer as there were here; we often jumped them when going to picket the horses, within a quarter of a mile of the tent, and found fresh tracks in the snow almost every morning, where they had been even nearer than that. One day, when out with Fishel, we passed a tumble-down cabin, Fishel remarking that this was where the "greenhorns" wintered, and when I asked him what he meant, he told me that two years before, deer-skins being then worth more than usual, he and a partner had wintered in these mountains, skin-hunting, and had good luck, getting more than thirteen hundred deer; and that, hearing of this, two other men came and put up a cabin near them, but had made a failure of it, only killing about four hundred deer and hardly paying their expenses. So that the four men had actually killed more than seventeen hundred black- and white-tailed deer for their skins alone, beside all those they wounded and did not get. Since then deer-skins had become of so little value as to be not worth taking off, fifteenpence being the outside price, and the deer were as plentiful as ever.

We put a bear-bait about four hundred yards from camp, in a small ravine with precipitous sides, fastening three deer to a strong rope and staking them down just under a large rock, which made a grand place to shoot from, being about twenty feet above the bait. Bears do not care for meat until it is high, so that for several days none came; but at last we found that one big one had supped there, so we tossed up for first chance, and the Colonel won, so he and Fishel went about half an hour before the moon rose and took up a position on the rock. We sat round the fire and waited, and about half an hour after they left we heard the Colonel's rifle, and then two loud reports, made by my ten-bore shot-gun, which Fishel had taken loaded with buckshot. Half an hour later they returned, having killed a fine grizzly, which, on skinning it the next morning, had, we found, a ball between the shoulders, passing close to the heart, and seven buckshot in the head, about enough for any bear, I fancy.

The next night the waggon-driver and I went out, and had an hour to wait, when, although we heard nothing come, we saw something grey moving on the bait, so we both fired together, and there was a great commotion, earth and stones flying in all directions for a few moments, after which all was still, and on descending we found that we had got a fair-sized bear, with a beautiful skin, one ball having taken him in the hind quarters and one breaking the spine in the middle of the back. This firing from above is very deadly, and we never failed to get a bear hit in this way. The Colonel went the following night, and got a third bear, after which they got shy, and did not come to the bait again while we remained there.

We were going to dinner one day when Tendoi and one of his men, who acted as a kind of *aide-de-camp*, rode into camp, and were very much astonished to see four large bear-skins pegged out round the tent, as the killing of a grizzly entitled an Indian to call himself a warrior and ranked with the taking of a scalp. Of course they stayed for dinner, for which we happened to have made a large curry, a thing which neither of them had ever tasted before, and with which Tendoi was delighted, taking eleven helpings, though his companion did not like it. Tendoi told me that he had never eaten anything so good in his life, and after he had finished he sat against the waggon-wheel patting himself and saying, "Me feel heap a good, me!" and then he called me and, patting me on the back, held up two fingers, and told me that they represented himself and myself who were two brothers, adding that if anyone hurt me he would kill him, or, as he put it, "Me kill um, me!" Before leaving us Tendoi told us that the Crows were coming to his camp to dance the war-dance, and that he hoped we would come and stay with him and see it, which I promised to do, the Colonel preferring to remain in camp, having a great dread of an Indian lodge, the smaller occupants of it having a particular liking for him, and refusing to leave when once they had paid him a visit. I have said very little of Symonds, as he never accompanied us on our excursions, passing his time fishing or reading, and wondering how we could find any pleasure in camp-life.

Some days before Tendoi's arrival we had found some fresh moccasin trails in a small valley running at right angles to the one in which we were, so we asked him whether they were made by any of his men, and he assured us that they could not have been made by any of the friendly portion of the tribe, as none of them had, at that time, been out hunting, but that Indians were always going between his camp and the hostiles, and that some of these might have passed near us; and he assured us that when it was known that we were his friends, we need not fear for ourselves or horses. We heard afterwards from Bowles that the tracks we had found were made by some of a party of horse-thieves—white men and Indians—who were camped in the big Snowies, the next range to the one we were in. These men had been stealing horses from both whites and Indians for some months, and, shortly after we had left the Basin, a mixed party was sent against them, Tendoi and some of his men joining it. The horse-thieves were surprised, but fought well, most of them being killed, and a number of horses were recovered; however, Fishel's two were not among them. We heard nothing of such an expedition before we left, or we should have remained longer and joined it. From this time we always brought the horses in at night, picketing them near the waggon, this being always the difficulty when remaining long in one camp, as each horse has sixty feet of rope, and all the grass near camp is soon eaten off, consequently some of our horses had to be picketed a quarter of a mile away.

One night, after we had turned in, we heard horses galloping, and then a number of them went by the tent at full speed. I jumped out of bed, caught up my rifle, and was away after them in a moment, forgetting that I had nothing on but a shirt, and shouted to the men to follow me. I ran some way down the valley, crouching now and then, but could see nothing as it was very dark; so, after going about a quarter of a mile, I turned back, meeting the men on the way. We talked the matter over and decided that they had been stampeded by some animal, as, had it been Indians, we should have heard them, and in any case nothing could be done till morning, so we returned to the tents, my feet being a good deal cut by the rough ground and my legs by the thorns. On going into the tent I found the Colonel in bed, his idea being that, as they were gone, it was too late to do anything. In the morning we found that all had gone but the Colonel's pony, which he had happened to picket away from the others in a small side valley. We trailed up the others, and found them all tied in the brush about four miles from camp. They had galloped some miles, and had then begun to feed, soon tying the sixty feet of rope, which each had fastened to his headstall, round the bushes.

We had, a few days later, an opportunity of seeing how it originated, and found that it was all owing to my grey horse, which had evidently been brought up in a bad school. He would walk up to his picket-pin, shake the rope which was round his neck as low as possible, and then, putting down his head, he would go off at full speed, not seeming to mind being thrown down when he came to the end of his rope, for he would try it again till he had pulled the picket-pin out, when he would go off to the nearest horse and gallop round him, winding him up in the rope, and throwing him, the result being that he would get up and rush off, tearing up his pin, the grey going on to one after another until he had them all loose. I tried tying his rope to a halter, but he would still manage it, so I made a fetlock-strap and tied it to that when I had him, and he never got away afterwards.

It was now time to go to Tendoi's camp for the dance, so Fishel and I started, meaning to remain away five or six days. We got to the camp the same night, and Tendoi seemed glad to see us, and set apart a portion of his lodge for our use; and this time we had brought our own blankets, and had the lodge well swept out and fresh pine-boughs put down before making our beds.

The war-dance was coming off the next day, so we passed the interval in going round among the lodges, making the acquaintance of the principal Indians, and had to eat something in each tepe and smoke in most of them. The Crows had erected their lodges close to those of the Bannocks, and we went to see them also, finding them very busy painting one another for the dance, the toilet taking a full day. One of them had white rings round his eyes, and a white line following each rib, while another had red and black stripes running side by side the whole length of his body, no two Indians being alike. The squaws seemed as proud as their husbands in this dress, or rather undress, as a lady in civilization might be to see hers in a general's uniform. The following day the Crows got up a sham fight in our honour, forming sides and using Winchester rifles and knives. The fighting-ground was in the centre of the Bannock camp, a circle about a hundred and fifty yards in diameter; and here the fight was so furious and they got so excited that one might very easily have fancied it real. They charged one another, yelling their war-whoop, firing in the air as they came on, and then closed and wrestled on horseback, showing us some very fine riding; and the horses seemed to enter into the spirit of the thing quite as much as their riders. Most of them rode bare-backed and yet clung as if glued on, one of them being every now and then taken from his horse and carried off, when he was supposed to be scalped and out of the fight. It lasted about an hour, and no one seemed a bit the worse for it, though there were some bad falls and some very hard knocks given.

I went to the ranche and found Bowles and Reed at home, and for a wonder sober, so I stayed and had a long talk, and Reed told me of a very foolish thing which had been done by an Englishman the previous year on this spot. It seems that early in the spring the great chief of the Crows, "White Horse," had died, and, according to the custom of the tribe, he had been doubled up and put in a box, which had been placed on a stage close to the stockade, the only departure from the usual custom being in this case the use of a box, the bodies usually being merely wrapped in blankets. An Englishman passed through the valley during the autumn, and tried to buy the head of the chief as a curiosity; but of course the Indians were horrified at the idea, and refused at once, putting a guard on the grave. In some way the Englishman managed to elude the guard and steal the head, going off at once to Benton, whence he took the head to England. When it was found out that the head was gone, the indignation and horror of the Crows may be imagined, as, according to their belief, their late chief could never go to the "happy hunting-grounds," and it very nearly led to a rising of the tribe against the whites, and this was only averted by their agent saying that he would get the head restored; and some months afterwards he produced a head which he said was the same, and it was replaced in the box, and the Crows quieted down: the truth, however, being that the head came from another agency where the Indians buried their dead, and where this head had been dug up.

In the evening the dance came off. Fishel and I went rather late, so that by the time we got to a large tepe in which it was being held there was an immense crowd of Bannocks—men, women, and children—round the door. Tendoi had refused to attend, as he said that many of the hostiles would be present, and as they had disobeyed him he did not care to meet them. We pushed our way towards the door, and had just reached it, when an Indian took me by the wrist and, pulling me out of the crowd, said something to me in Bannock, which I of course did not understand, so I told him I was Tendoi's brother, having learned that much of their language on purpose, and this seemed to satisfy him and he let me go. I had my hand on my revolver, and could easily have shot him had he tried to injure me. On reaching the door again I found that Fishel had got us two places against the side of the tepe, the inside of which presented a curious spectacle. Round against the sides were squatted three rows of Indians, one in front of the other, as close as they could be made to go, while the Crows were dancing round a large fire in the centre, swinging their tomahawks in their right hands and holding knives in their left. Each man was given a chance of telling his exploits, the others joining in now and then with a loud note of praise, when any more than usually daring deed was recounted, and at the end of each man's recital all of them sang a sort of war-chant, striking with their tomahawks and using their knives as if scalping an enemy, dancing furiously in the meanwhile; and this went on till every man had made the most of his warlike deeds, when some whiskey which had been got from the ranche was handed round, and we then left, though we could hear them singing and shouting most of the night.

It gave one a very curious feeling to think that many of those present were declared enemies of the whites, and had probably been committing atrocities within the last few days, and that if they met us anywhere else they would attack us at once. I mentioned to Tendoi on our return what had happened to me, on which he said, "You safey; you my white brother!" and I really think that he would have killed the man who tried to kill me.

CHAPTER XXV.

Symonds leaves us.—I explore the Little Snowies.—Follow the trail of a grizzly.—Try to get back to camp.—A difficult road.—A fine view.—Plenty of game.—I enjoy a siesta.—An alarming awakening.—Peculiar rocks.—Mountain-sheep.—I bag a grizzly.—Good sport.—Meet a party of white men.—The Greenhorn.—Attempt to lasso the grey.—Indian attack defeated by Greenhorn.—Stories of grizzlies.—Sheep-ranches.

WHILE I was in Tendoi's camp, a lot of freight-waggons stopped at the ranche, on their way to Butte city, and it struck me that this would be a good opportunity for Symonds, who wished to go there; so I persuaded the "Boss" to wait a day or two, while I returned to camp and brought him back with me. I found Symonds very ready to go; camp-life was intolerably dull to one who had no taste for sport of any kind, and who was continually longing for a town. We parted good friends, although we had not fraternized much. I arranged for him to sleep in one of the waggons, and paid for his food as far as Butte, and we induced him to take the greyhound with him, as it had only been in our way, requiring to be tied up when we went out hunting, and often howling in the night, which might have brought the Indians on us.

A few days after getting back to camp I made up my mind

to explore the Little Snowies, making a tour of the range, and going up any likely-looking valleys which I might come across. I got the cook to make me enough camp bread for a week, and taking two blankets, a coat, and a few camp necessaries, I started due east, keeping well in the range and crossing numerous ridges and ravines. I do not think any kind of hunting comes up to the pleasure and excitement of these solitary rambles, where in many cases you carry your life in your hand, and rely for your daily food on your rifle, and never know from minute to minute what may turn up.

I passed some beautiful places for camps, and jumped a great many deer the first day, and came across one small bear, but it saw me first and made off up the mountain, and I let it go, as the ground was almost impassable. My first camp was in a pretty ravine at a spring, where I put up a rough shelter and made a fire, as the weather was very cold and there were several inches of snow on the ground. I was so far up in the mountains that no wolves came to serenade me, which was a great relief, for their howling is a very melancholy sound when you have no one to talk to. I rode Brownie, and a good companion he proved, coming and standing by me at the camp-fire, now and then rubbing his head against me. I never tied him up after the first night, and he was always somewhere near in the morning. I had trained him to stand very still when I fired off him, and to remain wherever I left him, and he was so intelligent that he learnt very quickly. On the morning of the second day I came on the trail of a large bear and cub, and as there was a great deal of fallen timber, I dismounted, and having removed the saddle and bridle, I left the pony loose with a short rope on him, taking the bearings of the place very carefully—a most important thing to do in a mountainous region, where the country is all so much alike. The trail led me over two high ridges straight for the top of the range, and I came then upon a very deep ravine, with almost precipitous sides, on the other side of which was the main range. I was by this time somewhat weary, for the ground was not only covered with fallen trees, but these were partially hidden under the snow, so that I was continually tripping and falling, so I sat down and ate some of my bread, and rested until I was too cold to remain any longer, when I began to descend, and found even this very difficult, as the ground was loose shale, which gave way continually, so that I slid down most of the way. The bottom of the ravine was one mass of fallen rocks and trees, and I made sure that I should find the bear in her lair under these, as the opposite cliff was almost perpendicular and looked impassable; but when I reached the bottom I found that she had gone straight up, and as it was shale and much steeper than the other side, I gave it up and tried to climb the side I had come down. This I found I could not do, as after getting up some yards, the shale would slip from under me in a mass, carrying the snow with it, and down I went. Finding I could not manage it, I made my way along the bottom, and the going was simply awful, for the rocks were piled up to a height of from ten to thirty feet. I tried several times to get up the side lower down, but always fell back again, and it ended by my having to scramble along that horrible ravine for more than three hours, feeling sometimes so utterly done that nothing but the certainty of being frozen to death if I remained where I was kept me going. At last I got to where the ravine ran out into the plain, and as it was now long after sunset, I had to walk about waiting for the moon to rise, before I could make my way to where I had left the pony. Fortunately I had marked this so well, that I found it even by moonlight. After this I never went without matches in my pocket, instead of in my saddle-bag, where they were on this occasion. Had I had them I should have camped for the night in the ravine, where there was any amount of wood. As it was I did not reach the pony till nearly ten o'clock, and I camped within a few yards of where I had left him, and ate an enormous supper, having only had a small piece of bread since the morning. Brownie seemed to be quite glad to see me, neighing when he first heard me and coming a short distance to meet me.

The next day I reached the end of the range, and had a fine view of the country away towards the Mussel-shell river, a distance of about twenty miles. There were several small bands of buffalo in sight, and one old fellow was just at the edge of the timber below me, but I must have wasted all the meat, so I would not kill him. There were not so many tracks of bears here as near our camp, as the berries were scarce, owing to the country having been recently burnt. That morning I shot a young black-tailed deer for meat and also a wild cat, using a solid ball. Deer were very plentiful, and so tame that one lot of five would not go away though I was within seventy yards of them, and I had to shout and throw up my hat to startle them.

I was now on the opposite side of the range to that on which our camp lay, and where the scenery was not nearly so beautiful, as the mountains came down very abruptly on my side, and there was much less broken ground at their base, and I had to ride along in the open. It was very hot in the sun in spite of the snow, so after my mid-day meal I thought I would take a siesta, and finding a very large fallen tree, which lay at a convenient angle, I lay down on it, and stood my rifle against the tree close to me; but it was not comfortable where I was, so I moved to the other end of the log, about forty feet away, forgetting to take my rifle with me, and soon fell asleep with my blanket over me. I must have slept for some time, when I was awoke by a noise, and, looking up, saw a row of shining copper-coloured faces round me, some of them being within two feet of mine. I do not think I was ever so startled in my life; but an instant's reflection showed me that I must pretend to be cool, so I raised myself on one elbow and held out my right hand, and all of them came forward and shook it. Then I got up slowly and strolled towards my rifle, feeling more comfortable when I had it in my hands. I feared that they might be one of the hostile bands of Bannocks, who were out under Peggee, but they turned out to be Crows from the large camp, and some of them knew me, from having seen me when there with Fishel, when looking for his stolen horses. They had plenty of meat with them, and I had to sit down and eat some of it, although I had already dined, or they would have been offended; so that it was nearly four o'clock in the afternoon before I got off, and I camped that night on the prairie, where there was a beautiful spring and good food for the pony. The change had done him good, and, in spite of the weight he had to carry, he was much fatter than when I started; the grass was brown, but it is a peculiarity of Montana that the hay cures without being cut, and will fatten a horse quickly long after it has lost its colour.

The next day I reached the other end of the Range, and turned the corner towards our camp, having a rather curious

Page 336.—I saw a row of shining copper-coloured faces.

experience. I was riding late in the afternoon, and had just passed a small band of elk, when I came to what looked like the remains of an enormous gateway. It was the entrance to a small valley, running up towards the main ridge, and the rocks on each side were so perpendicular as to be exactly like the remains of a work done by the hands of man; I thought I would see where the valley went to, so, getting off my pony, I led him up a narrow deer-path, through pines and brushwood, and after going a hundred yards, I came out into a small oval prairie, having in the middle what at first resembled the remains of a very high church-tower, and I began to think I had got among some gigantic ruins, which had not yet been discovered by anyone else. A second look, however, showed breaks in the outline, but it was still an extraordinary rock, standing as it did nearly in the middle of the prairie. It must have been two hundred feet high and about four feet wide, retaining this width to the top. About halfway up was a hollow in the surface of the front, which might have been the hole where a clock had once been. There was splendid grass here, so I camped on one side of this rock, which, by the way, lost all resemblance to a tower when seen from the side.

My usual camp on that trip was a mackintosh sheet put up as a lean-to, in front of which I lit a fire, and when I took the trouble to put about six inches of small pine-boughs under the sheet, it was a first-rate bed and shelter. An equally good and much lighter one can be made of a large sheet of common cotton-drill, and if stretched properly it is nearly as waterproof. I remained in this camp two nights, and found lots of game, and I think I could have killed twenty or thirty deer a day had I wished to do so. On the second day I climbed the main ridge on foot, starting early, and had barely reached the top when I saw three mountain-sheep. They were on a lower ridge on the other side, and a long way off, but the wind was right, and I determined to try for one of them. I had a very steep descent of four hundred feet, and some rocky ravines to cross, then came a climb, where I had to use my hands as well, after which it was all crawling, and I managed to get within a hundred and twenty yards of them, when I saw they were two sheep and a young ram, with well formed but short horns. I had pushed the safety-bolts of my rifle forward, and now, as I thought, drew them back; but when I tried to full cock the hammers, I found that I could not do so, and I took my knife-handle to push the bolts further, when off went the right barrel, and the sheep did the same, and I had my long scramble for nothing. On my way back I shot a deer, choosing one which I started close to the valley, so that I could come again for more of the meat.

On the morning of the next day I was off again, being now, I calculated, only one day's journey from camp, and I was riding down a ravine when I saw an immense bear coming up it. I jumped off at once and got behind my pony, hoping that the bear had not seen me, but he had done so, and turned up a side ravine. Leaving my pony I crossed two small ridges which lay between me and the ravine he was in, and arrived just in time to see him go into a thick patch of dead thorn bushes. These, as I have said before, are very common in that part of the Montana; fire at some time has killed them, and the bark has come off and the wood become very hard, but the thorns remain as sharp as ever, creepers grow over them, and they are a very favourite lair for bears. This patch was about sixty yards long by about half as wide, and by standing on the hill above I could easily see if anything left it. Here I stationed myself, and the ground being stony, I began to throw in all the big ones I could find, now and then hearing a grunt and seeing the bushes move, which showed that I had gone near him. This went on for some time, and I was nearly out of big stones, when the bear broke cover on the opposite side and I gave him a shot from behind, when he rolled over backwards into the cover again. Almost all the bears I have shot have done this when hit, and until you know better you think you have made a splendid shot; the truth is, that they bite at the wound, and in doing so roll over, but are up again and off in an instant, unless the wound is really mortal. The bear now sulked, and stones were evidently of no use, so I had to make up my mind to go in and tackle him in his den. This was all the more awkward, as I had disabled one barrel of my rifle, the base of a brass cartridge having come off, leaving the remainder in the barrel. Had there been any spectators looking at me I think the task would have been easy, but I walked round the place and did not like the look of it at all. It was very thick, and to go in one would have to crawl, and be in a very awkward position for shooting as the bear charged. I fear I was a long time before I made up my mind to do it, and I then found the largest hole I could and began to creep in, pushing my rifle in front of me. I had got in perhaps twelve feet when I saw something moving up and down, and on looking closely, for the light was bad inside, I saw that it was the bear's jaw. He was evidently hit in the stomach, and was lying with his head on his paws breathing hard. I brought up my rifle, and aiming at the centre of his forehead fired, just as he was rising to charge me. The smoke hung so that I could see nothing, and thinking that perhaps I could see better outside, I retired in such haste that I left some skin and part of my clothing on the thorns. On getting outside and finding that the bear had not followed me, I allowed time for the smoke to clear away, and then went in again, and saw him lying in much the same position, and evidently dead. I had desperately hard work turning him over and opening him, as he was the largest bear I had yet killed; the thorns too were very dense, and it was almost impossible to cut them with a common butcher's knife; however I managed it at last, and having carefully taken the bearings of the place, and blazed several trees leading to it, I rode off towards camp, but did not get in till the next morning, as the bear-fight occupied some time.

I found that the Colonel had killed three bears, though none of them were as large as my last, and he had also had good sport with deer and elk. There were certainly more bears near our camp than anywhere in that range, and many more elk, and I have often noticed, as a very curious thing, that two parties of hunters will hunt the same range, some miles apart, and while one will have no sport at all, the other will have as much as they want.

One of the Colonel's bears had been killed in an unusual manner. He had seen the bear out in an open place, and by keeping behind him and walking very cautiously had got within thirty or forty yards, killing him at the first shot. At the beginning of the trip the Colonel used solid balls in a single Sharp's rifle, but seeing my express balls and the execution they did, he sent into Helena, the capital of Montana, and had an express mould made, and from that time used express balls with excellent results; his rifle was a ·45, with a charge of a hundred grains of powder, the accuracy being quite as good as with the proper bullet, which was a long conical one.

We remained in this camp another fortnight, getting three more bears, of which I shot two, and one of them was nearly as large as the one I have spoken of, the weight of which we calculated to be about eleven hundred pounds. The second large one I got when out on foot. I saw him enter some bushes, and having grown bold from seeing how many stones it took to dislodge the other, I walked very confidently to within four yards of the bushes and then threw in a large piece of rock. I suppose it must have gone very near the bear, if it did not actually hit him, for out he came at once; I had no time to raise the rifle, so I fired from the hip, both barrels at once, and then having business at the top of the hill which would admit of no delay, I made "capital time" for about a hundred yards, turning when near the top, and when my rifle was loaded, to find that the bear had not stirred, but was lying where I had fired at him, and yet I could have declared that he was smelling at the calves of my legs all the way up the hill. Both bullets had taken him in the top of the head, and he had died almost immediately.

A few days after this we left this camp for Martinsdale, going out of the mountains by a new way, and had very hard work to get the waggon across the numerous watercourses we met with, as our team was a weak one. The day we left we saw a grizzly bear feeding on the ridge on our right, so having halted the waggon, the Colonel and I tied up our horses and climbed the ridge, and on looking over the top we saw the bear feeding not more than fifty yards from us, with his head down in the long grass rooting. We fired together and he rolled over, dying in a few minutes, and we found that he was small, but had the best coat of any we had killed.

We stopped about three miles from the ranche, and found a party of men camped near us, who had been into Carroll for their winter supplies. One of them, who was a baker, was the butt of the party, and they were telling him of all the Indian atrocities that they could remember or invent, as he was a greenhorn and had only just come from the east. They moved their camp close to ours, and we remained a few days there, as the feed was good.

One day I was bringing in my grey horse, intending to ride him, when he managed to slip the rope over his head and gallop off. I got another horse and chased him, several of the men joining me, but he was so crafty that we could not catch him. He had evidently been lassoed before, and knew how to avoid the rope. When you thought you must have him, and had thrown the noose so that it fell just where his head should be, he immediately lowered it, and the rope slipped along his back, when he would raise his head again. Bowles happened to come into camp just as we were thinking of giving up the chase, and as he prided himself on his roping, he laughed at us, and asked us to let him do it, and of course we were only too glad. He started very confidently, and ran his horse down, trying to get his rope over, but without succeeding, and had to give it up at last, and we were obliged to drive the horse to the ranche, in the yard of which we roped him.

As our horses looked somewhat better we all started together, camping in the pass between the Little and Big Snowies the first night, and as we were to separate here, the other party tried to persuade us to pass another night, but being in a hurry to get our letters we left the next morning, a fortunate thing, as we heard afterwards, as on our arrival at Martinsdale we heard that the party we had just left had been attacked by the Indians that night, who had fired at the tent to frighten them, and had then tried to stampede their horses. But the greenhorn had frustrated the attempt by rushing out and firing rapidly at them with a repeating rifle, all the other men remaining in the tent. Had we been there we should probably have lost all our stock, as our horses were only picketed, while theirs were also hobbled. The Indians had cut the picket-ropes, but in the darkness had not noticed the hobbles, which prevented the horses from going off.

At Martinsdale we introduced ourselves to Mr. Clendenin, a brother of Colonel Clendenin, who owned one of the two houses of which the place was composed, and were hospitably entertained by him. Happening to speak of bears, he told us that he had just returned from a timber camp which he had in the mountains, and that while there a large bear had come into the camp one night, and opening the mess chest had eaten all the bread, sugar, and butter it contained, not attempting to touch anyone. He told us, too, that when his brother was on his way the year before between Benton and Berthold on horseback, two large grizzlies had come down close to his camp, where he and his companions were sitting by the fire, and had evidently wished to carry off a deer which was hanging up. They had only one small-bore rifle with them, which would only have irritated the bears without doing them much harm, so they did not fire, managing at last to drive them away with firebrands. This was in the winter, when the snow was deep and the bears savage from hunger. I heard of one which came into a cowshed, close against the back of a ranche, in broad daylight and carried off a calf. These, however, are exceptional cases, and although I have killed seventy-four grizzlies, most of them by myself, but some in company with other men, I have only had two of them charge me unprovoked, and one of these I all but rode over. They always seem to be in a great hurry to get away, though they will turn and fight if wounded and you are near them at the time.

We remained two days at Martinsdale, the whole talk being of sheep, which were then beginning to be introduced into that part of the country. When I visited the Judith Basin in 1884 I found the whole of it a mass of sheep-ranches, and not at all improved by the change, a sheep-ranche being a very unpleasant place to stop at, the immense number of sheep tainting the whole air. Soon after I left, on that occasion, began what was almost a war between the cattle and the sheep men, the one industry interfering with the other, as cattle will not graze on ground where sheep have been. I believe there is now peace once more, the district having been divided; but even yet the "cow man" has not a good word to say for the "sheep man," and I have often been warned by the former never to stop at a sheep-ranche, as they would feed me badly and charge hotel prices. Having received great kindness from both, I need hardly say that this is all prejudice.

The day is fast coming when these large ranches must disappear, as from the cattle and sheep remaining on the same ground all the year round the grass is giving out, and already very large districts in Wyoming, Montana, and Dacotah have had to be abandoned.

When I was in the last-mentioned State four years ago there

were many thousands of cattle on the Little Missouri, and now nearly all of these have disappeared and have been replaced by small bands of horses, which stand the cold better, and, being of course not so numerous as cattle, allow the grass a chance of recovering itself. The large ranches will eventually be succeeded by farms, where a certain number of cattle, sheep, and horses will be raised, and where, being fattened on corn, they will fetch better prices.

CHAPTER XXVI.

Visit Crazy Woman Mountains.—Difficult ravine.—Park-like country.—Narrow escape from a grizzly.—We make for the trade-road.—The end of my grey horse.—Some bragging hunters.—I part company from Colonel P—— and the men.—The stage waggon.—Dangers of stage-drivers.—A companion joins us. Queer story about him. I ride part of the way with him.—Arrival at Miles City.—I am offered quarters, which I decline.—Call on General Miles.—Stories of General Miles.—I leave Fort Keogh with the General.—Rough journey.—Yellowstone Kelly.—Arrival at Fort Abraham Lincoln.—Kindness of American officers.—Road agents.—More anecdotes of General Miles.—Arrival at Chicago.—The present state of my old hunting-grounds.—Conclusion.

From Martinsdale we travelled towards the Crazy Woman Mountains, which are said to have been so called because the Indians found a white woman wandering in them, who was crazy from hunger and exposure. Our way lay through a beautifully hilly country, well wooded and having numerous small streams running through it. Wishing to explore as much of it as possible, I took a line of my own, about two miles further south than the one taken by the waggon. It was, in those days, entirely uninhabited, Indians and now and then a stray prospector being the only people you were likely to meet, and these last were very scarce then, as the danger from Indians was so great.

While riding across a small prairie lying at the foot of the mountains, I found a great number of elk-horns which had evidently been shed, some of them being very old, and some only shed the year before, and among these I picked a beautiful little pair of horns of a deer which is now almost extinct—the fantail. They were very much like the horns of the black-tailed deer, but about a quarter the size; from the state they were in, I should say that they had been there about two years.

I rejoined the waggon at night and heard that the Colonel had killed three blacktails during the day; I had seen several, but as we had plenty of meat I had not fired at them. On the second day we reached the Crazies, and found ourselves on the edge of an immense ravine about three hundred feet deep, and filled with a dense mass of trees and underbrush, and there was no way by which the waggon could cross. It was too late to go any further that night, so we camped, and had to carry water for ourselves and animals through the dense brush and up a bank at an angle of 45°, doing most of our labour in the dark. We had been told that we should come across a hunter's cabin on reaching the mountains, but we must have wandered out of our proper course, as we could find no traces of it. It was most unfortunate, as the owner of the cabin had lived in it for many years and knew the whole country, so that we could have got valuable information from him.

The next morning the Colonel and I rode along the edge of the ravine to find a crossing, and at last came to one which might be made to do, needing, however, a good deal of digging and brush cutting; so we went back and brought the waggon to the top of it; and then all of us set to work, and by evening we had a fair road down, and it took us till the middle of the next day to make one up on the other side, and even then we had to chain both hind wheels going down, and unload the waggon and carry everything up to enable the team to take the waggon over, and our want of proper tools made the work much harder, as we had only one shovel and pick.

The country on the other side was worth all the trouble we had taken to reach it. It was very much like a fine English park—open glades and clumps of fine trees, with patches of brush scattered about, where we could always jump deer. Bear-sign was, however, very scarce, and what we found was old, showing that they had left this part of the country, and we only saw one small one in the eight days we remained here. We were a little tired of deer-shooting, so we determined to move on again, which we did, going about fourteen miles to where the Crazies ended, as there were some fine valleys running into the range from there. The day after we reached our new camp the Colonel had rather a close shave with a grizzly. He was out hunting on horseback, and dismounted to stalk an elk, when he came on a large bear drinking at a stream. He managed to crawl up to within about sixty yards when he fired, striking the bear far back, as there were a good many bushes in the way and it was difficult to see him. The bear immediately charged, and the Colonel, having some trouble in getting a fresh cartridge in, scrambled up a steep bank which was behind him; the bear sprang twice at it, but each time fell back, the wound having crippled his hind quarters; and it was trying a third time, when the Colonel managed to get the cartridge in and fire, killing the bear. This was a very powerful animal, though not so large as some of the others we had shot, but the muscles of the forearm were so much developed that the men always spoke of it afterwards as the prizefighter.

One day the Colonel and I started for a long ride into the mountains to explore some very likely-looking ground for elk and bears, passing through some lovely country, but seeing nothing but black- and white-tailed deer till we reached a high point, when we got our glasses and soon made out some mountain-sheep above us, and some of them seemed to have fine heads. It necessitated a long climb, so the Colonel agreed to hold the horses while I went after the sheep. I had to descend some way, as there was no cover above us, and make a long detour, ascending again when I was round the end of the mountain, fallen timber making the walking very slow and tiring. I had got up higher than where the sheep were, when I saw two Indians going along the mountain-side above me on foot, and as there was no way of telling to what tribe they belonged, I lay down in the brush for fully an hour to let them get well away, when I continued my stalk, and on turning the point of the mountain again I saw that the sheep had moved and were coming my way, so I got behind a large tree and waited about twenty minutes, by which time they were only about a hundred and twenty yards from me. All I could see were sheep or young rams, so I let them enter a thicket, where they lay down, and my patience was nearly exhausted when two fine rams came up at full speed, giving me a snap shot, when I hit the hinder one, and had a run of about two miles over awful rocks before I could get in a second shot and finish him. The horns were a very perfect pair, but not so large as I had fancied, being only thirty-five inches long and eleven inches round the thickest part.

I found that the Colonel, tired of waiting and thinking I had gone after something else, had moved and shown himself, and his doing so had started the rams. We separated now, arranging where we were to meet. I was to take the high ground while the colonel skirted the base of the mountains, and soon after leaving him I saw a large band of elk feeding on the opposite side of a valley which lay below me. I let them feed over the ridge and then led my pony down and picketed him in the valley, climbing the hill on foot. It was necessary to be careful now, as I was going in the same direction that the Indians had taken, and they might have heard my shots at the ram and might be lying in wait somewhere near. I had nearly gained the ridge over which the elk had gone when I saw two young bulls watching me, so I lay still, hoping they would go away; but this they did not seem inclined to do, for they would pretend to fight and butt at one another, and then come a little nearer to have a look at me. Getting tired of this, I waved my handkerchief to and fro, when they trotted off, and I climbed to the top of the ridge and found myself within forty yards of a large band of elk: most of them were lying down; but I could see no fine heads, so I thought I would risk it and jumped up suddenly, when there was an extraordinary commotion, the elk going in all directions, some of them running against others in their confusion; but as I did not want meat, and did not see a single fine head, I did not fire, though they were so stupid that I could easily have killed two or three. The bulls must have fed on ahead, as I did not see a single large one as they went off. I rejoined the Colonel towards evening and found that he had killed a good ram, with finer horns than the one I had got, the horns being nearly two inches longer and one and a half thicker; he had seen a great many deer, but no sign of a bear.

As it was now late we rode as fast as we could for camp, but were so hindered by the roughness of the ground that we found we could not do it, not knowing the country well enough to travel through it in the dark; we therefore selected a small sheltered hollow and put up a bough shelter, made a big fire in spite of Indians, using very dry wood so that the smoke should be less dense, and were soon very comfortable, consuming a good supper of mountain mutton and water, after which we turned in. Our only covering was one saddle-blanket, but by lying close to each other we got through the night pretty well, having now and then to make up the fire; and in the morning, after a breakfast of more mutton-steaks, we reached camp by midday.

Fishel and I made another round through the mountains on the following day, and managed to lose ourselves, as this part of the country was new to both of us; but came at last to an old road. It was raining hard and very dark, so we got off to feel the road for tracks, as we had passed over one like this in coming to our present camp; and after groping about for some minutes we found some tracks which we followed, and soon saw an immense fire which they had lighted in camp to guide us. We got in just as supper was ready and did ample justice to it.

As bears seemed to have left this part of the country, and we did not care for any more deer-shooting, we decided to make for the stage-road between Bozeman and Fort Keogh, I intending to take the stage for the latter place, while the Colonel meant to drive to Bozeman and sell the outfit, going on to

2 A

Helena for the winter. During the day we passed a small river, and on stopping to let the horses drink, the Colonel's pony lay down, rolling him off into the stream, which was very cold, so we camped on the bank and lit a fire to dry him. The whole thing was so comical that I could not help laughing; and very shortly after I was punished for doing so, as the grey bucked as I was sitting sideways talking to the Colonel, and so bucked me off for the second time, though he did not lash out at me as he had done before. Some men passed us late in the afternoon, and I sold him to them for rather more than I gave for him, and was very glad to get rid of him. I heard afterwards that he got loose when on the prairie, near the large Crow camp, and joined a band of buffalo, so that no doubt the Indians got him again.

These men told us that during the previous winter they drove a band of elk into a small valley in the Crazies, from which there was no exit, closing the mouth of it with trees and brush, and had then killed the whole band, taking nothing but their skins and tongues; happening to visit the valley some weeks later, they found that most of the bodies had been eaten by bears, which had been there in such numbers that the whole place was trampled by them, some of the tracks being very large.

We struck the stage-road on the following day and drove down to the place where the stage changed horses, and found an old man and his wife in charge, who seemed to think nothing of the danger they ran from Indians. They told us that the stage was due in the morning, so we camped by the house, and while at breakfast two long-haired, very-much-fringed individuals drove up and dismounted, and after the usual questions as to who we were, where we were going to, &c., they began to pull about our collection of horns, asking why we took home such poor things, one of them saying to the other, " Why, Bill, they are not much more than half the size of those we got last week!" On our asking him how big those were, he said that he had held the head up, with the points of the horns on the ground, and that his companion, who was over six feet, had walked under the head without stooping. I had heard these stories so often that I thought I would test this one, so I took out fifty dollars and offered it for the head if they would bring it in. Seeing him hesitate, I took out another fifty dollars and offered them both for it, when the first speaker said that perhaps after all it might be hard to find the place where they had thrown them, and that they had not time to go there, after which they mounted and rode off.

The stage came about eleven o'clock and proved to be an ordinary farm waggon, with short springs under the seat. The driver was a rough-looking fellow, but turned out to be better than he looked. There was no cover of any kind, so I spread my mackintosh sheet over my things, as we now had snow or rain every day. There were five large mail-sacks in the back of the waggon already, which, with my bedding and horns, quite filled it. Now came the good-byes, which are the most unpleasant part of all trips, four or five months in camp making men better friends than years in civilization, after which we parted.

I found that the driver had been at this kind of life for many years, and was a pleasant companion. He had on several occasions been attacked by Indians, and had more than once to desert his mails, and to ride off on one of his team; but for the last two years he had had no trouble, though he still carried a repeating rifle and a brace of revolvers in case of necessity. He told me that he feared white desperadoes more than Indians, as they could so easy pretend to be friendly and shoot him unawares. Once, when he was known to be carrying a good deal of money, one of them had met him on the road, and had ridden alongside of the waggon for some time, asking questions as to the country, and then, dropping behind, had fired twice at him with a revolver, missing him but hitting one of the horses. He had at once thrown himself down in front of the seat, and, his team bolting, had given him time to get at his rifle, with which he had fired at the man, driving him away, though he had not hit him, as he was unable to take any aim on account of the roughness of the road.

I found that we had about three hundred miles to do, and should be five days doing it, as our team was only two small ponies which were to be changed twice each day. The day's journeys were of very unequal lengths; the first and second were about sixty miles each, and then came one of ninety-six, while on each of the last two days we were to do forty miles.

On the second day a young man, riding a cast cavalry horse and leading a second, joined us, whom my driver knew, asking him as he came up, "how it had gone," the answer being that it was all right; and most of what followed was about mutual friends, after which the man left us and rode on. I asked who he was and what he meant by its "being all right," and was told that the man kept a saloon at Miles City—a place which was springing up near Fort Keogh—and that some months before he had been joined by a partner from the East who had brought a good deal of money with him for investment. The two men had occupied one room over the saloon, and one morning the partner had been found with his throat cut, while his money had disappeared. This man said that he found him dead on awaking in the morning, and that the window of the room was open. He was arrested and taken to Bozeman, where he was tried for murder and had just been acquitted, though my driver seemed to think him guilty.

When we stopped for the night I had a long talk with this man, whose name was Moss, and at the end of it he told me that my next day's drive was ninety-six miles, and that although we were supposed to get in that evening, we should really be going all the next day, as the team was only changed once, so he offered me the use of his second horse if I would ride with him, in which case we should be in by seven and be in time for supper. I accepted the offer, and then took the driver aside to ask him what he thought of it. He advised my going, as I should avoid a very tedious drive, and he thought that Moss had now had a good lesson and would hardly risk hanging, which would be a certainty were he tried again on the same charge. To make sure I borrowed one of his revolvers, not having one with me.

We were off before daylight, and breakfasted under a very curious rock, covered with Indian carvings, about twenty miles from the stage station, having done this in something over two hours and a half. We rested an hour, turning our horses out to feed, and started again about eight o'clock, making forty miles by dinner time, having dinner at a stage station where the waggon was expected to arrive in about three hours. The remaining distance we managed easily by half-past six, without the horses having suffered at all. We had gone at a hand-canter nearly all day, Moss leading, and I had found him a very pleasant companion, as he had lived a long time in the West and had a great collection of stories connected with it. Of course I said nothing of what I had heard, nor did he allude to it. He left us the next morning, intending to be in Miles City by night, offering to take me with him; but I preferred arriving with my things, as I wished to make myself presentable before calling on General Miles, to whom I had a letter of introduction. As there was no hotel, Moss offered me a bed at his saloon; but this I declined with thanks, as I should hardly have felt comfortable there, so I promised to look him up if I came to Miles City, which he said was about two miles from Fort Keogh, on the opposite side of the Yellowstone River. The two following days I rode on the stage, through a very uninteresting country, reaching Fort Keogh early in the afternoon of the second. Here I went to call on General Miles, who was in command; but my appearance, I fear, was anything but prepossessing, as I had a four months' beard, long hair, and was very much tanned; my clothes, too, were not in first-rate condition, and my boots had not been blacked since I left Bismarck.

The General received me very kindly, and said that he would put me up as long as he remained at the post; but he was on the point of going East on leave, after which he would be transferred to another command, so that he was selling off everything and did not know how much furniture I should find in my room, nor how long what there was would remain there. I was soon comfortably established, finding a good bed, wash-stand, some chairs, and a carpet; and it was a great source of amusement during my stay, as we inquired each morning what articles had disappeared since the day before. The first thing to go was the bed and bedding, when I came to a mattress on the floor; then this went, and I put my buffalo-robe in a corner and slept on that; then all the rest of the things except the basin went, and that I emptied out of the window and hid every day under my robe, the General faring in the same way. One of the officers drove me to Miles City; but I found it was a miserable little place, containing about a hundred inhabitants, most of them keeping saloons, the soldiers being their customers; and yet, when I heard of this place four years afterwards, it was from a young lady who had just been by rail to a ball there, and it was then a fine and rapidly-growing place of several thousands, with stone houses, a town-hall, and a Mayor and Councilmen.

While at the Post I heard several stories of my host, who was said to be the best Indian fighter in the American army; and this was because he imitated their tactics, travelling with very little baggage, and starting at once on hearing news of Indians. It was not at all uncommon for the bugle to blow in the middle of the night, and when the officers and men were mustered the General would tell them that his scouts had brought him word that a war-party was near the Post, on their way to attack some settlement, and that a hundred men, with mules in proportion, must be at his quarters ready for a four or five days' scout in thirty minutes. The mule-master was in despair, assuring me that it was impossible for him to keep his mules in good condition, as they were nearly always away on these expeditions, and would come back mere bags of skin and bone, and in many cases not come back at all, having been left on the road, as they could not keep up, when the Indians got them.

On one occasion the General had started with a party of ladies to the Yellowstone Park, three or four officers and an escort going with them, and while on their way some of his Indian scouts met him, and told him that a war-party of Sioux under a noted chief was only about a day's ride from where they then were, returning from a raid. A consultation was held, and the General decided to send the ladies to Fort Ellis in charge of a corporal and two men, and to go himself with the remainder of the escort in pursuit of the war-party, sending for help from Ellis. The distance to the fort was sixty miles, and the ladies were in despair, doing all they could to alter his decision, but to no purpose, as they were at once sent off, the General and his party, consisting of thirty-seven men all told, going in the opposite direction. The scouts represented the "hostiles" as being about one hundred and thirty warriors, though they were not at all sure of this, and recommended waiting for reinforcements from Ellis; but this the General would not hear of, so they pushed on, and were close to the camp by night. The plan of attack was that a Captain Bennett should take one half of the men round to the opposite side, and that at the report of a pistol they should all close in, no prisoners being taken. This was carried out and a furious fight ensued, the Indians, though surprised, fighting well, and it ended in most of the Sioux being killed, a few escaping in the dark. On the side of the troops, though several men were wounded, there was only one man killed, the first shot fired by the Indians hitting Captain Bennett in the forehead, killing him so instantaneously, that the cigar he was smoking lay close to his mouth when he was found. A number of scalps were found, many of them those of women and children, justifying what had been done. General Miles had the best scouts in America, and got them in a very unusual manner. Having beaten a large party of Sheyennes, about three years before I met him, he offered the survivors liberty on condition that they would come to Fort Keogh as scouts, when he promised to get them implements and seeds, and to build them houses, selling some of their ponies to raise the money. They came and made a permanent camp, getting their wives and children from their homes, and, when I was at Keogh, were doing so well that they supplied the fort with most of the grain, vegetables, &c., that it needed, besides making the best scouts that the General had ever had. They had orders to disturb him at any hour, day or night, and did not hesitate to do so, and always spoke of him as their white chief.

As the time drew near for the General to start, he very kindly offered to take me with him, which of course I accepted with much pleasure, as otherwise I should have had more than four hundred miles in the waggon in which I had arrived. When it was known that I was going with the General, I was condoled with by my friends at the Fort, and was told that I should have to do the four hundred and twenty miles without getting a single night's rest, travelling incessantly, as relays of mules would be sent on under escort from Keogh halfway to Fort Lincoln, others being sent from there for the other half. We were given a grand "send off" supper by one of the officers, arrangements having been made to start at twelve o'clock that night, but a very heavy snow-storm coming on while we were at supper, our departure was postponed to the same hour the next night, when we were given another supper by the doctor of the post, and this time we really did get off. We were a party of eight in two ambulances, each drawn by four mules, and had two men on the box of each, besides an escort of a corporal and six men, as there was a possibility of being stopped either by Indians or "road agents." Our baggage was carried in a light waggon behind. We made fifty miles by morning, changing mules once, and before doing so had to cross a river, on the other side of which was a camp, where we were to find fresh mules and our guide, a celebrated scout, who went by the name of "Yellowstone Kelly." We drove into the river, which at the ford was not more than two feet deep, but as it was very dark we crossed a little too high up, and the ambulance getting into a quicksand began to go down. The mules, after struggling for a few minutes, lay down and refused to try any more, as they always do when frightened. It was very dark and we could see nothing, but could feel the water coming into the bottom of the ambulance. The General shouted to the escort, who came alongside and took us out one by one, seated behind them on their horses' backs.

On landing I found myself in a small camp, and as all the men had to turn out and help, I took possession of some blankets and was soon fast asleep. It took them nearly three hours to get out the ambulance and put everything straight, and I pitied the soldiers as they had to work up to their waists in ice-cold water. We ate a hasty breakfast and started again, and by twelve o'clock had done ninety miles, halting for dinner in the middle of a prairie, where there was water but no wood, the General telling us that he gave us an hour in which to cook and eat our dinner. We had brought plenty of steaks with us, but they were raw, and there was no wood or substitute for it within miles. Our guide showed us some bushes which were just visible on the edge of the prairie, about two miles away, and some of the escort were sent off at full speed to fetch some of them. We had barely time to cook half the steaks and bolt them, when the order was given to start again. We got one night's rest after all on the way down, one relay of mules being behind time, and the General and I turned in on the seats of the ambulance, which were made to fold down to form a bed, and as we were both of us pretty big men, it was an uncommonly tight fit, one being obliged to turn when the other did.

And now a few words as to our guide, Yellowstone Kelly, about whom enough stories have been told to fill a dozen "penny dreadfuls." He was said to have killed dozens of Indians, and to have had hair-breadth escapes without number. I had several talks with him, and found him to be a very quiet, unassuming man, who had very little to say about himself. I asked him if he had ever killed seven Indians in one fight when quite alone, as I had been told; he replied that he had never killed more than two, and that only once. He had been riding with despatches from one Northern Post to another, when he was waylaid by two Indians, who fired at but missed him. Not knowing how many there were, he threw himself from his horse and lay as if dead, when the two Indians walked up to him, and as they got near him he shot one and killed the other with his clubbed rifle. He said that he had been in a good many Indian fights, but had only once been wounded, a bullet having taken off a portion of one of his ears. His chief exploit was watching Sitting Bull's camp for six weeks without being discovered, though there were nine hundred Indians in it at the time, and discovery meant death. His duty was to bring word to General Terry at Fort Benton of any contemplated raid over the American frontier, as Sitting Bull was then in British territory.

Nothing of any consequence occurred until we reached the Big Heart River, which was frozen over, but which the guide thought would not bear the ambulance. The General, however, told the driver to "go ahead," and we drove on to the ice, which gave way under us, and we went down suddenly about two feet, the mules remaining on the ice; they struggled desperately to get us out again, but instead of doing so went in themselves, and all was now confusion—the mules tumbling over one another, the driver beating them, and the General shouting to "go ahead"; and our difficulties were much increased by its being a very dark night. The whip was kept going on the team, and by breaking the ice all the way across we reached the bank at last, and had to halt to repair damages, as some of the harness was broken.

Shortly after getting under weigh again, when crossing a deep and narrow watercourse, the pole of our ambulance was run into the opposite bank and broken off at the base, but the mules managed to take us safely out of it. Here the General showed what he was, as he took off his coat and spliced the pole himself, making a very good job of it. A few hours after this we drove into Fort Abraham Lincoln. I found in command here the General Sturgiss who had been so kind to me at Fort Belknap in Northern Texas in 1878, and who now pressed me to stop with him; but I could not accept his kind invitation, as I wished to return to the east for Christmas.

Nothing can exceed the kindness of American officers to

anyone going to one of the Western Posts. He receives so many offers of hospitality, that he is at a loss which to accept. I once stayed for two months at Fort Wadsworth, in Dacotah, and had the use of an ambulance and of any of the horses belonging to the Post at any time, having merely to say what I wanted and when.

General Miles was also in a hurry to go east, and I wished to travel with him, so we crossed to Bismarck and took the train for St. Paul's, the General and his guide being the observed of all observers, and I must have been asked fifty times to introduce men to the former. During the journey I was surprised to find Kelly reading Pope's Homer's Iliad, and when I expressed astonishment, he told me that he had not been brought up to be a scout, but had been made one by circumstances.

On reaching St. Paul's, the General got a telegram telling him that two ambulances full of officers, who had left Keogh only one day after us with an escort of six men, had been "held up," as it is called, which means stopped by "road agents," whose cry is always "hold up your hands," when they proceed to examine your pockets, some of the party keeping their rifles aimed at you. It seems that the escort was nearly a mile ahead, and that the ambulances were travelling slowly, when four men with repeating rifles sprang into the road shouting to the escort to hold up their hands, which they did at once as their carbines were fastened to their saddles. They were searched and their weapons taken from them, and they were then conducted into a ravine, where one man was left to guard them. The other three then returned and stopped the ambulances, and went through the party, getting a thousand dollars (£200) from one officer, who had in consequence to give up his leave and return to the Post. They took all the guns and ammunition, and cutting the traces and the soldiers' saddle-girths, they rode off, and so far as I could hear were never captured, though parties of soldiers scoured the country in all directions. These men might very easily have done the same thing to us, as our escort always rode with their carbines in slings beside the saddle, and we were so tightly wedged in the ambulances that though the corners bristled with weapons, as I knew to my cost when I nodded, we could never have got them out in time; the only man of our party who was ready was Kelly, who carried his rifle across the front of his saddle.

At St. Paul's we were given a grand dinner, and from Bismarck to Chicago we were not allowed to pay for our railway tickets, everyone wishing to honour the General on account of his Indian exploits. I heard one of these which may interest my readers. He had been pursuing White Cloud, the great Sioux chief, for some days, and at last found him camped in a deep ravine, where he evidently meant to make a stand. A scout was sent to summon the chief and his warriors to surrender, when the answer was, that if the white men wanted them they must come and take them. The General had some mountain howitzers with him, and with these he shelled the Indians' position, they returning the fire as well as they could. This went on for two days, when the chief sent to say that he would surrender, as the white men were too strong for him. White Cloud and his warriors then came out of the ravine, bringing their wounded with them, and marched slowly to where the General was. They shook hands and sat down for a talk, and the chief asked to be allowed to go away for eight days, that he might take his wounded to their home and make some necessary arrangements with his tribe, promising that he and his warriors would return at the end of that time and give themselves up. Most of the officers present were opposed to this, saying that if he were allowed to go he would not come back; but the General granted his request at once, and the Indians left, returning on the appointed day and surrendering themselves as prisoners. It turned out at their trial that the tribe had been more sinned against than sinning, and they were only sent back to their Reservation.

At Chicago I said good-bye to the General, as our respective routes diverged here, and so ended one of the pleasantest trips I ever made.

I have now come to the end of what, I fear, is a rambling account of my experiences in the Great North West, and their only interest, if interest they have, is in their depicting a kind of life which has now become a memory, and a very dear one to those who have once enjoyed it. I have paid several visits to my old hunting-grounds since 1878, and in many cases did not recognize them, so much had ranches and enclosures changed the face of the country. The whole of the Judith Basin is now a mass of sheep-ranches, and with the exception of a stray antelope or deer all big game has disappeared, though on my last visit I saw, even in these matter-of-fact days, something which reminded me of old times. Five Sioux Indians had made a horse-stealing raid on the Bannock camp and had run off some ponies; they had been closely pursued, and had taken refuge in a cattle corral, where they had all been killed. This happened in July, and I saw the bodies in November, and I thought it a most convincing proof of the beauty of the climate of Montana that these bodies were not in the least unpleasant, but had simply shrivelled up.

The whole country was covered with cattle and cowboys, very poor substitutes, in my eyes, for buffaloes and Indians; and I could not help regretting the days when I had ridden over that beautiful country, my rifle across the front of my saddle, depending on it for my daily food, and never knowing how soon I might have to use it in self-defence. Texas, too, was changed even more: towns have sprung up all over the prairies, wretched little Henrietta being now quite an important place, and Granville a city, while the scene of the Custer fight is now enclosed as fields.

While writing the foregoing chapters I have lived again in the past, remembering none of its drawbacks; and if I have given my readers a portion of the pleasure which I have felt myself, my task has not been in vain.

THE END.

PRINTED BY TAYLOR AND FRANCIS, RED LION COURT, FLEET STREET.

www.ingramcontent.com/pod-product-compliance
Lightning Source LLC
Chambersburg PA
CBHW030408230426
43664CB00007BB/799